AGlobal genda

Issues Before the United Nations
2010-2011

Edited by Irwin Arieff
Foreword by Sir Brian Urquhart

Published by the United Nations Association of the United States of America, New York, New York
Production of "A Global Agenda" was made possible by a generous grant from Korea University
facilitated by the World Federation of United Nations Associations

UNITED NATIONS ASSOCIATION, USA Inc.

Published in the United States of America
by the United Nations Association of the United States of America.
801 Second Avenue, New York, N.Y. 10017

ISBN 978-0-9845691-0-6

Printed in the United States of America

Advisory Board: Ayca Ariyoruk, Suh-Yong Chung, A. Edward Elmendorf, Bonian
Golmohammadi, Stephen Schlesinger, Courtney B. Smith, Sir Brian Urquhart

Consulting Editor: Barbara Crossette

Senior Editor: Dulcie Leimbach

Editor: Irwin Arieff

Articles Editor: Betsy Wade

Senior Researchers: Mirva Lempiainen, Simon Minching

Associate Researcher: Hilary Novik

Photo Editor: Joe Penney

Designer: Laurie Baker, Cohoe Baker Design cohoebaker@nyc.rr.com

Indexer: Simon Minching

Front cover: Helmet and flak jacket of a UN peacekeeper in the Democratic Republic of
Congo, from South Africa's 1 Parachute Battalion.
UN Photo/Marie Frechon.

Back cover: Sandra Doinita Visan, a UN peacekeeper from Romania, pays tribute to women
peacekeepers as part of a ceremony in Dili, Timor-Leste, in May 2009.
UN Photo/Martine Perret

Contents

Introduction *A. Edward Elmendorf*   iv

About UNA-USA   vii

About Korea University *Dr. Ki-Su Lee*   viii

About WFUNA *Bonian Golmohammadi*   x

Editor's Note *Irwin Arieff*   xii

Contributors   xiii

Foreword

Reinventing the United Nations Again? *Sir Brian Urquhart*   xxii

Chapter 1 Taming Chaos: Strategies for Global Security   1

Rebooting the Global System *Jayantha Dhanapala*   2

UN Counterterrorism: A Rising Stock? *James Cockayne*   4

In Search of New Momentum on Disarmament *Jayantha Dhanapala*   8

Arms Bans: Working Around Weaknesses *Marie Isabelle Chevrier*   11

Chapter 2 The Trials and Errors of Modern Peacekeeping   15

Peacekeeping Boom: Here to Stay? *Jean-Marie Guéhenno*   16

Congo to UN: Time Is Running Out *Hélène Gandois*   20

Haiti Quake Smashed 20 Years' Progress While Revealing   26
It Was Paper-Thin *Nathanial Gronewold*

The Middle East: What Can the UN Do? *Samir Sanbar*   29

A Weak Link in a Chain of Responsibility *Sarah Trefethen*   32

Women Peacekeepers: Not Tokens but Essential Workers   35
Veronica Haglund

continued

Given a Single Purpose, Peacekeepers Find Other   37
Tragedies They Can't Confront *Shin-wha Lee*

Chapter 3 The Evolving US-UN Relationship   41

Washington and Turtle Bay: Restarting the Dance of Diplomacy   42
Jeffrey Laurenti

Susan Rice: Obama's Policy Voice in the UN Halls *Evelyn Leopold*   48

An Interview with Ambassador Rice *Evelyn Leopold*   51

Chapter 4 Aid: Finding a Path for the Future   55

Development Aid: Is It Worth the Money? *Abigail Somma*   56

Afghanistan: Rapid Changes that Presage More Difficulty   62
Robert P. Finn

From Farm to Market to Sustainable Development   67
Susan Blaustein

Iraqi Reconstruction: Behind a Veil of Violence *James Wurst*   70

Primary School: Not Yet for Everyone *Dulcie Leimbach*   72

Pursuing Peace in Nigeria's Troubled Delta *Musikilu Mojeed*   74

Chapter 5 Fresh Start on Human Rights?   77

The Human Rights Council: Smoke and Mirrors   78
Jacques Fomerand

Washington's First Rights Review *Edward R. McMahon*   86

A Mandate to Protect *Tendai Musakwa*   88

Coaxing Europe to Welcome Two-Time Refugees   92
Indra Baatarkhuu

Chapter 6 Seeking Common Ground on Climate Change   95

After Copenhagen, Climate Dealers Shuffle the Cards   96
Karen Freeman

The Secretary-General's Point Man on Climate Policy   104
Karen Freeman

Help, My Island Is Sinking! *Mirva Lempiainen*   107

Chapter 7   Perfecting the Pursuit of Global Atrocities   111

International Criminal Court: Growing Up *Matthew Heaphy*   112

'Ignorance is the Worst Enemy' - A Profile of ICC's President   116
Suh-Yong Chung

Chapter 8   Changing with the Times   121

Healing the UN: A Prescription *Thomas G. Weiss*   122

The Reform Agenda *David E. Birenbaum*   125

G20: In Need of a UN Embrace *Park Soo Gil*   129

New UN Women's Agency Sets Sail on Uncharted Course   131
Barbara Crossette

Appendices   135

A. Important Dates in United Nations History   136

B. The UN System   140

C. Composition of the Secretariat   141
Compiled by Simon Minching

D. Operations and Budgets *Compiled by Simon Minching*   142

E. Acronyms and Abbreviations   154

F. Glossary *Compiled by Christopher J. Tangney*   163

G. Nobel Prizes   178

Charts and Tables   181

Peacekeeping Missions   182

Top Contributors of Peacekeeping Funding   184

Top Contributors of Uniformed Personnel   185

Global Summary of the AIDS Pandemic   186

Consolidated Appeals   187

Millennium Development Goals and Targets *Max McGowen*   188

Index   190

UNA-USA Membership Application   195

Introduction

A. Edward Elmendorf
President and chief executive officer, UNA-USA

It is with great pleasure that I introduce the 2010-2011 issue of UNA-USA's flagship publication, "A Global Agenda." We at UNA-USA are delighted that "A Global Agenda" was published this year through the first year of a five-year grant from Korea University, facilitated by the World Federation of United Nations Associations.

As I observe the vast and often poorly understood worldwide enterprise that the United Nations has become, I look for common themes in its work. This book reflects many such themes in the hopes and sometimes the fears of millions of people across the globe. A central idea for me, however, in "A Global Agenda" is performance—a huge challenge, given that it presumes a common knowledge of what the UN tries to do. Yet these understandings can be as varied as the alphabet soup of agencies and other bodies carrying out the UN's many mandates. Nevertheless, it is possible to discern changes that could improve effectiveness, including the suggestions in the book that could lead in this direction.

In discussing challenges to international security *["Rebooting the Global System," P. 2]*, Jayantha Dhanapala, a former UN under secretary-general for disarmament affairs, sees great opportunities for increasing the effectiveness of the UN and improving its global responses to world problems. Echoing a theme of President Obama, Dhanapala calls for nuclear weapons to be outlawed worldwide and eliminated verifiably. Climate change, in his view, can be remedied only through intense international cooperation with the UN at its center.

Reviewing the current rise in peacekeeping *["Peacekeeping Boom: Here to Stay?" P. 16]*, Jean-Marie Guéhenno, a former under secretary-general for peacekeeping, reports that peacekeeping forces have quadrupled instead of the expected modest increase since the release of the landmark Brahimi report in 2000. Like Shin-wha Lee's ideas on balancing peacekeeping and humanitarian responsibilities *["Given a Single Purpose, Peacekeepers Find Other Tragedies They Can't Confront," P. 37]*, Guéhenno perceives peacekeeping's future in the management of conflict within societies rather than between nations. He finds inadequate resources and capacity to be a growing problem for both peacekeeping and peace-building missions. Yet, increasing peacekeeping's effectiveness will inevitably raise questions about national sovereignty, a situation that has recently occurred in Chad and in the Democratic Republic of Congo, as Hélène Gandois reports *["Congo to UN: Time Is Running Out," P. 20]*.

Guéhenno observes that in a world where threats are becoming transnational, weak states can become as much of a threat as aggressive powers. Peacekeeping's growth reflects an awareness of this shift, but the national security systems of individual UN members have yet to adjust. Efforts to draw upon a government's responsibility to protect people living in the country, as explored by Sarah Trefethen *["A Weak Link in a Chain of Responsibility," P. 32]*, may be part—but only part—of the answer. To improve its own usefulness, the UN must begin to look beyond New York to work directly with the national security staffs of its members.

Looking to improve the UN's role in the Middle East, Samir Sanbar *["The Middle East: What Can the UN Do?" P. 29]* suggests that a secretary-general's personal diplomacy is crucial. With so many hot spots, it may no longer be possible for a secretary-general to engage in every crisis, so his special representatives could increase in importance. Are they adequately selected and supported? Are their mandates realistic? Paying more attention to their experiences could yield handsome dividends in their effectiveness.

Abigail Somma *["Development Aid: Is It Worth the Money?" P. 56]* highlights the raging debate over the value of international aid. Dambisa Moyo, a scholar from Zambia, made sharply critical observations in her 2009 book, "Dead Aid," putting development practitioners on the defensive. The problem often lies in a failure to understand what is meant by effectiveness and to specify the objectives being pursued and the time horizon to accomplish them.

Critics on both sides of the aid argument often focus only on foreign assistance and fail to fully recognize the larger amounts of local resources that are being spent by the countries receiving outside aid. Supplementing specific domestic resources with small amounts of foreign financing for highly targeted tasks could make a huge difference. The UN could provide a stunning example of its effectiveness at the country level by facilitating reviews of development spending from all sources and monitoring their follow-up.

Discussing the progress made by the UN Human Rights Council, Jacques Fomerand sees "smoke and mirrors" *[P. 78]*. He argues that the relatively new council (2006) is no less politicized than its discredited predecessor, the Human Rights Commission. It was hoped that choosing members by secret ballot would help the new entity's reputation, but the UN practice of presenting pre-selected regional slates of candidate countries has prevented competitive elections.

Fomerand considers the council's outside experts and investigators to be one of the most productive mechanisms for protecting human rights, but they face continuous threats from politically motivated national representatives. As for the council's periodic reviews of each UN member's rights performance, Fomerand writes that some countries have accepted recommendations from the reviews while others have not. When the council undergoes its five-year review in 2011, the UN and rights groups should focus on lessons for future effectiveness rather than on scoring political points by exposing the weak human rights records of irresponsible leaders and fragile states.

In his essay on fixing the UN *["Healing the UN: A Prescription," P. 122]*, Thomas G. Weiss contends that the UN is paralyzed. Rigid regional blocs, overlapping jurisdictions of UN bodies, weak leadership and the absence of central financing all contribute to this sense of immobility. Weiss suggests that reframing the concept of national sovereignty is a crucial remedy to the problem.

To drive such reform and improve management, the General Assembly and the Secretariat must maintain a meaningful dialogue on their own responsibilities. But David E. Birenbaum *["The Reform Agenda," P. 125]* sees little progress there. Birenbaum nonetheless hopes that the secretary-general will persist in his efforts at human resource management reform, which could certainly improve the inner workings of the UN. Yet to overcome bloc voting, efforts must be made to increase trust among the key players in the assembly and its budget group, the Fifth Committee.

Considering its size and the complexity of the world and its own diversity, the UN actually functions well, providing critical services in difficult environments. As a former World Bank staff member for 30 years, I know that meetings and bureaucracy can cripple ambitions. The UN continues to function despite its inefficiencies and occasional lapses. The Security Council is constantly engaged in managing world crises. The UN delivers aid in humanitarian emergencies—think of Haiti after the January 2010 earthquake—sends peacekeepers to war zones, provides health care to enormous numbers of desperate people, mobilizes governments to pursue disarmament, safeguards the environment, helps poor countries with development strategies and programs and performs so many other correctives that it is no wonder the UN suffers from its own flaws. It is an institution we love to pick on, but it is also an institution that the world—people, governments, nongovernmental actors and our beleaguered planet—needs to have at its side. ▦

About UNA-USA

The United Nations Association of the United States of America (UNA-USA) is a nonprofit membership organization dedicated to building understanding of and support for the ideals and work of the UN among the American people. Its education, policy, publications and advocacy programs emphasize the importance of cooperation among nations and the need for American leadership at the UN. UNA-USA is affiliated with the World Federation of United Nations Associations, which began in 1946 as a public movement for the UN.

As a center of policy research , UNA-USA focuses on international peace and security, health, development and human rights. UNA's Business Council is a leading catalyst for innovative opportunities between member companies and the UN. Its Global Classrooms program attracted 2,500 students this year. UNA's publications department publishes an annual book, "A Global Agenda: Issues Before the United Nations"; an online newsletter, the World Bulletin (www.unausa.org/newsletter); and a recently introduced online version of its venerable magazine, The Inter-Dependent (www.theinterdependent.com), featuring blogs and articles on the UN.

With about 12,000 members nationwide, UNA-USA combines broad grass-roots outreach with policy studies involving scholars and government officials from many parts of the world, identifying areas of potential cooperation. Through programs, publications and its network of chapters and divisions, UNA-USA continues to pioneer efforts to involve the American public in the discussion of foreign policy priorities as well as to provide information and educational materials for Congress, the executive branch, corporations, nongovernmental organizations, the general public and the media.

UNA-USA's 130 community chapters and divisions, 93-member Council of Organizations and National Council enable it to reach out to millions of citizens who want their voices heard in Washington and at the UN. With its headquarters a few blocks from the UN in New York and a Washington office, UNA-USA is financed primarily by foundations, corporations, individuals and membership dues. UNA-USA has long worked closely with the UN Foundation and other organizations, and a formal alliance with the UN Foundation is being elaborated as this book goes to press this summer. ■

About Korea University

Dr. Ki-Su Lee, President, Korea University

Korea University's commitment to excellence in education extends beyond the classroom and the campus to the world. In South Korea and abroad, it strives to prepare students and faculty to help solve important social and humanitarian problems.

That is why Korea University has worked with the United Nations Association of the United States of America to support publication of the 2010 edition of "A Global Agenda." The book is an indispensable guide to the UN and the crucial international challenges it faces.

Korea University was established in 1905 with the guiding principle of "national salvation through education" and is dedicated to independent learning and modern education.

Since its founding, the university has been at the forefront of every major turning point in Korean history. Countless graduates have served as leaders in every sector of society, giving the university the status of a beacon for the nation.

The university's main campus in Anam-dong, a neighborhood in north-central Seoul, was built in 1932 under the guidance of its then-president, Kim Sung Su. The Anam Campus now covers 8.5 million square feet; a second campus in Sejong, in the province of Choongchung Nam Do, is 4.3 million square feet in area. As it matures, Korea University is also growing academically; it currently comprises 20 colleges and divisions and 20 graduate and professional schools. Its enrollment includes 27,000 undergraduates and over 10,000 graduate students, with 3,043 faculty members renowned in their fields and devoted to research.

Korea University can compete with the world's best. Its excellence has been widely recognized, most recently in the 2009 rankings of the national newspaper JoongAng Ilbo, which rated Korea University No. 1 in domestic comprehensive private universities.

Korea University is also in the forefront of the globalization of higher education in Korea. It has international exchange agreements with 710 institutions in 72 countries, and in the past year, 1,070 of its students went abroad to study as part of exchange or visiting programs. This year, 1,880 foreign students from 73 countries have come to Korea University.

Korea University has student exchange programs with, among others, the University of British Columbia in Canada, the University of Pennsylvania and University of California-Davis in the United States, Royal Holloway University of London, Griffith University in Australia and Renmin University in China.

Yearly the university's International Summer Campus—a program conducted entirely in English—serves as an educational hub where students from around the world gather to experience Korea and engage in intercultural dialogue.

In May 2008, Korea University launched "Vision 2030," an ambitious development plan to increase its international competitiveness and propel it, in the next 20 years, into the ranks of the world's greatest universities. With a special focus on training top-notch global leaders, this plan aims to provide a holistic education with equal emphasis on acquiring knowledge, practical skills and a humanitarian spirit.

In recognition of its exertions, the institution has become the first Korean university to be accepted by Universitas 21, a network of 21 leading research-intensive universities in 13 countries, and the Association of Pacific Rim Universities, with 42 members.

The university is rigorously expanding its horizons at home. Its Division of International Studies and Graduate School of International Studies conduct all their courses in English. A distinguished faculty directs courses in international commerce, international relations, trade and security.

The Division of International Studies has also hosted a model United Nations with the UN Development Program and the UN High Commissioner for Refugees and a model meeting of the Group of 20, among other international activities. Housing the UN Development Program policy office in the International Studies Building will significantly contribute to the development of international studies research and education.

To provide its students with the best possible education, the university provides an innovative general curriculum. Its new Office of General Education is aiming for a broader range of subject matter. The Korea University Social Service Organization was set up to advance knowledge and nurture future leaders of society.

With a frontier spirit and broad ambitions, Korea University is well on its way to becoming a leading world-class institution. ▪

About WFUNA

Bonian Golmohammadi, Secretary-General,
World Federation of United Nations Associations

For the United Nations community, the year 2010 has been characterized by complex global challenges, such as the devastating earthquake in Haiti, as well as hopeful instances of progress including the unanimously adopted outcomes of the Nuclear Non-Proliferation Treaty Review conference. Each of these recent events clearly shows the necessity of approaching today's interconnected challenges and opportunities from a cooperative multilateral perspective. Furthermore, these events highlight the UN's central role in confronting global problems and managing multi-sectoral responses.

The World Federation of United Nations Associations is a global nonprofit organization representing and coordinating a membership of over 100 national United Nations Associations and their thousands of constituents. Guided by our vision of a UN that is a powerful force in meeting common global challenges and opportunities, WFUNA works to strengthen and improve the UN. We achieve this through the engagement of people who share a global mindset and support international cooperation—global citizens.

WFUNA is pleased to be, for the first time, a partner in the publication of "A Global Agenda." This edition covers a wide range of topics that are of special interest and relevance to our work and the work of our UNAs worldwide. The publication serves as a valuable resource providing reliable and up-to-date expert analysis and information that our members and partners can use in their outreach, advocacy and capacity-building. Its contents are relevant for a wide range of readers, including academics, students, diplomats, government officials and nongovernmental activists—the constituency represented by our UNAs.

Based on the premise that we are all united through the UN's core values, in 2009 WFUNA launched the "Global Citizen Campaign," a series of targeted programs and activities that underscore the interconnectedness of global issues; promote cooperative and democratic problem-solving; and educate and engage the youth of today to be leaders and global citizens. The programs of the campaign are guided by the three pillars of the UN—peace and security, sustainable development and human rights—and engage civil society in these key areas through education, advocacy, and action.

In the area of peace and security, WFUNA has a special focus on the Responsibility to Protect, the rule of law and nuclear disarmament and nonproliferation. Through our project "Responsibility to Protect—mobilizing public and political will," we aim to provide citizens around the world with a framework for holding nations accountable in the face of genocide and mass atrocities. On disarmament, we are currently running a global youth design competition.

In the sustainable development focus, WFUNA is building two main programs: "Go beyond" (focusing on climate change) and "YOUth Impact Africa" (centering on the Millennium Development Goals). Through the "Go beyond" program, WFUNA will work with companies to alter the consumption behavior of individuals towards a climate-responsible lifestyle and promote a grass-roots response through UNAs. "YOUth Impact Africa" aims to contribute to the achievement of the Millennium Development Goals in the region through youth-led community service projects and education through Model UNs.

Finally, in the human rights issue area, our program "Civil Society in Action for Human Rights" increases the advocacy capacity of national UNAs through training, capacity-building and ongoing technical support from WFUNA. We have a Web site entirely dedicated to human rights.

In addition to our core programming, WFUNA has further initiatives and campaigns focusing on youth engagement, grass roots capacity-building and campaigns on special topics. One such campaign, "The UN in the G20," focuses on formalizing the UN's participation in the Group of 20 and establishing appropriate channels of communication and exchange between the UN and that group. The relationship between the UN and the G20 is explored in an article in this edition of "A Global Agenda," by Park Soo Gil, WFUNA's president and a former Korean ambassador to the UN *["G20: In Need of a UN Embrace," P. 129]*.

Global citizenship has been an ongoing theme for WFUNA in the past year. Every individual who is a part of our network is a global citizen. We are all committed to the ideals of the UN, express an acute interest in today's global issues, and are working towards a world of peaceful cooperation, sustainable development and human rights for all people. "A Global Agenda" is truly a publication for the global citizen. ■

Editor's Note

The tens of thousands of people who work at the United Nations know firsthand that there is no shortage of pain in the world. It is the nature of their work to be confronted by disease, poverty, war, natural disaster and human misery of every sort.

It is many UN staffers' everyday job to try to make things better. There is no question things do not always work out—in too many places, it may seem as if nothing ever works. But only the UN has a presence in nearly every hot spot and a legitimacy conferred by having every country as a member.

"A Global Agenda, Issues Before the United Nations 2010-2011" explores the UN'S constantly shifting fronts, evaluating a range of programs with a critical yet hopeful eye. The book's central assumption is that much international problem-solving these days requires international cooperation. It aims to make the case that every nation should at least be offered a place at the table, an opportunity to help formulate strategy and translate talk into action.

As the book's authors make abundantly clear, multilateral approaches often offer the best promise of solving urgent and complex world problems, and the UN, while far from perfect, best embodies multilateralism by offering every country a voice and a role.

Excluding this or that nation or class of nations, for whatever reason, may make it easier to reach an agreement. But what good is "unanimity" if some parties are not at the table? A better game plan is not to exclude or divide but to give everyone a greater stake in a successful outcome. And all must look beyond their own immediate interests and seek the greatest long-term benefit for everyone.

This book is bound by these basic beliefs. I am grateful to our many authors for giving so generously of their time and wisdom to ensure its success. I also want to acknowledge the invaluable contributions of UNA-USA interns, past and present, including in particular Hilary Novik, Mirva Lempiainen and Simon Minching. Dulcie Leimbach, the UNA-USA publications director, deserves special recognition for her unstinting help and support. And special thanks to our copy editor, Betsy Wade; photo editor, Joe Penney; consulting editor, Barbara Crossette; and our designer, Laurie Baker, for doing so much to help this book come together. ■

–*Irwin Arieff, New York, August 2010*

Contributors

Irwin Arieff is a writer and editor who worked for Reuters for 23 years in Washington, Paris and New York before leaving daily journalism in 2007. He served in the Reuters UN bureau for seven years; other postings included chief US political correspondent, White House correspondent and science and medicine correspondent. He has written for several UNA-USA publications. Arieff earned a master's degree in journalism from Northwestern University and did his undergraduate study at the University of Pennsylvania. He also served three years in the Peace Corps, specializing in rural development in Senegal and Mauritania.

Ayca Ariyoruk is a senior policy associate at UNA-USA, responsible for the association's research and policies on human rights, strengthening the UN and UN reform. She serves as the association's representative to the UN in New York and formulates concepts for UNA-USA programs and events. In partnership with Seton Hall University's John C. Whitehead School of Diplomacy and International Relations, Ariyoruk organizes annual seminars on the UN for graduate and undergraduate students. She was earlier a research fellow at the Center for UN Reform Education and a Marcia Robbins International Young Scholar at the Washington Institute for Near East Policy. Ariyoruk received her master's from the John C. Whitehead School and bachelor's in political science from the University of Nebraska.

Indra Baatarkhuu is a George Soros scholar at Bard College, majoring in International Relations. From Mongolia, she has interned at the UNA-USA and the International Institute of Rural Reconstruction.

Laurie Baker is a partner in Cohoe Baker, award-winning graphic designers for many leading publications including UNA-USA, The New York Times, The Wall Street Journal, Andersen Consulting and Mercedes-Benz of North America. Baker has worked as a designer and/or art director for Storey Books, New York University's Center for Global Health, Travel Holiday magazine, the Leukemia

Society and the Metropolitan Museum of Art. She holds a master of fine arts from the University of Michigan.

David E. Birenbaum was the first US ambassador to the United Nations for Management and Reform, serving from 1994 to 1996. He is of counsel to the law firm of Fried Frank Harris Shriver & Jacobson; he retired as a partner in 2000. Birenbaum is senior scholar at the Woodrow Wilson International Center for Scholars. He is the author of numerous publications, many of which concern UN reform issues. The founder, and chair from 1996 to 2000, of the Emergency Coalition for US Financial Support of the UN, he is a board member of a number of nongovernmental organizations.

Susan Blaustein is co-founder and co-director of the Millennium Cities Initiative, a project of Columbia University's Earth Institute established to help sub-Saharan cities achieve the Millennium Development Goals. She previously worked on conflict prevention with the International Crisis Group, pursued independent study into the roots of the Rwandan genocide, and was a foreign correspondent in Southeast Asia. Prior to this, Blaustein was on the faculty of Columbia University, a Junior Fellow at Harvard University and a lecturer at Yale University, where she also earned her doctorate. She has received awards from the American Academy of Arts and Letters and the Guggenheim Foundation and serves on the board of the nonprofit Millennium Promise, the lead UN partner in the Millennium Villages project.

Marie Isabelle Chevrier is professor of public policy and political economy at the University of Texas, Dallas, where she directs the master's program in public policy. Her primary areas are negotiations to ban the possession and use of biological and chemical weapons, their impact on proliferation and the threat of bioterrorism. In 2004, she received a Fulbright fellowship to teach at the Nelson Mandela Center for Peace and Conflict Resolution at Jamia Millia Islamia University in New Delhi. She is a member of the Scientists Working Group on Biological and Chemical Weapons in Washington, and the chair of the board of directors of the BioWeapons Prevention Project in Geneva. Chevrier holds a Ph.D. in public policy from Harvard.

Suh-Yong Chung is an associate professor of international law in Korea University's Division of International Studies. He is a member of the Compliance Committee of the UN Basel Convention and has participated in activities of international organizations, including the UN Industrial Development Organization, the Yellow Sea Large Marine Ecosystem Project of the UN Development Program-Global Environmental Facility, the UN Environment Program's Northwest Pacific Action Plan, and the UN Economic and Social Commission for Asia and the Pacific. He has been an adviser to the South Korean government, including the Presidential Committee on Green Growth, the Ministry of Foreign Affairs and Trade, and the Ministry of Environment. Professor Chung holds degrees in law and international relations from Seoul National University, the London School of Economics and Stanford Law School.

James Cockayne is senior fellow and director of the New York office of the Center on Global Counterterrorism Cooperation. An international lawyer by training, he has worked with governments, civil society, academia and businesses around the world on the regulation of violence, including in the areas of war crimes trials, organized crime, terrorism, peace operations and private security. Cockayne is a graduate of the University of Sydney and of New York University, a former chair of the editorial committee of the Journal of International Criminal Justice, and a former director of the Transnational Crime Unit of the Australian Attorney-General's Department.

Barbara Crossette is a regular contributor to UNA-USA publications and is also the UN correspondent for The Nation. She was UN bureau chief for The New York Times from 1994 to 2001 and earlier its chief correspondent in Southeast Asia and South Asia. She is the author of "So Close to Heaven: The Vanishing Buddhist Kingdoms of the Himalayas," "The Great Hill Stations of Asia" and a Foreign Policy Association study, "India: Old Civilizations in a New World." Crossette won a George Polk award for her coverage in India of the assassination of Rajiv Gandhi in 1991 and the 2010 Shorenstein Prize for her writing on Asia. She is a member of the Council on Foreign Relations and a trustee of the Carnegie Council on Ethics in Foreign Affairs.

Jayantha Dhanapala is president of the Nobel Peace Prize-winning Pugwash Conferences on Science and World Affairs and a member of the governing board of the Stockholm International Peace Research Institute. He was the UN under secretary-general for disarmament affairs from 1998 to 2003. As a Sri Lankan diplomat, Dhanapala served as its ambassador to the US from 1995 and as its representative to the UN in Geneva from 1984 to 1987. He also held diplomatic posts in London, Beijing and New Delhi and represented Sri Lanka at many international conferences, chairing a number, including the historic Non-Proliferation Treaty Review and Extension Conference of 1995. He was Director of the UN Institute for Disarmament Research from 1987 to 1992. Dhanapala has received many international awards and honorary doctorates, lectured widely and published books and articles in international journals. He speaks Sinhala, English, Chinese and French. His home is in Sri Lanka.

A. Edward Elmendorf is president and chief executive of UNA-USA, a post he assumed this year after 40 years' experience as an international and national civil servant. He started his international career in the US Foreign Service at the US Mission to the UN under Ambassador Adlai Stevenson. He later became a UN staff member and in 1970 began a 30-year career at the World Bank. After retiring, he taught at Johns Hopkins University and consulted for the World Bank, the World Health Organization, the UN Development Program and the US

Institute of Medicine. He served for 15 years as an officer or board member of the USA-UNA's largest local chapter, in the national capital area. He graduated magna cum laude with a bachelor's in German literature from Yale, has a master's degree in economics from George Washington University and a master's in public health from Johns Hopkins.

Robert P. Finn is Associate Research Scholar in the Liechtenstein Institute of the Woodrow Wilson School of Public and International Affairs and lecturer in the Woodrow Wilson School at Princeton University. He was the Ertegun Visiting Professor of Turcology at Princeton from 2003-2005. From March 2002 until August 2003, he served as the first US ambassador to Afghanistan in more than 20 years. Previously, he served as US Ambassador to Tajikistan and opened the US Embassy in Azerbaijan in 1992. Finn is the author of the book "The Early Turkish Novel," published in English and Turkish, and his poems and translations have appeared in the United States, Turkey, France and Pakistan.

Jacques Fomerand joined the UN Secretariat in 1977, where he followed economic, social and coordination questions in the Department of Economic and Social Affairs. From 1992 to 2003, he was director of the UN University office in North America. He now teaches at John Jay College of the City University of New York, Seton Hall University and Occidental College and has published widely on matters related to the UN. His latest book is "A Dictionary of the United Nations." He is completing a study on the practice of human rights.

Karen Freeman is a freelance journalist and educator involved with journalism education in Eastern Europe. She was an editor and occasional writer at The New York Times on the National, Technology, Science and Business desks before joining its Editorial Department, which she left in 2007. Before joining the Times in 1995, she was associate professor of journalism at Pennsylvania State University. Before that, she was the science editor at The St. Louis Post-Dispatch. She has a master's degree in neural science from Washington University Medical School. Freeman was a Knight International Journalism fellow in Moldova in 2006 and now lives in Dublin.

Hélène Gandois specializes in the study of security regionalism, with a focus on Africa, and is the author of "From Ploughshare to Sword: Regionalism," published in 2010 by LAP Academic Publishing. A visiting scholar at Columbia University from 2005 to 2007, she has previously worked for the UN University and for the Carnegie Council on Ethics and International Affairs. A graduate of the Institut d'Etudes Politiques de Paris, she holds a Ph.D. in international relations from Oxford. She is currently working on a freelance basis for the United Nations.

Bonian Golmohammadi is secretary-general of the World Federation of United Nations Associations. Previously, he served as secretary-general of UNA-Sweden. Since 2005, Golmohammadi has served as president of the UNA Europe Network.

Prior to joining UNA-Sweden, Golmohammadi worked with private businesses in the Czech Republic, including a publishing trust and a real estate firm.

Nathanial Gronewold is a reporter and New York City Bureau Chief for Environment and Energy Publishing, producers of the online news services Greenwire and ClimateWire. He traveled to Haiti in late 2009 to investigate environmental problems just before the devastating earthquake of Jan. 12, 2010. He returned later to cover the rebuilding plans. Gronewold researched foreign aid programs and policies in college and graduate school.

Jean-Marie Guéhenno is the Arnold Saltzman Professor of War and Peace Studies at Columbia University. As UN under secretary-general for peacekeeping operations, from 2000 to 2008, he led the largest expansion of peacekeeping in UN history, overseeing 130,000 staff members on 18 missions. Before joining the UN, he was director of policy planning in the French Ministry of Foreign Affairs, France's ambassador to the Western European Union and chairman of the French Institute of Higher Defense Studies. He is also a nonresident senior fellow at the Brookings Institution. He is a graduate of the Ecole Normale Supérieure, the Institut d'Etudes Politiques de Paris, and the Ecole Nationale d'Administration.

Veronica Haglund was an intern in UNA-USA's publications department in 2009. She is pursuing a bachelor's degree in media in communications studies and business at Uppsala University in Sweden, her home. She has worked as a volunteer for the nonprofit Indian Network for Development Exchange in Margao, Goa.

Matthew Heaphy is the deputy convener of the American Nongovernmental Organizations Coalition for the International Criminal Court, a post he has held since July 2006. Before joining the coalition, Heaphy was an associate legal officer in Trial Chamber I at the International Criminal Tribunal for the former Yugoslavia in The Hague and interned as a law clerk to Judge Anita Usacka at the International Criminal Court. He also worked as an antitrust litigation lawyer in San Francisco. In law school, Heaphy clerked in the litigation department of a Brazilian law firm and represented human rights advocates as a Frank C. Newman intern at the 59th Session of the UN Commission on Human Rights. A graduate of Wesleyan University and the University of San Francisco School of Law cum laude, Heaphy has been a member of the California Bar since 2003.

Jeffrey Laurenti is senior fellow and director of foreign policy programs at The Century Foundation and a member of the Council on Foreign Relations. He was UNA-USA's executive director of policy studies until 2003 and currently serves on its board. He was deputy director of the United Nations Foundation's initiative in support of Kofi Annan's high-level panel on global threats, challenges, and change in 2003-04, candidate for the US House of Representatives in 1986, senior issues adviser to Walter Mondale's 1984 presidential campaign, and from 1978 to 1984 was executive director of the New Jersey Senate. He is the author of numerous monographs and articles on international peace and security, terrorism, UN reform and other topics. Graduated Phi Beta Kappa and magna cum laude in government from Harvard University, he earned his master's in public affairs from Princeton University's Woodrow Wilson School of Public and International Affairs.

Ki-Su Lee is the president of Korea University, a position he has held since 2008. He has served since 1984 as professor of law at the Korea University College of Law, and since 2002 as a Distinguished Visiting Scholar at the University of Wisconson-Madison Law School. He has a bachelor of law degree from Korea University, a master of law from Seoul National University, a Ph.D. from Germany's Tübingen University, and an honorary doctor of law degree from Waseda University in Japan. He has also been a visiting professor at Mainz University Law College, München Max-Planck Institute and Marburg University Law College, and a visiting scholar at Harvard Law School. The Korea Bar Association has awarded him the Korea Legal Culture Award and the Korean Arbitrators Association has given him its Grand Award.

Shin-wha Lee is a professor in the Department of Political Science and International Relations at Korea University in Seoul. She received her Ph.D. from the University of Maryland at College Park and was a post-doctoral fellow at Harvard. She has served as a special adviser to the UN Rwandan Independent Inquiry, an adviser to the chair of the East Asian Vision Group, a visiting scholar at Princeton University's East Asian Studies Program, a member of the Trilateral Commission, a board member of the Academic Council on the United Nations System, a visiting professor at Columbia University's School of International and Public Affairs, and coordinator of the Unesco Chair on Peace, Democracy and Human Rights.

Dulcie Leimbach is publications director of UNA-USA, where she edits The InterDependent, an online magazine focused on the United Nations, and the World Bulletin, an online newsletter featuring information on UNA. She is the senior editor of "A Global Agenda" and a former editor at The New York Times, where she worked for more than 20 years. She holds a bachelor's degree in journalism from the University of Colorado and a master of fine arts from Warren Wilson College.

Mirva Lempiainen is a freelance journalist and a recent graduate of the international reporting program at the City University of New York Graduate School of Journalism. Her work has been published in the US, Finland and Australia. She spent the summer of 2010 training young journalists in the Maldives while on a grant from Davis Projects for Peace.

Evelyn Leopold is a freelance writer and regular contributor to the Huffington Post, based at the United Nations, where she served as UN bureau chief for Reuters for 17 years. She chairs the Dag Hammarskjöld Scholarship Fund for Journalists and is a member of the Council on Foreign Relations. She was awarded a gold medal for UN reporting in 2000 by the UN Correspondents Association, received an Alicia Patterson Fellowship, and was co-author of a book in German on women in East Germany. At Reuters she also served as a news editor for North America, the Africa region editor and associate editor worldwide. She was a reporter in London, New York, Washington and Bonn.

Max McGowen is a senior at George Washington University, majoring in political science, and entering a master's program in legislative affairs. He works as a research assistant to the Eleanor Roosevelt Papers project and was an intern in the Publications Department at UNA-USA in 2008. Most recently he completed an internship with U.S. Rep. Steve Rothman of New Jersey.

Edward McMahon holds a joint appointment as research associate professor in the University of Vermont's Department of Community Development and Applied Economics and its Department of Political Science. McMahon also serves as a senior research associate at Freedom House. He was Africa Regional Director with the National Democratic Institute for International Affairs from 1989-98 and served for 10 years as a US diplomat. In addition to his journal articles and book chapters, he was co-author of "Piecing a Democratic Quilt: Regional Organizations and Universal Norms," published by Kumerian Press in 2006. He was co-editor of "Democratic Institution Performance: Research and Policy Perspectives," published by Praeger in 2002.

Simon Minching is a master's candidate at the University of Chicago, specializing in international security studies and analytical methodology. A former UNA-USA policy intern and contributing author in 2009, Minching has a bachelor's in government and politics from St. John's University.

Musikilu Mojeed, a Ford Foundation International Fellow, is studying international reporting at the City University of New York Graduate School of Journalism. He is a deputy investigative editor at Nigeria's NEXT newspaper, currently based in New York, and has written extensively on politics, corruption and human trafficking for other major Nigerian newspapers and magazines, including The News, Tempo, Tell and The Punch. His work has also appeared in the Huffington Post and on the New York City News Service. Mojeed was a member of the board of the Forum for African Investigative Reporters, based in South Africa, and a member of the US-based Investigative Reporters and Editors.

Tendai Musakwa was a publications intern with UNA-USA in 2009. He is pursuing a master's degree in Chinese studies at Oxford, and is a recent graduate of Vassar, where he received a bachelor's in Chinese and political science.

Hilary Novik is an intern in the UNA-USA's publications department. She will receive a bachelor's degree with honors from Trinity College in Hartford in May 2011, with an international relations major and Hispanic studies minor.

Park Soo Gil is president of the World Federation of United Nations Associations. He is also a professor at Korea University's Graduate School of International Studies, teaching on the subject of international organizations and the UN. Between 1984 and 1998, he served as South Korea's ambassador to Morocco, Canada, the UN in Geneva and the UN in New York. From 1963 to 1998, he held a variety of positions at South Korea's Ministry of Foreign Affairs and Trade, including director-general of treaty affairs, deputy minister for political affairs, and chancellor, the Institute of Foreign Affairs and National Security. He also served as a member of the UN Sub-commission on the Promotion and Protection of Human Rights.

Joe Penney is a photographer who has worked on assignment for Reuters, the McGill Daily and Montreal Mirror. His photographs covering the Guinea-Bissau presidential election in 2009 appeared in The New York Times. His work is currently featured in an exhibition at the Musée National du Sport in Paris. He is a recent graduate of McGill University in Montreal. His photos can be viewed at joepenney.com.

Samir Sanbar is executive editor of www.unforum.com, a Web forum he started after retiring from the UN. While at the UN, he served as assistant secretary-general for public information and head of the Department of Public Information, launching the official UN Web site http://www.un.org in 1994. A graduate of the American University of Beirut, he worked for several Middle East media organizations before joining the UN in New York as special assistant to the secretary-general. From 1975 to 1982, he headed the Information Center in Beirut while helping to establish the UN Interim Force in Lebanon. He later headed the network of 78 UN Information Centers around the world. He also served as director of the Department of Public Information's External Relations Division, and as the secretary-general's special representative to oversee the referendum in Eritrea.

Stephen Schlesinger is an adjunct fellow at the Century Foundation in New York City and a former director of the World Policy Institute at the New School. In the early 1970s, he edited and published The New Democrat Magazine. Thereafter, he was a staff writer at Time Magazine, served as Gov. Mario Cuomo's speechwriter and foreign policy adviser and worked at the United Nations at Habitat, the agency dealing with global cities. He is a co-editor of "Journals 1952-2000 by Arthur Schlesinger Jr." and the author of three books: "Act of Creation: The Founding of the United Nations," which won the 2004 Harry S. Truman Book Award; "Bitter Fruit: The Story of the U.S. Coup in Guatemala" (with Stephen Kinzer), which was listed as a New York Times notable book for 1982 and has sold over 100,000 copies; and "The New Reformers." Schlesinger is a frequent contributor to magazines and newspapers, including The Washington Post, The Los Angeles Times, The Nation and The New York Observer.

Courtney B. Smith is associate dean of the John C. Whitehead School of Diplomacy and International Relations at Seton Hall, where he is also an associate professor and director of the UN Intensive Summer Study Program. His teaching and scholarship focus on international organizations, specifically the UN. Smith has published articles or book chapters on global consensus building, Security Council reform, the secretary-general, peacekeeping, the US-UN relationship, the UN Year of Dialogue Among Civilizations, peace-building, human rights and teaching about the UN. His book, "Politics and Process at the United Nations: The Global Dance," has been honored by the Academic Council on the United Nations System and Choice: Current Reviews for Academic Libraries. Smith earned his Ph.D. at Ohio State University.

Abigail Somma is a freelance writer, editor and playwright. She has completed assignments for the UN Development Program; the UN Children's Fund, Unicef, and the World Bank as well as various think tanks and media outlets. She has a master's degree in International Relations and Economics from Johns Hopkins University's School of Advanced International Studies and a bachelor's from Villanova University. Her first play, "Beneath the Hush, a Whisper," is expected to be produced in 2011.

Christopher J. Tangney was the communications assistant in the Publications Department at UNA-USA from 2008 to 2009. Previously, he was an editor and writer at IAG Research and worked in various editorial positions at The Boston Globe. He has a master's degree in applied sociology and a bachelor's in political science from the University of Massachusetts, Boston.

Sarah Trefethen was the online editor of The InterDependent magazine, a UNA-USA publication providing independent news coverage of the United Nations. She holds a master's degree from the City University of New York Graduate School of Journalism, where she specialized in international reporting.

Sir Brian Urquhart was the second person to be recruited for the Secretariat of the Preparatory Commission of the UN after six years of wartime service in the British Army. He was personal assistant to Gladwyn Jebb, the executive secretary of the Preparatory Commission, and then to Trygve Lie, the first secretary-general. From 1954 to 1971, he worked with Ralph Bunche on conflict control, including the organization and direction of peacekeeping operations in the Middle East, Kashmir, Cyprus, Lebanon, Congo and elsewhere. He was also involved in organizing the first and second International Conferences on the Peaceful Uses of Atomic Energy and in setting up the International Atomic

Energy Agency. In 1972, Sir Brian succeeded Ralph Bunche as under secretary-general for special political affairs. He retired from the UN in 1986, and until 1995 was scholar in residence with the international affairs program of the Ford Foundation. His books include "Hammarskjold," "Ralph Bunche: An American Odyssey" and "A Life in Peace and War," a memoir.

Betsy Wade is a freelance editor and writer. She formerly headed the New York Times foreign copy desk, was a news editor in the Times's UN bureau and wrote its Practical Traveler column. She is now a licensed New York City tour guide and co-author of "Opening the Way," a women's history tour of Downtown New York.

Thomas G. Weiss is presidential professor of political science at The City University of New York Graduate Center and director of the Ralph Bunche Institute for International Studies, where he is co-director of the United Nations Intellectual History Project. He was president of the International Studies Association in 2009-2010 and chairman of the Academic Council on the UN System from 2006 to 2009. He also served as research director of the International Commission on Intervention and State Sovereignty and research professor at Brown University's Watson Institute for International Studies. He has written or edited extensively on multilateral approaches to international peace and security, humanitarian action and sustainable development. His essay in this edition of "A Global Agenda" is based on his latest book, "What's Wrong with the United Nations and How to Fix It," published in 2009 by Polity Press.

James Wurst is a veteran journalist on international security issues, having been based at the UN since 1987. He has been a reporter for The InterDependent, UN Wire, Global Security Newswire and the Inter Press Service, and a contributor to the Bulletin of Atomic Scientists, Arms Control Today and In These Times. He is a former editor of Disarmament Times and Disarmament Campaigns, a newsmagazine based in The Hague. He has also worked as a consultant on arms control issues for the Global Security Institute, the Council on Economic Priorities, the Arias Foundation for Peace and Progress, and the Lawyers' Committee on Nuclear Policy. ■

Foreword
Reinventing the United Nations Again?

Sir Brian Urquhart

In its first 65 years, the United Nations has been called many things—"a permanent partnership ... among the peoples of the world for their common peace and common well-being" (President Harry Truman); "ce machin" (Charles de Gaulle), and a "cesspool" (a mayor of New York). In the memoirs of a recent US ambassador to the UN, we find the heading, "There Is No Such Thing as the United Nations." While surviving these and countless other characterizations, the UN has somehow continued to reinvent itself, never to the total satisfaction of anyone. The current demand for reinvention is as pressing as any the organization has faced.

The idea of giving the leaders of the victorious wartime alliance—which had been fighting since 1942 under the collective title "United Nations"—the task, as permanent members of the Security Council, of securing and if necessary enforcing the peace seemed a logical course in 1945. With the onset of the cold war, however, it became a formula for political paralysis. In the next decade, the organization improvised a new method, peacekeeping operations, to contain brushfire conflicts that might otherwise touch off an East-West confrontation. It also provided a forum where the contestants in the ideological and nuclear arms races, the two superpowers, could meet without loss of face even during the most heated crisis, to stave off the ultimate horror of nuclear war.

The UN was the catalyst for decolonization, a process that went much faster than its founders anticipated. Many of the new members that brought the membership from the original 50 to the present 192 were nations that had just gained their independence. Economic and social development became the predominant task of the UN and the specialized agencies and programs that make up the so-called "UN system." Not surprisingly, the new members were intensely protective of their newly acquired sovereignty.

Different War, Different Peace

When the cold war ended, it seemed for a while as if the UN might at last be able to work as its founders had originally intended. However, the nature of both peace and war, as well as the other challenges facing the organization, were sharply different from those that governments thought they were facing in 1945 when the UN Charter was written. The bloody conflicts that the public assumed should be the responsibility of the UN—in former Yugoslavia, Somalia, Cambodia, Sierra Leone and East Timor, for instance—were within the borders of a country rather than between countries.

So-called "global problems"—issues that no government can successfully deal with by itself—were virtually unknown in 1945. Now they include nuclear proliferation, the deterioration of the environment and global warming, international terrorism, pandemics, and a probable future shortage of such necessities as clean water. As a universal organization, the UN should be uniquely suited to provide leadership and to coordinate action on such matters, but the ability of its members to use it as a place to cooperate on dangerous global problems has been limited and disappointing, as was recently shown at the Copenhagen meeting on climate change, where no agreement could be reached going forward.

Since 1946, scarcely a year has gone by without having the subject of UN reform surface in one way or another, and from time to time useful reforms, including the addition of new agencies and programs, have been made. Events have occasionally driven the UN to adopt new principles. The horror of the 1994 Rwandan genocide, for instance, impelled then Secretary-General Kofi Annan to put forward the concept of "responsibility to protect." This concept, cautiously approved in principle by the heads of state summit in 2005, opened a possible door for the international rescue of groups in unbearable misery or under lethal harassment in their own country. (So far, the counter-principle of the primacy of national sovereignty, in places like Zimbabwe or Myanmar, for instance, has kept the door firmly shut.)

Still No Standing Force

Peacekeeping, an improvisation not mentioned in the UN Charter and controversial in its early years, is now universally accepted. More than 120,000 peacekeeping soldiers are at present deployed across four continents, although no progress has been made toward a standing UN rapid deployment force; in an ideal or even rational world, this would be the obvious way to provide for the speedy initial deployment of well-trained troops and civilians in an emergency.

These are major efforts, both conceptual and practical, to deal with the world as it is, and to enable states and international organizations to deal cooperatively with some major problems. At present, however, the UN and its members are still very far from the goal of establishing a stable, peaceful and unthreatened international society in an age of potentially terminal global problems.

It is often said that the UN is becoming marginalized in the affairs of a globalized world. The global threats to the preservation—even the survival—of organized life on the planet demand a much more effective global organization than has hitherto been thought necessary. The UN lives to a considerable extent in a political past where independent national sovereignty was the gold standard of international affairs. What is needed now is to reconcile national sovereignty with the demands of human survival and decency in the astonishingly dangerous world we have absentmindedly created.

If organized life on the planet is indeed seriously threatened by even one of the often cited potential global catastrophes, it would seem reasonable for the member governments of the UN to try to upgrade it to a level at which it could be a leading, even a decisive, factor in managing such problems. If such an effort involves sensitive and fundamental political questions, the stakes are now surely high enough for governments to take that risk. ▧

(This essay first appeared in longer form on May 27, 2010, in The New York Review of Books)

For the 101 peacekeepers
and civilian staff of the UN
and its agencies who
died in the Haiti earthquake

International Security Assistance Force photo

Afghan National Army tanks conduct a road-clearing exercise at the Kabul Military Training Center in September 2009.

Taming Chaos: Strategies for Global Security

2 Rebooting the Global System
Jayantha Dhanapala

4 UN Counterterrorism: A Rising Stock?
James Cockayne

8 In Search of New Momentum on Disarmament
Jayantha Dhanapala

11 Arms Bans: Working Around Weaknesses
Marie Isabelle Chevrier

1

Rebooting the Global System
Jayantha Dhanapala

In the two decades since the end of the cold war, an enormous opportunity for international peace and security under the United Nations Charter has been squandered. Instead the world has been propelled into a succession of calamities —political, economic and social. This period has been characterized by general rejection of international cooperation as a way to find durable global solutions to global problems.

We now have a unique opportunity to reaffirm multilateralism and global inter-dependence, by recognizing that global security is a blend of military security, development and human rights, and a fusion of international security, national security and human security. This is, in essence, an opportunity to "reboot" the global system and change the narrative of international relations radically. Unless global responses become a common approach, we are likely not only to return to the "Great Games" of the 19th century and the politics of balance of power, but also, more dangerously, to imperil the future of our planet through nuclear anni-hilation or a disaster in the climate, or both.

International cooperation is the key to combating terrorism as a global problem. International politics was dominated by nationalist competition for land and resources until World War II, when the UN was established in hope of eliminating "the scourge of war" and ushering in cooperation for freedom, peace, development and human rights. Today, nationalism has been rekindled, with a multiplicity of ethno-nationalist groups all seeking statehood. This again jeopardizes international cooperation.

Established nations, large and small, continue to defend their national security interests. Dangers arise from the covert support for terrorism by some countries in support of international rivalries or claims for lost territory.

Encouraging groups that use terrorist means—by recognizing them or supply-ing arms—violates global strategies against terrorism, however the encouragement may be disguised. It can also be self-destructive as terrorist groups created for one purpose remake themselves to strike elsewhere, even at their own creators.

Pitfalls of Demand

With globalization, we have consumerism as a very important driver of the inter-national economy. Since the arrival of mass production, consumer demand has grown into a global phenomenon. Demand lubricates markets. The welcome growth of a number of large economies in the South—particularly in Brazil, China, India and South Africa—has empowered their people and led to a demand for increased energy supplies and other commodities, bringing a rise in prices. However, the "bottom billion" continue to be left behind and the Millennium Development Goals remain a mirage. We are no longer able to continue using fos-sil fuels to satisfy world consumer demands. The reports of the Intergovernmental

Panel on Climate Change irrefutably argued that case. To ignore them would be supreme folly.

But the case against the carbon fuels is leading to a fresh demand for nuclear energy—the "nuclear renaissance." Article IV of the Nuclear Non-Proliferation Treaty guarantees that countries without nuclear weapons will have an "inalienable right" to use nuclear energy peacefully. But the world has awakened to the perils of this promise, both in terms of proliferation of weapons and the need to keep nuclear materials and facilities out of terrorist hands, unless nuclear weapons are outlawed globally and eliminated verifiably.

The fusing of the crises facing the world is increasingly evident. Nuclear-weapon proliferation arises largely from the demand for national security in a world where each country can define its own national security interests. Climate change continues to be caused by global consumption patterns and can be remedied only through intense cooperation in converting to new sources of energy and a fair-minded remaking of rules on international trade that currently favor wealthy nations and restrict the access of developing nations to world markets.

Ultimately, the response must be through multilateralism—effective and cooperative multilateralism with the UN at its epicenter. ▓

US Marine Corps photo/Cpl. Andres Escatel

A US marine fires a Javelin anti-armor missile at a Taliban position near Marja, Afghanistan, in February 2010, during an operation to clear Taliban fighters from the town.

UN Counterterrorism: A Rising Stock?

James Cockayne

In the almost 10 years since the attacks of Sept. 11, 2001, multilateralism has increasingly become accepted as a useful approach to counterterrorism. United Nations bodies have long played a key role in global counterterrorism efforts.

The General Assembly has for decades served as the forum for negotiating counterterrorism agreements; it has produced 16 universal legal instruments, including conventions governing problems from aerial hijacking to terrorist financing, as well as the 2006 Global Counter-Terrorism Strategy. Its work continues with painstaking effort on a comprehensive convention on international terrorism. This 17th instrument, however, is stalled over differences on a definition of terrorism and it seems unlikely to be concluded any time soon.

The Security Council has also sought to limit support for international terrorism, imposing sanctions on Libya in 1992, Sudan in 1996, and the Taliban and Al Qaeda in 1999. This culminated in the creation of global strategies governing national efforts to combat terrorism, its incitement, and the proliferation of weapons of mass destruction. The UN's operational agencies, notably the Office on Drugs and Crime, have also long been active in this field, helping countries develop counterterrorism abilities.

Yet for years after 9/11, a cloud of antagonism hung over these activities. The extensive reporting requirements set by the council were viewed with particular skepticism, if not outright hostility, by many developing countries that saw them as unwarranted, over-reaching and unnecessarily burdensome intrusions into their sovereign territory. At times the council and the assembly seemed to be traveling on separate tracks, rather than pushing in the same direction. And human rights proponents—supported increasingly by decisions of regional and national courts—voiced deep concern about whether the council's terrorist listing and delisting procedures adequately respected the rights of the people involved.

These clouds now seem to be lifting. While this may appear to coincide with the start of the Barack Obama administration, which has abandoned polarizing terminology such as "Global War on Terror" and expressed enthusiasm for pragmatic multilateralism, this momentum has been building over a longer time. The evolution of the UN's counterterrorism agenda has been steady, if subtle, over the last decade.

The Security Council's Counter-Terrorism Committee, established in 2001, created an executive directorate in 2004. After a slow start getting staffed and operational, in the last three years or so the directorate, and a second council committee set up to help prevent the spread of nuclear, biological and chemical weapons, have been working to make their deliberations more transparent. They hold regular briefings for UN members, offering countries earlier assessments of how well they are fulfilling their counterterrorism obligations, making greater use of their Web sites and scheduling frequent field visits.

In December 2009, the Security Council adopted important reforms to the Al Qaeda and Taliban delisting process, creating a post for an independent ombudsman to help give listed individuals a voice in the council's deliberations. Canadian Judge Kimberly Prost was appointed to the position in June 2010. And there are strong signs of improved coordination between the Counter-Terrorism Executive Directorate and other UN bodies working in this area, through joint country visits and collaboration in specialized working groups. These working groups are organized under the UN's Counter-Terrorism Implementation Task Force, set up to carry out the General Assembly's strategy. This task force was in turn boosted by the creation in 2009 of a support office in the UN Secretariat's Department of Political Affairs.

Overall, the UN's counterterrorism efforts have moved to a more cooperative footing. There has been a subtle but important shift towards more collaborative approaches in deliberations and programming, with the UN increasingly comfortable bringing together disparate groups to tailor solutions to particular challenges.

Legitimacy through Cooperation?

This spirit of cooperation means there will be little appetite for major reform when the Counter-Terrorism Executive Directorate and the Global Counter-Terrorism Strategy are reviewed in 2010. Any reforms are likely to be incremental: how to strengthen further the legitimacy of the UN's work in this area, through further improvements in transparency, protection of human rights, and efficiency; how best to foster common responses to threats and conditions that may encourage terrorism; and how to deal with connections between terrorism and other transnational threats such as drug-trafficking.

One priority will be strengthening cooperation between the UN membership and the council's various counterterrorism bodies. There may be a push for regular briefings for members, or for closer cooperation with ad hoc groupings of countries, for example, regional and donor groups, on specific projects.

There is recurring support for streamlining reporting requirements and encouraging information-sharing among the council's counterterrorism bodies. There are also continuing appeals to the council to affirm more clearly the central role of human rights in counterterrorism. These might result in UN approval for additional human rights positions or council approval of more ombudsmen, particularly if ombudswoman Prost's tenure is widely seen as a success. There may also be consideration of some informal way for the General Assembly and the Security Council to consult on how best to carry out the global strategy in specific cases.

Attention will also increasingly move from discussion to implementation. Both governments and outside experts will want evidence that the UN's efforts are strengthening governments' capacities to do the job. As a result, the main counterterrorism bodies are likely to emphasize more strongly assessing—and facilitating—operational activities, such as cross-border law enforcement cooperation and regional efforts to repair the conditions in which terrorism flourishes. Given their limited operational capacity, these bodies will work more and more closely with external partners: civic and religious groups, the private sector, regional organizations, specialized agencies such as the International Maritime Organization and the World Customs Organization, and UN agencies dealing with matters ranging from development aid and human rights to education and refugee assistance.

Joint responses will increasingly become the order of the day. Already, there is evidence of a trend in this direction, with the Implementation Task Force in 2008 establishing a working group to help countries (currently Madagascar and Nigeria) carry out the global strategy within their borders. This is UN counterterrorism's version of the "Delivering as One" initiative encouraging greater cross-agency coordination.

Promoting Rule of Law

As UN efforts move in this direction, some may ask how they differ from projects to improve governmental capacity in other areas. Privately, some officials answer: "Not much." The truth is that in many quarters, "counterterrorism assistance" is more easily provided if it is delivered under some other label. That makes it no less effective. In fact, there are already signs that UN efforts in counterterrorism will increasingly be framed as part of a broader response to a range of transnational threats emerging in areas where the rule of law is weak.

For example, Security Council statements issued on Dec. 8, 2009, and Feb. 24, 2010, called on the secretary-general to focus routinely, in all UN peace-building and conflict-prevention efforts, on such transnational threats as terrorism, corruption and illegal trafficking. These statements reflect growing concern on the part of the UN membership that criminal and terrorist networks flourish in zones of conflict and instability where the rule of law is particularly weak. In Afghanistan, the UN is confronting an insurgency and terrorist activity that is clearly sustained by an entrenched opium economy sustained by governmental corruption. In western and north-central Africa, there are growing signs that Al Qaeda offshoots are becoming entwined in a regional economy that incubates the smuggling of drugs, humans, oil and weapons, with sidelines in kidnapping and extortion—and military coups. And the fragmented economy of the Horn of Africa is increasingly penetrated by transnational criminal and terrorist networks profiting financially and politically from piracy, extortion and smuggling.

UN responses to these situations seem increasingly to be based on efforts to promote the rule of law, often through tools that have much in common with those used in counterterrorism. In response to terrorist attacks in Lebanon, Baghdad and Pakistan, the UN has supported international investigations. In Guatemala, the UN has supported an International Commission Against Impunity, which is working with Guatemalan prosecutors and the police to unravel the grip on Guatemalan politics of clandestine criminal networks, financed by transnational drug trafficking.

To deal with piracy off the coast of Somalia, the UN has backed a contact group of concerned nations and specialized agencies, including the International Maritime Organization and the UN Office on Drugs and Crime, which helps coordinate military, law enforcement and public-information responses. In West Africa, parts of the UN—including its peacekeeping department—are building transnational crime units. And throughout Africa, UN sanctions bodies are tracking illicit cross-border transactions that sustain conflict economies.

Shaping Strategy

Developing these tools, and finding ways to help them work together, will take on an increased urgency through 2010 and 2011, as resistance to the UN's traditional conflict-management tools—especially the pushback against consensual peacekeeping currently being led by Sudan, the Central African Republic and the Democratic Republic of Congo—forces the UN to look for new, lighter-footprint configurations for its conflict-management work. This will lead to an increased reliance on the kinds of tools the UN has developed in recent years in the context of counterterrorism: sanctions, listing, and especially technical assistance and initiatives to strengthen the rule of law.

Maintaining strategic clarity as these tools develop may prove difficult: the components are scattered among numerous UN agencies, each responding to different governance arrangements. Three potential solutions seem possible.

First, there may be a need for stronger strategic direction—both in specific cases, and to guide the system-wide development of these tools—from senior levels of the UN. There is already a mechanism that might be adapted to this purpose —the Rule of Law Coordination and Resource Group, chaired by the deputy secretary-general. But such an adaptation would mark a significant change. At present, that group serves more as an information-exchange mechanism than a strategy-setting body. Consideration of these issues within the secretary-general's Policy Committee may also be warranted, as this could establish common policies for dealing with these issues across the UN Secretariat.

Second, consolidation of the disparate sources of UN assistance on the rule of law—now scattered across numerous agencies—into one stand-alone office may gather support in time. Needless to say, such a proposal would be highly controversial both within the organization and amongst the membership, as agencies sometimes act as competitive rivals rather than harmonious partners.

Third, members might choose to use the Rule of Law Coordination and Resource Group, or some other body, as a vehicle for steering and perhaps also carrying out large-scale assistance projects through a pooled fund, like those increasingly favored in the development, health and humanitarian assistance spheres.

Whichever—if any—of these options emerge in time, the emphasis on the UN's counterterrorism and related efforts seems likely to be increasingly on its ability to bring together a range of interested parties to assess assistance needs and then match supply to demand. This is indeed the direction things are already heading. That promises an approach to terrorism more explicitly based on the promotion of rule of law and less explicitly on "counterterrorism," which now seems a loaded term. Almost a decade after 9/11, that is none too soon. ▧

In Search of New Momentum on Disarmament

Jayantha Dhanapala

The regulation of conventional weapons is fundamental in the United Nations Charter. Barely six weeks after the founding document was signed, nuclear weapons were used on Hiroshima and Nagasaki. Thereafter, the first resolution of the UN General Assembly, in January 1946, called for the elimination of weapons of mass destruction and this too has been a goal of the UN ever since.

Twenty years after the end of the cold war, nine countries have nuclear arsenals. The five permanent Security Council members—Britain, China, France, Russia and the United States—are recognized as nuclear-weapon states in the context of the Nuclear Nonproliferation Treaty, which came into force in 1970. The four others with nuclear weapons—India, Israel, Pakistan and North Korea—remain outside the treaty. Among the nine are a total of 23,300 nuclear weapons, 95 percent in US or Russian hands.

A new momentum for nuclear disarmament has developed as a result of a 2007-2008 appeal by four US elder statesmen: two former Secretaries of State, George P. Shultz and Henry A. Kissinger, a former Secretary of Defense, William J. Perry, and a former Senate Armed Services Committee Chairman, Sam Nunn. They pressed for a world free of nuclear weapons, a call endorsed around the world and now, significantly, by President Obama. A new US-Russian Strategic Arms Reduction Treaty has been signed and a US nuclear-posture review announced, with a reduced role for nuclear weapons and restricted possibilities for use. In addition, a nuclear security summit meeting has been held with specific commitments to safeguard materials and facilities.

Toward a Nuclear-Free Middle East

With this improved political climate, the 2010 Nuclear Nonproliferation Treaty Review Conference in May adopted a final document by consensus aimed at strengthening all three of the treaty's pillars—nonproliferation, disarmament and peaceful uses of nuclear energy—through a 64-point action plan. Diplomats attending the month-long meeting also agreed to convene a conference in 2012 to negotiate a Middle East region free of weapons of mass destruction. With delegates from Iran, Cuba, Venezuela, Libya, the five permanent Security Council members and the countries of NATO and the European Union all in the room, consensus was no mean achievement.

The Charter concept of a collective and integrated security contrasts with the weapons-based security on which most military doctrines and national strategies are based. As a consequence, global military spending in 2009 totaled $1.5 trillion, according to the Stockholm International Peace Research Institute, of which the Security Council's five permanent members accounted for 61.1 percent. At the very least, security must be achieved at the lowest possible levels of arms spending.

Targeting Conventional Arms

A timely proposal, originally made by a group of Nobel Peace Prize laureates, for an arms-trade treaty to bind countries to common standards in regulating the arms trade, has made progress and is being negotiated in an open-ended working group, with a conference to agree on a treaty scheduled for 2012. UN mechanisms encouraging countries to register their conventional arms transfers and disclose their annual military budgets, laudable as they are, remain voluntary and participation is by no means universal.

Major differences in levels of conventional weapons are causing deep insecurity. Parallel drives to regulate or restrict both weapons of mass destruction and conventional arms are needed. Precision guided missiles and other advanced

Secretary-General Ban Ki-moon meeting with Goodluck Ebele Jonathan, then acting president of Nigeria, now president, at the Nuclear Security Summit in April 2010 in Washington. The summit, hosted by President Obama, brought participation by over 40 nations.

weapons have not, ironically, reduced the mistakes made on battlefields and the number of civilian deaths. The Conventional Armed Forces in Europe Treaty, which set ceilings for air and land forces, also needs to be revisited and reductions in conventional weapons should be negotiated in areas of tension.

The proliferation of small arms and light weapons is an area in which the UN has taken the lead. Progress in carrying out a program of action adopted in 2001, which was intended to end the illegal trade in these arms, will be reviewed this year for the fourth time in nine years. The size of the problem is visible in a handful of statistics: The global small arms trade is valued at $5 billion a year, one fifth of it illicit; 640 million small arms are in circulation, enough for one weapon for every 10 people on earth; 8 million new guns are manufactured every year by at least 1,249 companies in 92 countries, and 10 to 14 billion units of ammunition are made each year, enough to kill every person in the world twice over.

The 1997 convention to ban antipersonnel land mines and the 2008 convention to ban cluster munitions resulted from a rare coalition of civic groups and nations. They quickly entered into force. Two additional areas in which the UN must now register progress are in missiles and space.

Missiles are essentially vehicles for weapons and not in themselves weapons. The absence of rules governing their production and use has led to their proliferation. UN expert groups have produced studies on this problem without arriving at a consensus on going forward because of conflicting interests of nations. At a minimum the UN must adopt measures aimed at easing tensions, building on the 2002 Hague Code of Conduct Against Ballistic Missile Proliferation.

Ballistic missile defense systems—once hailed as "star wars" mechanisms—have now been limited to theater missile defense systems but they remain an irritant and are likely to provoke a new arms race, consuming vast resources.

On space, the "last frontier," which is militarized but not yet weaponized, UN efforts to prevent an arms race remain inconclusive.

Disarmament and peace education, on which the Secretary-General's Advisory Board on Disarmament Matters has done admirable work resulting in a UN study and a General Assembly resolution, remain hamstrung by lack of resources. Disarmament must ultimately receive support at the grassroots level. Education is crucial to replace a culture of weapons and violence with a new culture of peace and disarmament. That is where activists and public interest groups must step in. ▪

Arms Bans: Working Around Weaknesses

Marie Isabelle Chevrier

Many international agreements seek to outlaw entire classes of weapons. The Biological Weapons Convention, the Chemical Weapons Convention, the Protocol on Blinding Laser Weapons, the Mine Ban Treaty and the Cluster Munitions Treaty require the ratifying governments to destroy existing stockpiles of specified armaments and pledge never again to produce, acquire, retain or transfer such weapons.

These treaties are in contrast to the nuclear arms control treaties limiting nuclear forces or, in the case of the Nuclear Nonproliferation Treaty, creating a bargain between nations that have nuclear weapons and those that have vowed not to acquire them. Despite the grand scope of these treaties, each has weaknesses that enable some countries committed to them to skirt obligations. All face the problem of countries that remain outside the treaty.

Biological Arms: Who's Complying?

The Biological and Toxin Weapons Convention, which entered into force in 1975, was the first international treaty to outlaw a class of weapons. Biological weapons include any consisting of disease-causing bacteria or viruses, while toxin weapons involve the action of poisons produced by living substances. Sidestepping arguments that possessing biological or toxin weapons could improve a nation's security, the countries embracing the treaty describe their use as "repugnant to the conscience of mankind."

Nevertheless, the cold war origins of the treaty, its wholesale violation by the former Soviet Union and the failure of 1995-2001 negotiations to strengthen the treaty have kept it from ensuring that nations are not making such weapons clandestinely. The convention has been ratified by just 163 of the 192 United Nations members, fewer than have joined the treaties on nuclear proliferation and chemical arms. And enforcement has been lackluster, since there is no mechanism for on-site verification of its requirements; calls for governments to act with greater transparency have often been ignored. Indeed, fewer than half of the convention's members have complied with the membership's call for annual declarations describing their biodefense programs and national capacities in the biological sciences.

Because the US in 2001 aborted negotiations to add compliance measures to the treaty, its parties have been meeting annually since 2002 to discuss how it is working and how to improve it. Governments will have an opportunity at a conference in 2011 to consider steps to make it more effective and increase its reach. Initial discussions among governments, academics and other interested groups have proposed updating the annual declarations and expanding the duties of the three-person unit created to help governments fulfill the treaty's obligations. This unit processes and disseminates the annual declarations, coordinates assistance among treaty parties, works to increase treaty membership and provides other administrative support. New duties could include helping countries carry out the convention and analyzing their declarations. Canada has proposed that members get together on a regular basis to describe how they have met the responsibilities imposed by the treaty.

Chemical Weapons: Destroying Stockpiles

The 1993 Chemical Weapons Convention outlaws the development and possession of chemical weapons. The Organization for the Prohibition of Chemical Weapons, an independent international organization that works with the UN, is responsible for carrying out the convention, including verifying the destruction of declared stockpiles, and weapon-production facilities. The organization also inspects facilities capable of weapon production and assists countries in carrying out the treaty. Just seven countries—Angola, North Korea, Egypt, Israel, Myanmar, Somalia and Syria—still have not joined it. Nevertheless, the crucial goal of achieving a universal commitment to rejection of all chemical weapons has yet to be achieved.

While the pace of destruction has picked up recently, Russia and the United States are unlikely to destroy successfully their entire chemical agent stockpiles by 2012, the deadline set by the treaty. According to the Organization for the Prohibition of Chemical Weapons, more than 57 percent of the declared global stockpile had been destroyed as of Jan. 31, 2010. Destruction of munitions, the devices that carry and disperse the chemicals, has been slower and there are concerns that existing munitions could be refilled with banned chemicals if they are not destroyed. Governments are likely to disagree on a response if the 2012 destruction deadline is missed.

In December 2009, a coalition of disarmament groups and other interested private organizations launched the Chemical Weapons Convention Coalition in The Hague. Modeled in part after similar coalitions that campaigned for bans on land mines and cluster bombs, the group said its mission was to achieve "the safe and timely elimination of all chemical weapons, preventing the misuse of chemicals for hostile purposes and promoting their peaceful use."

Land Mines and Cluster Bombs

The conventions banning land mines and cluster munitions—deadly weapons consisting of clusters of bomblets that break apart when they explode—represent a new approach to disarmament. They were adopted on the principle that these weapons cause unacceptable harm to civilians, while previous treaties were based on the extent to which weapons limitations or disarmament contributed to a country's security. Moreover, both of these treaties were negotiated using a new strategy. Countries supporting the treaty held meetings and invited only countries and other advocacy groups specifically in favor of banning these weapons. Consequently, progress could not be halted by countries that were opposed to eliminating these weapons.

The mine ban treaty, in force since 1999, was widely celebrated around the world but is weakened because many influential countries are among the 37 that have not yet ratified. The United States, however, is reconsidering its refusal. The

US did not sign the treaty originally, in part because of the extensive use of mines along the border between North and South Korea. Recently, however, 68 US Senators, more than enough to secure Senate ratification of the treaty, have urged President Obama to agree to the terms of the ban. During its first 11 years, more than 44 million landmines have been destroyed. Clearing existing mines has led to fewer casualties, and fewer landmines are in use. Jordan, for example, has been clearing mines along its border with Israel, in part because Queen Noor has championed the ban.

The treaty calls for its members to assist people who have been injured by landmines. Such assistance, however, has fallen short of expectations. When financing has been available it has been used mainly for medical care and physical rehabilitation rather than promoting economic self-reliance and social integration of the injured into their communities.

Israel used cluster bombs extensively in its 2006 war with Hezbollah in Lebanon. At the time, Israel argued that their use conformed to international humanitarian law. Israel's rationale for the use of cluster bombs angered countries that opposed all use of these weapons and drove them to draft a treaty banning their use, manufacture, possession and transfer. The Cluster Munitions Treaty was completed in 2008 and is scheduled to enter into force in 2010. So far 109 nations have signed it.

Taken together the momentum behind these pacts has moved beyond a focus on weapons of potential mass destruction to encompass weapons such as landmines and cluster munitions that disproportionately kill and injure civilians. Yet much remains on the agenda. Trade in arms, especially small arms that cause such destruction in regional conflicts and civil wars, remains a controversial topic. Ending the production of the raw material for nuclear bombs is also under consideration. During the last fifty years nations have committed themselves to arms control and disarmament measures that would have been unthinkable in the first half of the 20th century. Momentum is in place to continue this progress towards a safer world. ▪

**Private Linda Mensah
of Ghana patrols the city
of Buchanan, Liberia,
in April 2009. Mensah
is one of 41 women in
a Ghanaian battalion
participating in the UN
mission in Liberia.**

The Trials and Errors of Modern Peacekeeping

16 Peacekeeping Boom: Here to Stay?
Jean-Marie Guéhenno

20 Congo to UN: Time Is Running Out
Hélène Gandois

26 Haiti Quake Smashed 20 Years' Progress, While Revealing It Was Paper-Thin
Nathanial Gronewold

29 The Middle East: What Can the UN Do?
Samir Sanbar

32 A Weak Link in a Chain of Responsibility
Sarah Trefethen

35 Women Peacekeepers: Not Tokens but Essential Workers
Veronica Haglund

37 Given a Single Purpose, Peacekeepers Find Other Tragedies They Can't Confront
Shin-wha Lee

Peacekeeping Boom: Here to Stay?

Jean-Marie Guéhenno

United Nations peacekeepers are on patrol in four continents, with a budget of $8 billion and more than 120,000 personnel—troops, police officers and civilians—deployed. This marks the peak level of activity for UN peacekeeping. Can we be confident that the UN has entered a new phase and that peacekeeping has become an accepted and important instrument in the toolbox of international peace and security?

UN peacekeeping is undoubtedly on more solid footing than it was at the end of the 1990s, as the institution struggled to recover from failure to halt the tragedies of Yugoslavia and Rwanda. In 2000, a landmark report by a panel led by Lakhdar Brahimi, the chief UN troubleshooter under several UN secretaries-general, laid the foundations for the renewal of peacekeeping, setting clear principles and recommending a significant increase in the resources committed to it.

Expectations were however for a modest and cautious growth, not the quadrupling of deployed personnel that followed, which makes by contrast the concurrent doubling of headquarters staff look modest indeed. This extraordinary comeback of UN peacekeeping raises big questions.

In many places, peacekeepers make a huge difference, as we see in Haiti, where the international recovery effort would be impossible without the efforts of the UN peacekeeping mission there. And yet, in other missions, from Darfur to the Democratic Republic of Congo, peacekeepers seem to be struggling. Does that mean that the present boom will be inevitably followed by another bust, as was the case in the '90s?

Peacekeeping is a barometer of the climate of the international system, and the quality of the response it provides to evolving challenges is largely a function of the degree of harmony in the international community. During the cold war, peacekeeping generally remained at a low level, but played a useful role in preventing local crises from escalating. The world is today less divided, which has made possible a considerable expansion of the activities of the Security Council. But the growing number of civil wars and other internal conflicts has created new challenges for the UN. As peacekeepers have been called upon to support fragile peace processes in countries devastated by civil war, it creates a controversial role requiring new answers. The ability of the international community to forge a consensus on dealing with civil wars is critical to the future of peacekeeping. Three challenges need to be addressed.

Gray Area

The first challenge is operational. As peacekeepers are deployed in the aftermath of civil wars, the mantra of peacekeeping—"no peacekeepers where there is no peace to keep"—is a central issue. The distinction between war and peace that is applied to conflicts between states loses its clarity in internal conflicts, where the actors are militias and rebel groups with uncertain chains of command or fluid contours.

Peacekeepers increasingly operate in a gray area between war and peace. Sometimes major actors have signed a peace agreement, but spoilers remain to challenge that agreement. Whether spoilers can be deterred through a show of force, or even a robust but limited use of force is difficult to judge, blurring the traditional separation between peacekeeping and peace enforcement.

At the same time, the range of activities expected from peacekeepers is expanding. Crucially, they are often expected to protect civilians in unsettled situations. The gap grows ever larger between the available resources and what a professional military would normally require to provide effective protection. The risks increase for forces that are expected to be more pro-active and mobile. Night patrols in dangerous areas, deployment in precarious mobile operating bases and urban warfare against gangs have in several missions become normal peacekeeping tasks.

But the peacekeepers often lack the abilities required to perform such tasks effectively and with manageable risks. The better-resourced forces of the most developed countries are absent from the most difficult operations. Developing nations, which continue to provide the bulk of peacekeeping troops, resent it that three of the five permanent members of the Security Council—France, Britain and the United States—appear willing to adopt increasingly ambitious and risky mandates, but are reluctant to contribute soldiers to the task.

The lack of significant troop deployments from developed countries—with the notable exception of Lebanon—reflects in part those countries' overstretched armies, and in part a lack of confidence in UN command and control. These issues need to be addressed to reverse the trend towards an ever-widening gap between resources and needs.

Coherence Is Crucial

The second challenge is institutional. In a country recovering from civil war, peacekeepers can provide a vestige of security, but re-establishing trust among the people, as well as between the people and the institutions of the state, requires a much broader effort. Peace-building has to accompany peacekeeping; the security provided by peacekeepers will be short-lived if the police are not transformed and there is no credible system of justice.

Basic public services need to be restored or created, the economy needs to be energized and jobs need to be provided. Thousands of young men have just disarmed, and they will go back to war if they have no prospect of making a living.

In recent years, the UN has responded to this new challenge by deploying "integrated peacekeeping operations." Under the leadership of the secretary-general's special representative, these missions are expected to harness all the resources of the UN system. But the UN's institutional arrangements are based on a clear separation between the Security Council, the 15-member body responsible for peace and security, and the General Assembly, where each of the 192 UN members has a seat. The creation of the peace-building commission is an attempt to bridge that divide.

Meanwhile, agencies, funds and programs as well as bilateral donors pursue their own priorities. There are inevitable and legitimate tensions between the priorities of a peacekeeping agenda driven by political deadlines, the apolitical approach of humanitarian workers and the longer-term priorities of development.

The varying sources of funds further undermines the coherence of international efforts. While paying for peacekeeping is an obligation of UN members, peace-building efforts largely depend on voluntary contributions, which often reflect the members' diverging priorities. In the absence of institutional reform, an integrated approach effectively combining peacekeeping and peace-building remains dangerously dependent on ad hoc arrangements.

The third challenge is political. As noted, the UN is an organization of states respectful of their sovereignty. Such cardinal principles of peacekeeping as impartiality and consent of the parties reflect respect for the principle of sovereignty, but they were elaborated when peacekeeping was a response to conflicts between states.

Hospitality—or Hostility?

What happens in an internal conflict? Does impartiality mean equidistance between the authorities of the state and rebel groups? Or should the peacekeepers become the auxiliary of the new authority emerging from a peace accord? Is the role of the peacekeepers to help press to the margins those who challenge the institutions of a state emerging from conflict, or is it to help broaden the political base of the state by drawing challengers in?

Should the international community try to take an active role in such issues as economic governance, as it does in Liberia with the Governance and Economic Management Assistance Program, the vetting of police officers, as it did in Bosnia, or the political implications of a reform of the security services? There is no one answer to such questions.

But as peacekeeping mandates become more ambitious, and peacekeeping missions more intrusive, host countries increasingly challenge them, sometimes signaling in no uncertain terms that the UN has overstayed its welcome, as Chad and Congo have recently done.

Meanwhile, there is little agreement among key countries on an expanded definition of peacekeeping, and therefore little support from the Security Council when missions are challenged by the government of the country peacekeepers have come to help. While the international community can agree on the overall goal of stabilization, there is no consensus on what constitutes stabilization.

For instance, is consolidation of the rule of law a critical element? The creation in 2007, in the Department of Peacekeeping Operations, of an Office of Rule of Law and Security Institutions may signal an emerging consensus. But there is still a wide range of views on the practical implications of a rule-of-law priority, and there are conflicting interpretations of what respect for sovereignty means.

Some countries in the West accept that preservation of an international system based on the sovereignty of states may in some circumstances require active and sometimes intrusive support from the international community to fragile states that lack the capacity to exercise their sovereignty effectively. But many other countries, among them China, are wary of such engagement. The complex peacekeeping operations that have been launched in recent years may face growing difficulties unless a genuine and more substantive consensus is forged on their ambitions and on the posture of the UN in fragile states recovering from conflict.

Will the international community rise to the challenges it faces? Morality and good strategic sense should point to a positive answer. Civil wars generate immense suffering, and UN peacekeepers are often the best hope for helping countries escape an otherwise never-ending cycle of violence. And in a globalized world, the despair of people who see no end to their misery can have dangerous consequences leading to terrorism.

For centuries, states have defined security as the defense of their borders, and national security has been about balancing power with power. In a world in which nation-states remain the primary providers of security, but in which threats are becoming transnational, weak states can become as much of a threat as aggressive power.

The rapid growth of peacekeeping reflects that new awareness, but national security systems have not yet adjusted. The political support and material resources provided by the international community are not commensurate with the heavy responsibilities it has conferred on peacekeeping. It is now urgent to create a consensus on what is expected from peacekeeping, and to support those ambitions with adequate resources. ■

For a detailed look at UN peacekeeping costs, please see Appendix Table 2 on P. 148. For information on ongoing peacekeeping missions, please see the chart on P. 182. For a chart showing which countries contribute the most money to the peacekeeping budget, please see the chart on P. 184. For information on which countries provide the most peacekeeping troops, observers and police, please see the chart on P. 185.

Congo to UN: Time Is Running Out

Hélène Gandois

The Democratic Republic of Congo, host since 1999 to what has become the world's largest peacekeeping operation, surprised the United Nations late in 2009 with a push to phase out the United Nations mission and restore full power in the country to its own military and government.

However, the plea by President Joseph Kabila for the UN to begin withdrawing troops by June 30, 2010—the 50th anniversary of Congo's independence from Belgium—quickly ran into resistance from the Security Council.

In December 2009, the council, while renewing the mission's mandate for just five months rather than the usual year, said much remained to be done before a drawdown would be possible "without triggering a relapse into instability."

The government, arguing that the situation was sufficiently improved after more than a decade of UN help, asked the council in March 2010 to wrap up its peace-keeping mission entirely by August 2011. The council partially heeded the govern-ment's request, ordering the withdrawal of 2,000 of the mission's 20,000 troops by June 2010 and transforming the remaining peacekeepers into a stabilization force with a mandate to stay in the country until June 2011 unless renewed.

The UN launched its intervention in 1999, a year after the start of a five-year war in Congo that eventually became known as "Africa's first world war." Before it ended in 2003, the conflict pulled in nine African nations and numerous militias, both foreign and domestic, driving an estimated total of 3.4 million people from their homes and killing 5.4 million people, in combat, or by starva-tion and disease.

Although the fighting largely subsided after the civil war ended, sporadic vio-lence has continued, particularly in some remote parts of the mineral-rich eastern Congo. The UN mission, whose name was changed in July 2010 to Monusco—the acronym for its French title, la Mission de l'Organisation des Nations Unies pour la Stabilisation en République Démocratique du Congo—had grown over the years to a force of more than 20,000 troops and with a $1.3 billion budget. The mission has been focusing in recent years on protecting civilians against armed groups terrorizing the east, including the Hutu-dominated Democratic Forces for the Liberation of Rwanda, whose leaders have been incriminated in the 1994 Rwandan genocide, and the Lord's Resistance Army, a Ugandan rebel group noto-rious for its brutality—slaughtering of whole villages and sexual enslavement of women and children.

The mission has worked with Congo's army in trying to hunt down these armed groups, but the fighters of the Lord's Resistance Army—roaming freely between Congo, the Central African Republic and Sudan—and Rwanda rebels have proved elusive enemies. The US-based Human Rights Watch charged in March 2010 that 321 people were massacred in a Resistance Army attack in Congo's remote north-east in December. And John Holmes, the UN emergency relief coordinator, said in

May that the UN was investigating reports of a Resistance Army slaying of 100 people in the same area in February.

The mission's work has been complicated by a large presence of former rebels accused of human rights violations and war crimes in the Congolese army. But overall, the situation in Congo improved with the organization of free and fair elections in 2006, better relations with neighbors that had intervened in the country in the past and greater success in getting some rebel soldiers to put down arms and return to civilian life.

Preparation of a responsible exit strategy acceptable to both Congo's government and the Security Council will be a major challenge for this mission, as the UN is well aware that there will be no stability in Central Africa without a stable Congo, and no stability in Congo without a stable Central Africa.

West Africa: Moving Away from War

Large expanses of West Africa, devastated by political disorder and civil wars that spilled over into neighboring countries, have become more stable in recent years with the help of concerted international intervention, military and political reforms and attempts to contain illegal drug trading, arms smuggling and the illicit diversion of valuable resources such as diamonds, lumber and crops. As a result, Liberia, Sierra Leone, and Côte d'Ivoire have been able, to varying extents, to start putting conflict and instability behind them.

In Liberia, the wounds of two civil wars that raged from 1989 until 2003, claiming the lives of nearly 250,000 and leaving a million people homeless, are slowly starting to heal. The release in 2004 of the final report of the country's Truth and Reconciliation Commission, which investigated gross human rights violations from 1979 to 2003, has helped Liberians to look to the future.

The UN Mission in Liberia, which assumed peacekeeping duties in 2003 from the forces of the Economic Community of West African States, is gradually drawing down although no end date is in sight. In September 2009, the Security Council extended the mission's mandate for a year and asked the mission to help Liberia with its 2011 presidential and legislative elections. Free and fair elections are a core condition for the mission's departure.

The current government has established a democracy and greatly stepped up efforts to fight the corruption endemic when Charles Taylor was president. He was forced to resign in 2003 and is now on trial on charges of war crimes, in a special tribunal in The Hague. Under President Ellen Johnson Sirleaf, Liberia has also made important progress in safeguarding its natural resources, the main source of its wealth. But it still faces significant security challenges in battling a continuing illegal trade in arms, timber and diamonds. Its economic challenges remain staggering, given its 85 percent unemployment rate and war-ravaged infrastructure.

For decades a beacon of stability in West Africa, Côte d'Ivoire was plunged into protracted civil strife after the death in 1993 of its founding leader, Félix Houphouët-Boigny. The political struggle escalated into civil war in 2002 when rebel soldiers attacked military installations in the official capital, Yamoussoukro, and in Bouaké, the second largest city of the country, ostensibly to protest against their planned demobilization in early 2003, but most likely in an attempted coup. The fighting soon divided the country into a rebel-held north and a government-controlled south. A UN peacekeeping mission, known by the initials Unoci, for the French title of UN Operations in Côte d'Ivoire, has since 2004 been working with the West African regional group and French troops stationed in the country to avoid any resumption of conflict, to help return soldiers to civilian life and hold elections.

The holding of elections has proved to be the main difficulty since 2002. Elections have repeatedly been scheduled and postponed, leading to a succession of peace deals. The latest accord, reached in 2007 in Ouagadougou, Burkina Faso, tried to address some of the root causes of the civil war, seeking, for example, to improve the conditions of military service and to specify what it means to be an Ivoirian citizen in a country with a large and enduring presence of foreign workers. Laurent Gbagbo, who became president in 2000 and remains in power though his term officially ended in 2005, postponed elections once again in February this year when he dissolved the government and the Independent Electoral Commission and set no new date for balloting. The country's seeming inability to hold elections appears to rule out an end any time soon to the UN peacekeeping effort.

For Sudan, a Pivotal Year

Since its independence, Sudan has suffered two civil wars between the central government and the oil-rich South, each as bloody as today's crisis in the western region of Darfur. The North-South conflict, which killed over 2 million people and left 4.6 million homeless, pitted Christian rebels against the Muslim-dominated central government in a fight over oil, land and political control. In 2005, a peace agreement was signed promising democratization of Sudan and an equitable distribution of oil revenues between North and South. The UN deployed a peacekeeping mission to support the enforcement of this agreement, provide humanitarian assistance and promote human rights. A crucial milestone falls in January 2011, when the South is scheduled to vote in a referendum on whether to remain a part of Sudan or secede.

The fighting that broke out in Darfur in 2003 between the government of Sudan and its allied Janjaweed militias and other armed rebel groups is estimated to have caused the death of 300,000 people and to have left 2.7 million homeless. While the crisis in Darfur has captured the attention of Western activists, that conflict developed partly because of incomplete resolution of the North-South war. Both conflicts arose from the same problem: regional discontent caused by exploitation of people and resources by the central government in Khartoum. The UN, in partnership with the African Union, deployed a separate mission in Darfur to protect civilians. Nevertheless, widespread atrocities, including killing of civilians and rape of women and girls continue, although they have abated.

Sudan's president, Omar Hassan al-Bashir, was easily re-elected in April 2010, confirming his hold on power despite a warrant for his arrest on charges of war crimes issued by the International Criminal Court, which later added charges of genocide. The elections, held as part of the fulfillment of the 2005 North-South peace agreement, were widely criticized as illegitimate and rife with fraud by both Western observers and Sudanese opposition groups. This does not bode well for the serious challenges still faced by Sudan. Most analysts expect the 2011 vote to bring a decision by the South to secede, creating a significant risk of a new armed conflict.

In Darfur, the odds of reaching a comprehensive peace agreement are higher since the signing in early 2010 of ceasefire agreements between the government and the region's two main rebel groups. But the Darfur crisis cannot be resolved separately from the more deeply rooted North-South confrontation. With the central government deeply concerned about the country's possible fragmentation, it is unlikely that any lasting solution will be reached in Darfur if the situation in the South unravels.

Chad, Sudan's neighbor, followed in Congo's footsteps in January 2010 in requesting the withdrawal of UN peacekeepers from its territory, asserting that the force had served its purpose and that the government would assume primary responsibility for the security and protection of civilians and refugees. The peacekeeping mission was established in 2007 to protect the thousands of refugees who had fled to eastern Chad from Darfur. The UN, which favored a gradual pull-out, agreed after protracted negotiations with Chad to trim the mission's military component and to schedule a complete withdrawal for the end of this year if the safety of civilians in the region can be assured.

Somalia: Pirates and Islamists

Somalia—a pirate haven devastated by factional fighting and without a functioning central government since 1991—remains mired in violence, and international efforts to improve the situation fail repeatedly. A traumatic intervention by Washington in 1993 in the capital, Mogadishu, which led to US casualties in the Black Hawk Down affair, left the entire international community—including the UN—extremely reluctant to intervene there.

In 2009, the Security Council "expressed its intent" to deploy peacekeepers but never did so. The situation is complex with several countries, both near and far, interfering and feeding tensions and mistrust. Among those intervening have been Ethiopia, which withdrew from Somalia in early 2009 after invading it with US backing to battle Islamist forces, and Eritrea, which also was widely reported to have funneled arms and troops into Somalia in support of the Islamists. Their confrontation on Somali territory could almost be seen as a proxy war between these two neighbors, who fought a deadly three-year war beginning in 1998, sparked by a border dispute. The Security Council in December 2009 imposed an arms embargo on Eritrea; a UN weapons ban has been in place on Somalia since 1992.

The internationally recognized central government representing Somalia's major clans has a very weak hold on power and is challenged primarily by Islamist insurgents known as Al-Shabaab. The African Union in 2007 deployed to Somalia its small African Union Mission, composed for the most part of Burundian and Ugandan troops, to monitor the security situation and help provide humanitarian assistance. The UN provides the mission with arms and logistical support, but no money. Overall, the mission remains small, is confined largely to Mogadishu, and has failed to end the fighting.

Chaos and lawlessness have spread to the sea. Somali pirates have attacked dozens of vessels with some including hijackings. Most attacks occur in the Gulf of Aden but the Somali pirates have extended their range and have attacked ships in waters as far south as Kenya in the Indian Ocean. Despite international efforts, ransom demands were estimated to cost shippers $90 million in 2009, demonstrating the futility of a solely sea-based approach. As of late April, 20 vessels ranging from small fishing boats to tankers were being held off the Somali coast.

There have, however, been several successful responses in which armed crew members or military ships fended off pirates. In April 2009, Capt. Richard Phillips, American skipper of the US-flagged Maersk Alabama, was freed when US Navy SEAL snipers shot three pirates dead as they sat in a lifeboat, holding him hostage.

The UN appears cautiously optimistic about Somalia these days. "The country is moving from being a failed state to being a fragile state," Ahmedou Ould-Abdallah, the secretary-general's special representative for Somalia, told the Security Council in January 2010. But Ramtane Lamamra, the African Union's commissioner for peace and security, pointed out that Somalia is still "seen through the lens of the trauma of its past experiences." In the absence of a concrete commitment and a determined international policy toward Somalia and its leadership, significant progress is unlikely. In the absence of decisive UN action and with humanitarian financing on the decline, the burden seems to rest squarely on the African Union and its mission, which is already spread too thin.

Regional Partnerships: Still in the Making

Secretary-General Ban Ki-moon has strong praise for UN initiatives to share the peacekeeping burden with regional organizations such as the African Union, the Economic Community of West African States, the European Union and the Organization for Security and Cooperation in Europe, from Honduras and Africa to Iraq.

In a January 2010 meeting of the Security Council, Ban called for closer cooperation with regional organizations in early warning, prevention, peacemaking, peacekeeping and peace-building. The UN "cannot afford to do without the benefits of cooperation and burden-sharing," he said. But the content of this partnership is still unclear. Indeed, many regional organizations are wary lest burden-sharing become burden-shifting. While some regional organizations are willing and able to handle some conflicts, they all—with the exception of the European Union and NATO—need the UN to pick up a part of the tab for weapons and logistics. The UN is still learning to do that and could also be tempted to disengage.

In the recent past, a pattern has emerged with regional organizations acting as first responders in a crisis, such as the West African group in Liberia, Sierra Leone and Côte d'Ivoire, and the African Union in Sudan and Somalia. Typically, the hope is for the UN, often unable or unwilling to act quickly, to step in later and take over.

But by intervening first, regional organizations take on a greater risk—both from a security and a political standpoint—should the UN refuse to take over, either because the situation seems too dangerous or complicated as in Somalia, or because governments won't or can't provide troops and money, or because the Security Council deadlocks.

There is currently little interaction between the UN Secretariat and the leaders of these organizations, a notable exception being the desk-to-desk exchange set up recently between the UN and African Union's political departments. There is thus a general dearth of knowledge about regional organizations and their capacities, typically limited. The increasing interest of regional organizations in cooperating with the UN and in taking on a security mandate cannot be doubted, but the practicalities of this cooperation are still in the making. So far, the moves have been improvised as crises unfold. There is still no coherent or deliberate UN policy toward regional organizations. Yet development of such a policy could radically change UN peacekeeping in the years to come. ■

UN Photo/Albert Gonzalez Farra

Playful children approach a UN soldier in Abu Shouk, Sudan, in December 2009. The peacekeeper, who serves with the joint African Union-UN peacekeeping force in Darfur, is on patrol in a camp for people made homeless by the fighting in the remote western Sudanese region.

Haiti Quake Smashed 20 Years' Progress While Revealing It Was Paper-Thin

Nathanial Gronewold

On January 12, 2010, one single catastrophe unraveled two decades of development work in Haiti. Luckily, in some sense, there wasn't much to unravel.

No question, the earthquake that leveled half of Port-au-Prince, Haiti's capital, brought destruction and death on an almost unimaginable scale. At least 230,000 were reported killed. More than 2 million were left homeless, with many sleeping under tarpaulins or makeshift shelters and tents. Virtually all administrative buildings collapsed. Entire towns crumbled to dust.

But the worst disaster ever to befall a country plagued by natural calamities and unrest also exposed how little development efforts have accomplished in almost 20 years. Corrupt dictators were hauled out, only to be followed by so-called champions for democracy maneuvering to take their place. Economic reforms wrecked Haiti's farms, endangering work for 60 percent of the population. Cheered on by the International Monetary Fund, World Bank, and the usual list of development banks and agencies, Aid Inc. and Haiti's self-absorbed leadership have been walking hand in hand on a treadmill for years, going nowhere while spending millions of the developed world's tax dollars along the way. Though many lives have been saved and improved, as a whole Haiti has seemed to get only poorer and more vulnerable.

The United Nations, effectively running all the nation's most important services since 2004—especially security but also health, education and job-creation— had hoped to turn a corner there. Haunted by setbacks in other peacekeeping and field missions, it was determined to have things turn out differently in Haiti, by putting it on a course to become one of its more successful enterprises to date, if not the most. Though they had enormously difficult jobs, the UN mission in Haiti, known by the acronym Minustah, for the French version of UN Stabilization Mission in Haiti, was brimming with confidence and optimism, and the local people felt it, too, creating glimmers of hope in what often seemed a hopeless situation.

Fuel Is an Abiding Problem

Those hopeful signs were small, but multiplying. A UN-financed experiment in urban recycling found a successful, cheaper alternative to charcoal (Haitians have stripped their forests bare to produce the essential wood fuel). A team of researchers was on a mission to restore forest cover, conducting surveys and laying the groundwork for replanting. Jobs were created by building storm protections to guard the poor from the frequent flash floods that still kill them. Local nonprofits were even farther ahead, leading experiments to build up alternative fuel sources, alternative livelihoods for the urban poor, and organizing communities to be more adept at cooperation than confrontation. The next 20 years were supposed to be different.

But the quake put an end to that. In Haiti the UN has been dealt its most devastating blow, not by terrorism but by plate tectonics. The lives of 101 staff members were lost there, including almost all the top leadership. Though the mission there has mostly recovered its bearings, trauma lingers. Now, after 20 years of effort in Haiti, it's back to square one—even lower, really, as the nation as well as the mission must first be dug out of the rubble.

And so begins what will likely become the largest, boldest and most expensive attempt at nation-building ever.

At the end of March, ambassadors, foreign ministers, aid workers and what's left of the Haitian government gathered in New York to unveil their grand strategy. It could be called "Extreme Makeover: Nation Edition." It includes $930 million for restoring buildings brick for brick, with a promise to adopt and enforce quake-proof building codes, and $230 million to fix the nation's dilapidated road network, most of which hasn't seen a maintenance crew since it was first paved. Money for farmers, finally, so Haiti can grow its food instead of begging for it. Clean water and sanitation for the slums, proper schools and education for the children, steady jobs for the unemployed. It's all there, a full menu of plans and strategies to the tune of $3.8 billion for just the first 18 months. A total of $10 billion may be required over the next decade. Unfortunately, enormous waste and overlap seem guaranteed; for instance, the government asks that $500 million of the $930 million rebuilding budget be used to lease and buy new land, most of which is controlled by the wealthy.

Language Sounds Familiar

Everyone involved is pledging to do all they can to avoid repeating the mistakes of the past: the scattershot project-based approaches to development where dozens of agencies and private groups tripped over each other and often duplicated work, sometimes even competing for opportunities to aid the poor. So long as Haitian authorities avoid a descent into corruption and disorder, they say, the international community can figure out what works and what doesn't, and pay for development that sticks rather than evaporates. Yet skepticism is warranted; the Action Plan for National Recovery and Development uses words and phrases such as "vision," "capacity," "cross-cutting themes" and others that echo the tired language of the development world. Success is nowhere near guaranteed, and what's even less certain is whether lessons from this strategy, if it does work, can or will be applied elsewhere, such as Africa, where the need is especially urgent.

For half a century the UN Development Program, World Bank, International Monetary Fund and various other foreign-aid bodies have been ostensibly on a mission to rid the world of the worst forms of poverty and human deprivation. But wherever development, real development, has managed to transform societies, the renaissance has had little to do with their efforts. Instead, effective government, properly designed policies and a flood of private capital eager for new frontiers has managed to lift hundreds of millions out of abject poverty. Market forces and mineral wealth are now changing places in the former Soviet bloc, with varying degrees of success.

This picture reflects poorly on the likes of the US Agency for International Development, the UN Development Program, the World Bank and others, once identified as "the Lords of Poverty" by the Scottish journalist and author Graham Hancock. Their successes have been incremental and piecemeal—a hydropower dam here, a paved road there, some wells dug elsewhere, with far too much money spent before it leaves a donor's borders. Meanwhile more than one-third of humanity scrapes by in areas devoid of the most basic sanitation, hotbeds for disease and death. After countless international conferences, reports, meetings, studies, working groups, pilot projects and millions of dollars spent, the world's aid professionals have hardly put a dent in the problem.

Granted, the conditions in which they operate are far from ideal. Many African governments are notorious for hostility to international donors because they bypass networks of theft and graft. Sovereign states must take charge first, of course. But foreign aid is still too often designed to benefit donor more than recipient—the US Agency for International Development, for one, routinely emphasizes this when asking Congress for more money. The rest seems merely intended as life support, hence the World Food Program's emphasis on donations rather than food production. Even the Food and Agriculture Organization, the UN body whose mission is to help farmers grow more food, has overseen a collapse of much Third World farming as it appears to focus more on statistics and research.

Haiti, first among the developing world to gain its independence, is now hoped to be moving in another direction altogether. If the government and aid officials can get their acts together there, demonstrating that foreign aid can achieve what intelligent bureaucrats and financiers have elsewhere, then perhaps the development community may possibly turn a corner as well. Otherwise we can look forward to watching another long, tragic journey on that treadmill. ▪

The Middle East: What Can the UN Do?

Samir Sanbar

Without the United Nations in a visible and credible political role, even an interim Middle East peace appears beyond achievement. But that would require a more active approach by the secretary-general, whose role has diminished since the early days of the UN, and a substantive operation by UN officials in the field, with sustained support from the Security Council, particularly its five permanent members: Britain, China, France, Russia and the United States.

Over 65 years, the UN has provided mediation, observer missions, peacekeeping and humanitarian support for millions of refugees and displaced people in the Middle East. It has also offered the only internationally palatable bases for negotiating a durable peace: resolutions from the General Assembly and the Security Council and guidance and leadership from secretaries-general who came forward as architects of reconciliation.

In the past, when the UN was smaller and secretaries-general exercised considerable freedom of action, leadership from the Secretariat and a pragmatic approach from the Security Council could mean the difference between saving lives and helplessly witnessing a senseless cycle of violence. While the UN presence may not have been noted at the time, its withdrawal could have led to war or renewed fighting, as in the 11 years after the 1956 Suez Crisis, when the first UN Emergency Force kept peace.

As a mirror of a constantly changing world, the UN itself evolves, though at a slower pace than its components. So does the role of the secretary-general, whose mandate in the UN Charter is vague. Despite their varied personalities, the first four secretaries-general—Trygve Lie, Dag Hammarskjold, U Thant and Kurt Waldheim—tended to deal directly with the relevant parties in disputes. One reason may have been that about two-thirds of the Security Council debates were centered on "the situation in the Middle East."

Bunche as an Early Hero

Special envoys—who were rarely appointed—were expected to accomplish specific tasks and then proceed elsewhere; they were not given indefinite terms. For example, Ralph Bunche, the most prominent American among high UN officials in the organization's early years, was given the task in 1948 of arranging indirect talks between Israel and Arab nations. When he succeeded the next year in reaching a ceasefire agreement between the Arab and Israeli armies (for which he was awarded the Nobel Peace Prize for 1950), he went back to the UN Department of Political Affairs.

The Swedish diplomat Gunnar Jarring was charged with following up on Security Council Resolution 242, a milestone text calling for "a just and lasting peace in the Middle East" that was adopted after the 1967 Six Day War and launched the famous formula of "land for peace." After seven tours in the region, he discovered that his mission had been paralyzed by a deliberate difference in interpretation of the words "territories occupied" in the resolution's two working languages, English and French. Unlike an envoy in another region who has been trying for a decade to find a name for the "former Yugoslav Republic of Macedonia," Jarring withdrew and returned to his diplomatic posting.

It was Hammerskjold who personally negotiated the establishment of the first UN Emergency Force in 1956, and who lost his life in Africa attempting to settle a dispute in Congo. It was U Thant who dealt substantively with the Egyptian President Gamal Abdel Nasser and the Israeli Prime Minister Levi Eshkol after the Six Day War. It was Waldheim who negotiated in detail the deployment of the UN Disengagement Observer Force between Israel and Syria in 1974.

Actively cooperative Security Council members have played important roles. It was Secretary of State Henry Kissinger who had worked out a deal with Prime Minister Golda Meir of Israel and President Hafez Assad of Syria that led to the disengagement agreement. But Kissinger recognized the value of employing a widely acceptable UN mission to enforce it. The outcome was one of the most successful international peacekeeping ventures in UN history. Over the last 36 years, despite fiery political rhetoric, not a single military skirmish has occurred across the Golan line.

The result was the same when a UN peacekeeping mission was established in South Lebanon to monitor Israel's withdrawal after its March 1978 invasion. Within days of the invasion, Ambassador Andrew Young of the US had spearheaded a Security Council resolution calling for the mission to be set up to help the Lebanese government re-establish authority over its territory until Israeli forces withdrew. Brian Urquhart, UN under secretary-general, took political charge of the operation. He dealt with key governments while a joint team (including myself) in Beirut helped in arrangements on the ground.

Two Ruptures on the UN's Watch

The resulting UN Interim Force in Lebanon was another example of an unheralded successful mission. Not only did it ensure the return of villagers to their homes but offered hope by providing needed support daily. Despite obvious tension and potential threats—and even armed confrontations—it has managed to maintain an atmosphere of peace in its area of operations with practical support by the Lebanese and Israeli governments. Two eruptions of violence have interrupted the peace maintained by the UN mission in Lebanon: Israel's 1982 invasion, which reached all the way to Beirut, and Israel's 2006 assault on Hezbollah, which was largely confined to southern Lebanon, the UN peacekeeping mission's area of operations.

Every secretary-general, from Trygve Lie to Ban Ki-moon, has recognized the central impact of the plight—and rights—of the Palestinian people as well as Israel's security needs and its right of survival, though the Israeli occupation of Arab territories in 1967 exacerbated the conflict and thwarted attempts at a fair and lasting settlement. Like in long-neglected wounds, occasional bandages would only cover more serious complications. Proclaimed negotiations over negotiations for the last two decades have achieved nothing significant, while giving ammunition to militants and extremists on both sides.

After a central role until the late 1980s, the UN Secretariat has become almost politically invisible in the region, despite frequent visits or reports from a host of envoys, sent by the UN and other countries. Surveys critical of Israeli actions in the West Bank and Gaza have come mostly from other UN bodies. Most recently there was the controversial Goldstone Report on potential Israeli—and Hamas—war crimes in 2008-2009 attacks on Gaza, written for the Human Rights Council at the request of member nations, not the Secretariat.

Secretary-General Kofi Annan, who commanded respect among Arab leaders, could perhaps have brought progress in the Middle East if he had not forgone a leadership role, possibly under pressure from Presidents Bill Clinton and George W. Bush, both of whom had hopes to bring agreements themselves. Instead, the secretary-general became one of a "quartet" of international mediators, along with the European Union, Russia and the United States. The Palestinian Authority, seen as weak at home, and a number of Arab governments went along with the quartet, which has done little more than meet occasionally and issue statements, which are generally ignored by both sides. A former British prime minister, Tony Blair, was appointed the quartet's representative in the Middle East, but he has apparently not been able to exert much influence recently.

US Direction May Be Crucial

There may be signs that the UN may take a role if the US decides to involve it more directly. President Obama has sketched out an international vision to solve problems in collaboration with others, particularly through the mechanism of the UN. He has also expressed a determination to deal with the Palestinian problem. Secretary of State Hillary Clinton has reflected similar views.

Foreign Minister Sergey Lavrov of Russia, who has served as his country's representative to the UN, repeatedly urged greater UN involvement. China would welcome an approach providing an opportunity to show its international standing. France and Britain would go along if appropriate appointments were worked out to their satisfaction. Other current nonpermanent members of the Security Council such as Brazil, Lebanon and Turkey would enthusiastically support a more relevant international involvement in the Arab-Israeli conflict.

The main initial prerequisite is for the UN Secretariat to re-examine its role and options, and prepare itself to take up the daunting challenge and unique opportunity. It is crucial that it regain its credibility not only among the UN membership but also with the people of the Middle East. ■

A Weak Link in a Chain of Responsibility

Sarah Trefethen

The United Nations Security Council holds the power when it comes to the humanitarian interventions called for under the Responsibility to Protect, the international community's framework for preventing genocide, war crimes, ethic cleansing and crimes against humanity.

But advocates of Responsibility to Protect, known for short as R2P, worry that when all else fails, the 15-member council—and particularly its veto-holding permanent members—Britain, China, France, Russia and the United States—might not be up to the task.

They worry that political forces in the council may prevent it from any action that goes against the interests of its powerful member nations, even if that action is meant to prevent or stop genocide.

Secretary-General Ban Ki-moon put it bluntly. "Within the Security Council, the five permanent members bear particular responsibility because of the privileges of tenure and the veto power they have been granted under the Charter," Ban wrote in a 2009 report. "I would urge them to refrain from employing or threatening to employ the veto in situations of manifest failure to meet obligations relating to the responsibility to protect . . . and to reach a mutual understanding to that effect."

One Recent Success

At times, the system works. When soldiers in Guinea, a West African nation ruled by a junta, attacked a stadium full of unarmed protesters, firing rifles and raping, in September 2009, the council met for informal consultations two days later. A statement, made public on the council's behalf by the US delegate, Ambassador Susan Rice, expressed concern about the killings and called on the government to end the violence.

A month later, the council issued a formal statement supporting regional mediation efforts and an investigation by the secretary-general of the attack. Both mediation and an investigation were already under way. Guinea held new presidential elections in June 2010; run-offs are due in September.

The council action on Guinea, however, may have been the exception rather than the norm. "The body's consistent attention and determination to uphold its responsibility to protect is far from certain," the New York-based Global Center for the Responsibility to Protect said in a recent report.

The R2P framework was formally adopted by the UN at a 2005 world summit. It helps governments and the UN decide whether something happening in a single country warrants UN intervention under international law.

The doctrine makes it clear that it is initially up to the government of the country in question to address the most heinous atrocities. The framework says that every individual nation "has the responsibility to protect its populations from genocide, war crimes, ethnic cleansing and crimes against humanity."

"This responsibility entails the prevention of such crimes, including their incitement, through appropriate and necessary means," the document says.

Wide Range of Responses

But it goes on to state that if a country is failing to protect its people from such atrocities, the international community must be "prepared to take collective action, in a timely and decisive manner, through the Security Council, in accordance with the charter." Under the charter, the response could range from a scolding statement to diplomatic or economic sanctions and even military intervention.

Inaction or even delay can have deadly consequences, and it can happen that a council member gives a lower priority to the obligation to intervene than to its own narrow interests.

China, for example, often opposes as unwarranted intrusion in a country's internal affairs a council action that is not supported by the targeted government. Russia typically sides with the Chinese in such disputes, and also routinely blocks council intervention in its breakaway republic of Chechnya, a source of charges of human rights abuses aimed at Moscow.

In the spring of 2009, tens of thousands of Sri Lankan civilians, including women and children, died under heavy artillery fire on an exposed beach, along with the rebel fighters hiding in their midst. This was the deadly climax of a four-year campaign by the Sri Lankan army to end a separatist revolt by Tamil Tiger fighters, during which the Security Council turned a deaf ear to multiple urgent warnings from rights groups and UN officials of the threats posed to civilians by both sides in the conflict.

Diplomacy and Business

China, Sri Lanka's strong ally and a major supplier of arms and financial support for the government's assault, played a central role in keeping the situation off the Security Council's agenda. Chinese contractors are also building a $1 billion port in southern Sri Lanka which, when completed, would serve as a refueling station for the Chinese Navy.

In 2007, China and Russia vetoed a draft resolution in the council that would have called on the government of Myanmar to halt human rights abuses including the suppression of democracy and the forced displacement of ethnic minorities. International watchdog groups consider Myanmar one of the countries at the highest risk of genocide in the world.

Sometimes, just the expectation of opposition from one of the council's permanent members can stop a draft resolution dead in its tracks. Speaking to the General Assembly during a debate on the implementation of R2P in July 2009, Rwanda's UN Ambassador, Eugene-Richard Gasana, raised the question of whether the doctrine would have halted the massacre of 800,000 people in his country during what he referred to as the "completely preventable" 1994 genocide.

At that time, New Zealand led efforts to persuade the council to deploy UN peacekeepers to stop the slaughter, according to New Zealand's UN Ambassador,

Jim McLay. But, McLay said, "some permanent members resisted even recognizing that genocide was occurring, and ultimately blocked any deployment of additional UN personnel." One of these was the US, which called for a rapid withdrawal of international forces from the country even as US officials privately warned of an imminent "massive bloodbath."

To its supporters, the Responsibility to Protect is the most recent expression of the quest for human rights, development and international security that led to the creation of the United Nations 65 years ago. The failure of the League of Nations on the eve of World War II was fresh in the minds of the UN's architects, and granting veto rights to the five victors in the war was the price paid to avoid the failing that brought down the League, McLay said.

"America wasn't there, Russia wasn't there, Japan had walked out, Italy and Germany had effectively disengaged," he said. "End result: World War II." ▣

UN Photo/Sophia Paris

United Nations peace-
keepers from Peru, joined
by US army officers, pro-
vide security at an aid
distribution point for the
UN World Food Program
in Port-au-Prince, Haiti,
in February 2010.

Women Peacekeepers:
Not Tokens but Essential Workers

Veronica Haglund

The number of female soldiers, police officers and civilian staff working for United Nations peacekeeping missions has increased steadily over the past decade. But the UN sees an opportunity for even more rapid gains as the number of peacekeeping personnel deployed over four continents soars to its expected record of more than 120,000 this year.

Peacekeepers work in some of the world's most inhospitable places, facing disease and violence on a daily basis and often having to spend long periods away from their families. But UN officials see great value in bringing more women into the forces.

UN missions have shown that women are better able than men to assist female victims in conflict zones and also act as positive role models for the women with whom they come in contact.

A Security Council resolution adopted in 2000 reaffirmed the importance of women's role in preventing and resolving conflicts and maintaining peace. That same year, the UN began assigning advisers on issues of gender to several of the larger peacekeeping missions. Ten missions, in the Democratic Republic of Congo, Sudan's western Darfur region, Haiti, Chad and elsewhere, now have such advisers.

"Gender is now a natural fit" in peacekeeping, according to Clare Hutchinson, a gender-affairs officer who was part of the UN mission in Kosovo before taking a job at UN headquarters in New York. While there has been good progress in hiring women as peacekeepers, she said, the UN "has a lot further to go."

Peacekeeping missions now have 13,000 police officers in the field, and the UN says it wants women to make up 20 percent of them by 2014, a sharp increase from the current 8 percent. Parallel efforts are under way to increase the number of women in the military and civilian staff employees. Women now make up 30 percent of the 19,800 civilian employees and 2 percent of the 88,000 military personnel working in peacekeeping missions.

They hold jobs in human rights, political affairs, legal affairs and public information as well as gender, police and military duties, among other lines of work. Two of the 15 current peacekeeping missions are led by women, Ellen Margrethe Loj in Liberia and Ameerah Haq in Timor-Leste.

The women on civilian staffs, most of whom are hired locally, come from many different countries. India, Ghana, Nigeria and South Africa are among the biggest contributors of female military personnel.

"We have noticed from several missions," Hutchinson said, that the impact of female peacekeepers on local women is "incredible." "One good example is the all-female police unit deployed in Liberia," she said, "whose presence has inspired

Liberian women to join the local police force. Since the unit was deployed in early 2007, the number of women officers in Liberia's own police force rose 15 percent."

The unit operating in Liberia is from India. A second all-female police unit, from Bangladesh, is stationed in Haiti.

A more subtle benefit surfaced in Darfur, where local women saw the peace-keepers driving and asked that they be taught to drive.

Women also enhance the effectiveness of investigations into gender violence in peacekeeping zones, including the reporting of sexual crimes committed by UN officers themselves. In some places, such as Sudan, women are discouraged from discussing sexual matters with males, making female officers especially important for an assessment of local problems. ■

UN Photo/Marco Dormino

Police officers from Bangladesh arrive in Port-au-Prince, Haiti, in June 2010 to help the country recover from the earth-quake five months earlier. The officers, part of a unit of 110 women, are one of two all-female contingents active in UN peacekeeping around the world. The other all-female group is an Indian police unit now serving in Liberia.

Given a Single Purpose, Peacekeepers Find Other Tragedies They Can't Confront

Shin-wha Lee

Defending a nation against external aggression protects its citizens. But armed conflict today is more likely to be internal rather than a clash with an external force.

Of the 128 conflicts between 1989 and 2009, only 8 involved warfare between nations. The overwhelming number of conflicts were based on ethnic, religious or regional differences within a single country, and these can also involve struggles for political power, economic resources or territory. Such conflicts become international if other nations provide weapons, money or troops. Refugee flows and cross-border support from kindred groups can further complicate the situation.

In such conflicts, civilians rather than soldiers often bear the brunt of the fighting, whether they are deliberately targeted by combatants or part of the peripheral damage, whether driven out of their homes by the fighting or felled by disease, starvation and gross human rights abuses. Since the end of the cold war, civilians are estimated to have constituted 90 percent of the casualties in internal conflicts.

Trapped in the fighting, civilians are deprived of food, water and shelter, and they suffer in the next cycle if they are later cut off from aid workers trying to restore those necessities. Their afflictions become even more lethal in "complex emergency" situations where civil wars coincide with large-scale displacement, extreme poverty, disease, lawlessness or an oppressive government. The most common United Nations remedy considered in such circumstances is peacekeeping. While that term does not appear in the UN Charter, peacekeeping has evolved into a crucial UN instrument.

Crises of a Different Sort Arise

Traditionally, peacekeeping operations were set up to stabilize a potentially volatile situation on the ground, often by monitoring a cease-fire agreement, troop withdrawal or buffer zone. Peacekeepers were invited in with the consent of the warring parties and were meant to act with impartiality and neutrality. But the changing nature of post-cold war crises has made the task more complex. Today's multidimensional peacekeeping missions may find themselves in the midst of a war, with no cease-fire or peace agreement in place, or working on national rebuilding and recovery after a civil war. They are increasingly involved in such nonmilitary tasks as humanitarian relief work and electoral assistance.

At the same time, UN planners may discover that, once a mission is approved by the Security Council, they can't come up with the needed troops, support personnel, helicopters and other logistical support, which must be volunteered by UN members who have their own military and budgetary needs to cope with. While the planners press UN members to be more generous, election day in the wartorn country grows nearer and preparations for voting must go forward. Civilians end up in unprotected settlements where they may die or suffer great hardships. When planners must spend a lot of their time rounding up enough troops, money and materiel, they may be too busy to pay enough attention to the evolving humanitarian situation on the ground.

For example, the peacekeeping mission in the Democratic Republic of Congo, the UN's largest and most costly, found itself powerless to act, lacking the appropriate mandate and resources, as local militias and rebel groups raped and murdered countless civilians over several years in the eastern towns of Bukavu and Bunia.

As UN peacekeepers looked on helplessly, unable to defend or shelter them, thousands of residents were forced to flee their towns for rebel-held territories or cross the border to Rwanda where they were less than welcome. The arrival of humanitarian relief agencies and the deployment of additional UN troops, with a stronger mandate as well as greater resources and a better strategy, eventually helped the mission deal more effectively with the attacks, but not before crowds of angry Congolese stormed several UN bases in protest.

Problems from the Best Intentions

Other problems can occur when peacekeeping intersects with humanitarian relief efforts. Peacekeepers traditionally try to remain neutral in a conflict, to earn trust from all sides. But charges of bias can surface when they support aid groups working with one side or the other, guard a site where food is distributed, negotiate with rebels to secure a right of passage through a battle zone for relief workers, or assist the government by protecting aid convoys from rebel attack. That can suck them into the conflict when all they hoped to do was facilitate relief work while keeping the peace.

The opposite can also occur. After a long civil war in Liberia, UN peacekeepers came under criticism from UN agencies as well as private aid groups for being incapable of helping aid workers do their jobs. The critics said the mission's coordination and control structures were too weak to prevent rebels from stealing aid intended for refugees and raping and looting at refugee camps.

Another unintended consequence of mixing peacekeeping and humanitarian assistance surfaced in Somalia beginning in 1992. Peacekeepers there were given an initial mandate to help ease starvation among the Somali people. However, during the mission, the mandate was expanded to encourage political reconciliation among warring factions. The goal was initially to establish a "secure environment" in the country and then to sideline Gen. Mohamed Farrah Aidid, a Somali warlord who was diverting food aid and had ambushed a Pakistani peacekeeping contingent.

To fulfill the new mandate, UN peacekeepers began working more closely with US forces pursuing the same goals, losing their impartiality and ultimately their ability to function. Rather than back down, Aidid and his supporters became more aggressive. Rising tensions in the capital, Mogadishu, eventually led to a street battle in which hundreds of Somalis were killed along with 18 American soldiers. US troops left the country shortly afterward, and the UN withdrew in 1995, with Somalia still mired in violence and lawlessness.

A Blind Eye in the Council

Then there is the role played by the Security Council, which authorizes peacekeeping missions but whose individual members may at times be driven more by narrow national interests than ensuring international peace and security, as required by the UN Charter. This clash of interests was visible in the tragic Rwandan genocide of 1994, when the Security Council turned a blind eye to the slaughter of 800,000 people, despite the presence of a peacekeeping mission in the country.

As the killing accelerated, council members failed to send in additional soldiers or even to order the peacekeepers already there to do what they could to stop it. Instead, they decided unanimously to draw down the peacekeeping presence to 270 soldiers from 2,539. Some of the most powerful UN members apparently saw the situation as being of little importance to their strategic interests, including the US, which was in addition reluctant to dispatch US forces to Africa after the deaths of its soldiers in Somalia.

In Rwanda, the mere presence of a UN mission presumably gave residents the impression that the peacekeepers would protect them, even if the mission's mandate did not call for the protection of civilians. They were unfortunately mistaken.

A similar situation unrolled in the 1992-95 war in Bosnia. In July 1995, UN peacekeepers stood by, failing to prevent the massacre in Srebrenica of 8,000 Bosnian Muslims by Bosnian Serbs, despite the town's UN designation as a safe zone.

Getting It Right

In response to such unintended consequences, the UN reviewed the way it plans and carries out complex peacekeeping operations. An independent panel, led by an esteemed UN diplomat, Lakhdar Brahimi of Algeria, called in August 2000 for a more comprehensive approach to each peacekeeping mission from its inception. It also called on UN humanitarian agencies to improve their planning and preparations for field operations. The Peacebuilding Commission, established in 2005, has also tried to improve coordination between humanitarian and peacebuilding operations after a peacekeeping mission has been wrapped up.

The UN should not be unduly influenced by narrow national interests in its peacekeeping and humanitarian work. The Security Council runs the risk of losing credibility when it bows to individual members rather than to the interests of the international community as a whole. This is particularly true in the case of its most powerful members, the five veto-wielding nations with permanent council seats: Britain, China, France, Russia and the United States.

To avoid unanticipated consequences, UN peacekeeping missions must be alert to the concerns of the humanitarian organizations and grassroots groups that they meet in the field. Every UN member, regardless of its power or stature, should gauge the gravity of each complex emergency on its merits and work collectively to address it. ∎

President Obama addresses the 64th session of the General Assembly in September 2009, eight months after moving into the White House. He praised the UN while denouncing its "broken politics" as allowing its members to "use UN processes as means to avoid action rather than a means to solve problems."

The Evolving US-UN Relationship

**42 Washington and Turtle Bay:
Restarting the Dance of Diplomacy**
Jeffrey Laurenti

48 Susan Rice: Obama's Policy Voice in the UN Halls
Evelyn Leopold

51 An Interview with Ambassador Rice
Evelyn Leopold

Washington and Turtle Bay: Restarting the Dance of Diplomacy

Jeffrey Laurenti

Many people—nowhere more than in Washington—were astonished when the Nobel Committee in October 2009 announced its Peace Prize was going to President Obama, who had been in office less than nine months. Obama himself publicly wondered whether the prize was premature, and to placate conservative critics at home he lectured his Nobel audience in Oslo about the occasional need to use military force, even unilaterally, a homily that seemed intended to confound the expectations of his listeners.

The Nobel committee cited Obama's "extraordinary efforts to strengthen international diplomacy and cooperation between peoples," adding that it attached "special importance" to his vision of and work for a world without nuclear weapons. In less than a year, the committee explained, Obama had created "a new climate in international politics."

"Multilateral diplomacy," the committee said, "has regained a central position, with emphasis on the role that the United Nations and other international institutions can play."

The change seemed particularly dramatic after the challenges that a fiercely nationalist and aggressively unilateralist American administration had posed to the UN Charter-based international order earlier in the decade. The willingness of the world's wealthiest and militarily most powerful nation to engage with great and small alike through UN networks and agencies has oscillated over the 65 years of the system's existence. Internationalist enthusiasms in the first two decades were circumscribed by cold war antagonisms, and opportunities for the UN in the two decades since then were constrained by US assumptions of indispensability if not global dominance.

Stand-Off for Survival

The determination of President George W. Bush to attack Iraq was widely seen as a challenge to the existence of the UN, with Kofi Annan, then secretary-general, warning that the "illegal" invasion had brought the community of nations to a "fork in the road" regarding the global order.

Though he was intensely disliked internationally for bellicose unilateralism, Bush did preside over a major reduction in America's dues delinquency to the UN. He embraced the call for increased financing for development in the world's poorer nations and pried substantial increases in financing for development assistance and HIV/AIDS control from a Congress that had dramatically pared US aid in his predecessor's administration. He led America back into Unesco, the Educational, Scientific and Cultural Organization, which his predecessor had conspicuously failed to do.

Yet Bush was most vividly identified as discrediting the UN's "relevance," both in word and deed—and not just regarding Iraq. Preferring to deal with a handful of partner nations it could dominate, the administration insisted on entrusting responsibilities for post-Taliban reconstruction in Afghanistan to a few Western governments rather than the UN and pressed unsuccessfully for a Western military force to supersede the UN peacekeeping force in Lebanon as Israel battled Hezbollah. Dealing with natural forces rather than military, it even tried to elbow the UN aside as leader of international relief efforts in the Indian Ocean tsunami at the end of 2004.

In 2002 he formally repudiated his predecessor's signature on the Rome Statute establishing the International Criminal Court, and in the national security strategy he presented later that year Bush saw no role for the UN, save as a partner to US policy in Afghanistan (though at least his preface acknowledged it as a "lasting institution").

Renewing US Standing

The Bush administration's adoption of harsh interrogation techniques—torture—against captives in contravention of international law evoked widespread revulsion. American allies were appalled in 2005 by his nominations of sovereigntist ideologue John Bolton as his UN representative and the Iraq war architect Paul Wolfowitz as World Bank president. Both were soon out of office. With this as the immediate historical context, the Nobel Committee—and, to judge by public opinion polling, the world—enthusiastically embraced Obama's steps in the other direction as change they could believe in.

The American public's own sense of its country's shattered global standing was a major issue for candidates of both parties in the 2007-08 presidential campaigns, and Obama was not alone in vowing to "renew American leadership in the world." He was unusual, however, in insisting, "No country has a greater stake in a strong United Nations than the United States" even as he denounced "the broken politics of the UN" that allowed its members to "use UN processes as means to avoid action rather than a means to solve problems."

As president-elect, Obama listed "strengthening international institutions" as among the three top priorities for his new secretary of state and he appointed his campaign's closest foreign-policy adviser, Susan Rice, as his representative at the UN. [See "Susan Rice: Obama's Policy Voice in UN Halls," P. 48]

The national security strategy he announced in May 2010 argued that the US had been successful in foreign policy when "pursuing our interests within multilateral forums like the United Nations—not outside of them." His strategy cited the UN 24 times (in contrast with Bush's two), affirming, "We need a UN capable of fulfilling its founding purpose—maintaining international peace and security, promoting global cooperation, and advancing human rights."

Some analysts have asked whether Obama's commitment to the UN is real rather than merely rhetorical. But in each area where his strategy calls for ensuring the UN is capable, the change appears real.

First and foremost, as Obama's strategy notes, "we are paying our bills." After a quarter-century of arrears, Obama made full payment of current as well as back dues a priority in Congress. In contrast with his predecessors, he insisted that a supplemental appropriations bill for Defense Department operations in Afghanistan and Iraq also include the US share of several UN peace operations. This came to $837 million, and Congress approved.

Washington's Bottom Line

Congress went on to provide full payment in the 2010 appropriations bill for the UN regular budget and peacekeeping, and spurned UN opponents' proposals to ignore UN assessments to pay for expanding veterans' benefits. He also rejected demands that payments be conditioned on US certification of UN "transparency" and that most of the UN regular budget be converted to voluntary payment.

Voluntary contributions from governments have long been the primary source of support for most UN agencies involved in social and economic development. The new administration ensured that Obama's commitment to increased development assistance—a key prong of his international security strategy—was reflected in appropriations for UN funds and programs. His first year's request for money for UN agencies' voluntary contributions was a hefty 27.3 percent above Bush's last request. Congress increased this, with the largest line items for the ever-popular UN Children's Fund, Unicef, $132 million, and the UN Development Program, $101 million.

As in previous years, Congress approved $55 million for the UN Population Fund, and the Obama administration actually paid the contribution to the family-planning program, which President Bush had blackballed. Washington's third-largest voluntary contribution in the UN system in Obama's first year was $65 million in supplemental financing for an independent UN arm, the International Atomic Energy Agency, whose nuclear nonproliferation mandate has traditionally had strong bipartisan appeal in Washington.

The Issue of World Survival

It is on nuclear weapons, in fact—the subject of the first UN General Assembly resolution in 1946—that Obama in his first year most dramatically altered the direction of US policy, something particularly noted by the Nobel committee. As a candidate and then as president, he affirmed the American commitment to nuclear disarmament—"a world without nuclear weapons," as he put it in Prague in April 2009. No American president has voiced this since the days of Ronald Reagan.

Obama launched a year-long negotiation with Russia, concluded in April 2010, on a new strategic arms reduction treaty. Cuts in the two countries' nuclear arsenals in this step signaled to the world that the cold war nuclear giants were moving on their disarmament obligations under Article VI of the nuclear nonproliferation treaty. Obama presided over a rare summit-level meeting of the UN Security Council in September 2009, which was convened to debate how best to deploy the council's powers to roll back nuclear weapons. The resulting resolution committed the council to "create the conditions for a world without nuclear weapons," urged ratification of the comprehensive nuclear test ban treaty by the handful of holdout states (the Bush administration opposed US ratification), and underlined the council's responsibility to deal with noncompliance with the nonproliferation treaty.

Obama followed these steps with announcement of a policy review that substantially narrowed the circumstances when US military planners could consider resorting to nuclear weapons, as well as with a nuclear security summit he held for top leaders of 38 countries. The careful set of steps to reduce nuclear weapons reached a crescendo at the nonproliferation treaty review conference in May 2010. The document created then represented global endorsement for Obama's two-pronged strategy of nuclear build-down and tightened monitoring and enforcement. (In 2005, Washington's refusal to acknowledge its prior disarmament promises torpedoed any conference agreement.)

Early Sounds of Endorsement

Significantly, the review conference set in motion a process toward negotiation of a convention to eliminate nuclear weapons and, more immediately, a treaty conference to create a zone free of nuclear weapons in the Middle East. The conference outcome, former top UN disarmament official Jayantha Dhanapala told United Nations Association delegates after its close, "was a tribute to the new political leadership of the United States." Indeed, Dhanapala suggested, in accepting Obama's compromises, most delegations "were voting for his re-election in 2012."

With this success in hand, Obama in early June won Security Council approval of a new round of mandatory sanctions against Iran's runaway nuclear program, with Russia and China voting with the council's Western members. This was a clear signal that Obama's commitment to international institutions and treaty law produces results, belying conservative assertions of multilateral weakness. It was an even clearer signal to Tehran that even its big trading partners were drawing the line on nuclear capability.

Western countries thwarted an Iranian move to renegotiate with Turkey and Brazil—nonpermanent members of the Security Council this year—a reprocessing agreement that Iran had negotiated with the council's permanent members and then reneged on. Stung by the permanent members' sidelining of their negotiations, Turkey and Brazil voted against the resolution, only to be humiliated as politically impotent when they could not persuade any other council member to join them against the Permanent Five: Britain, China, France, Russia and the US.

Israel: A Chronic Concern

The US had a harder time corralling its Israeli ally into the peace settlement with Palestine that Obama vowed at the outset of his administration to achieve. The Israeli retention of lands seized in the June 1967 war continues to generate trouble, with the US often virtually alone in buffering Israel against international condemnation, especially in the Security Council. Although Israel's increasingly conservative security establishment and fervent allies in America were worried that Obama's election might open the door to a less adamant American approach, the new administration did not see the UN as a strategic place to press for peace between Palestine and Israel.

Instead, the UN has been a place where issues considered by the administration to be distractions from its goal of Middle East peace keep getting in the way. It concluded in April 2009 that participating in the follow-up UN conference to assess progress against racism would bring too little in substantive gains against racism to be worth antagonizing the new rightist Israeli government, which it was pressing to halt settlement construction in the occupied territories.

Similarly, when the report on Gaza war UN crimes by a panel chaired by the South African justice Richard Goldstone infuriated Israel's defenders, the Obama administration was primarily anxious to keep the controversy from derailing its effort to restart peace negotiations, which Prime Minister Benjamin Netanyahu's government was threatening to scuttle. Rebuffing appeals from human rights groups to support Goldstone's recommendations for war accountability, the administration declared the report "deeply flawed" and bottled up in the Security Council calls to refer the charges of war crimes to the International Criminal Court.

Swimming Upstream

Gaza again took center stage in the Security Council in May 2010 with a botched Israeli commando attack on a Turkish vessel leading a so-called relief flotilla aimed at breaking Israel's blockade of Gaza. While the rest of the Security Council was quick to ascribe the shipboard deaths to the Israelis, the Obama administration balked, insisting on a resolution text that called for an "impartial" (but not explicitly a UN) investigation of what happened, and which condemned "the loss of life and injuries" without specifying who caused "the use of force during the Israeli military operation in international waters."

For decades, issues related to Israel and the Palestinians have taken up a huge amount of time and items on the agendas of UN human rights bodies, including the new Human Rights Council. Obama had pledged in his campaign to seek a seat for the United States on that council, vowing to insist on comparable scrutiny for other countries with dismal human rights records. Simply running for the council represented a break from the Bush administration's aloofness, though most observers saw simple pragmatism in the Bush decision not to compete in elections that an unpopular administration, one involved in torture of prisoners, was sure to lose. Obama's apologies for US violations of human rights during the so-called global war on terror, and his reaffirmation of US respect for international treaty obligations banning torture and governing war prisoners, made the US eminently electable to the council. Rebalancing the council's agenda once Washington gained that seat has proved rather more difficult. *[See "The Human Rights Council: Smoke and Mirrors," P. 78]*

Nonetheless, the administration promised full cooperation when the US comes up for its turn at "peer" review across the full spectrum of human rights by the council in late 2010. *[See "Washington's First Rights Review," P. 86]*

While it endorsed ratification of the Convention for the Elimination of All Forms of Discrimination Against Women, which President Jimmy Carter signed 30 years ago, the administration did not secure a place on the Senate calendar for a ratification vote. Obama proved more cautious, however, with the Rome Statute creating the International Criminal Court, which remains controversial in military circles. Not only did he not call for Senate consent to US ratification of the statute; he did not revoke the Bush-era letter repudiating President Clinton's lame-duck signature on the treaty. However, in contrast to the Bush administration's bristling hostility to the court and refusal to "legitimize" it by sending observers to the meetings of its governing body, Obama has had observer delegations present at its meetings. *[See "International Criminal Court: Growing Up," P. 112]*

Complex Divides

By the end of his term, Bush had come to acknowledge that something needed to be done about global warming, but his skepticism about the phenomenon and about government measures to confront it frustrated European governments as well as endangered island and coastal states seeking urgent action. Obama shared their sense of urgency, and long-stalled negotiations on a climate change agreement came quickly to life in 2009.

Still, good intentions alone were not sufficient to bridge the complex divides on economic, energy and climate issues by the time of the Copenhagen conference in December 2009. With the negotiations in Copenhagen breaking down, Obama made a dramatic 11th-hour personal appearance for a high-stakes negotiation of a North-South accord with his counterparts from China, India, Brazil and South Africa. The "meaningful agreement" they produced, as the administration spun it, was a political accord rather than a treaty, involving no binding targets for emission reductions or for compensatory energy assistance. But it picked up 138 subscribing governments in the ensuing months, ensuring that its parameters would be the framework for the delayed treaty commitments. *[See "After Copenhagen, Climate Dealers Shuffle the Cards," P. 96]*

It may be a coincidence, yet telling nonetheless, that Obama flew to Copenhagen just days after the formal conferral of his Nobel Peace Prize in Oslo. His personal leadership in the negotiations on "saving the planet" represented precisely the "multilateral diplomacy" and "new climate in international relations" that the prize committee believed he made possible in the UN system. ■

Susan Rice: Obama's Policy Voice in UN Halls

Evelyn Leopold

It was a Friday morning and Susan E. Rice, the chief United States representative at the United Nations, was in her office for an interview and not in Washington, where she often spends three-day weekends with her family.

"I am here as long and as hard as I need to be here—which this week is five days," Ambassador Rice said. "And I participated in meetings in Washington by video, as I often do. We are working on stuff that requires me to be here."

The "stuff" that day presumably was a forthcoming deal on a fourth sanctions resolution against Iran, which was endorsed by the four other permanent Security Council members—Britain, China, France and Russia—but announced in Washington by Secretary of State Hillary Clinton before Rice did the same in New York. Yet both she and other US officials say the two women are in harmony, despite Rice's role as Barack Obama's senior foreign policy adviser in his 2008 campaign against Clinton for the Democratic nomination.

"We're both in the Cabinet," Rice said. "We sit around the same table. Usually, if I am there we are next to each other. We have regular meetings. We talk on an ad hoc basis, if needed, so we are in quite regular communication."

When in Washington, she attends meetings of the Cabinet or other top officials —and tries to spend more time with her husband and two young children. It's a fast but not an easy commute. As a working mother, she says that the situation would be impossible without the help of her husband, Ian Cameron, the executive producer of the Sunday morning "This Week" program on ABC.

"I have a tremendous husband who has an important job of his own," she said. "And he also is a tremendous father. He works weekends. To be under the same roof, most weekends it would be in Washington."

Absence of Hostility a Relief

Rice is a welcome relief to her colleagues at the UN after what they perceived as outright hostility from John Bolton, a predecessor.

Athletic (a high school jock) and glamorous enough to merit a spread in Vogue, Rice moves quickly through UN corridors, surrounded by security guards. She addresses the press infrequently, as do most of her colleagues. During the UN renovation, barriers have been erected around the temporary Security Council chambers to guard against informal chats with correspondents, once a trademark of the Republican Bolton as well as the Democrat Richard Holbrooke. Consequently, many reporters find they must rely on briefings at the French and British UN missions for information.

But there is no doubt that Rice and the Obama administration have made a difference at the UN: the United States has paid its bills, played a leading role in environmental policy and lobbied intensively inside the often-dysfunctional Human Rights Council in Geneva rather than denouncing it from afar, as did Bush and Bolton.

On women's issues, the tone has changed appreciably. No longer does abortion dominate so many US statements, as it did during the Bush years, and reproductive health—birth control—is considered basic in discussing maternal mortality. Two of Rice's three deputy ambassadors are women, a first.

"We view this as an institution, despite its imperfections, that allows for a degree of constructive burden-sharing on international peace and security that we think is valuable in hot spots in the world," Rice said. "It is not the only vehicle we have but it is one that in many instances, whether it is dealing with issues like North Korea or Iran, is an important component of our foreign policy and our strategy."

Diplomats find Rice, who speaks in complete paragraphs, knowledgeable, straightforward and willing to engage in Security Council consultations and more informal talks. Heraldo Muñoz, Chile's veteran UN ambassador until recently, compliments Rice on her interest and "a good and constructive attitude." But he says actions speak louder than words and the evidence for him of change in Washington was US participation in the Human Rights Council, the payment of dues and action on nuclear disarmament, where Obama organized a Security Council meeting that envisioned a world without doomsday weapons.

'One Place at a Time'

Some say that she does not stand around the numerous receptions, where diplomats lobby as well as socialize, in the style of her immediate predecessor, Zalmay Khalilzad. Speaking of this reputation, she said: "Frankly, I don't know what you hear in corridors."

"You know I am a human being and am only able to be at one place at a time," she said. "Eighty percent of my time is here on average and sometimes a hundred percent is here."

Susan Elizabeth Rice was born in November 1964 in Washington to a university economics professor and a former member of the Federal Reserve. She earned her B.A. at Stanford University and was a Rhodes Scholar at Oxford, where she received a doctorate.

She spent eight years in the Clinton administration—as a member of the National Security Council staff (where she was director for international organizations and peacekeeping), and then was a special assistant to the president and senior director for African affairs.

In 1997 Rice was catapulted into the job of assistant secretary of state for African affairs, the youngest person to hold that post. She has said that her biggest regret during the Clinton years was not pushing hard enough to intervene in the 1994 Rwanda genocide, when 800,000 people were massacred.

Difficult Issue of Darfur

She has been outspoken on atrocities in Darfur, particularly when compared to Gen. Scott Gration, the US envoy to Sudan, who is often criticized by human rights groups for ignoring abuses by Khartoum. However, Rice said Gration had the right approach, particularly in southern Sudan.

But she said, "I have been working on issues related to Sudan for 15 years at least. . . . my own comments reflect my experience. And I have learned through hard experience that Khartoum responds to pressure more readily than to incentives. The United States needs to continue to be clear in acknowledging the failings of all parties."

Rice, who has been mentioned as a future national security adviser or a secretary of state, just smiled when asked if she would stay at the UN should Obama be re-elected. "I serve at the pleasure of the president," she said. ■

UN Photo/Marco Dormino

Susan Rice, the US ambassador to the UN, travels by helicopter to Gonaïves, Haiti, in March 2009 as part of a four-day Security Council tour of the impoverished nation.

An Interview with Ambassador Rice

Evelyn Leopold

Following are excerpts from an interview with Susan E. Rice, chief United States delegate to the United Nations. This rare interview was given to Evelyn Leopold in New York for "A Global Agenda" on May 14, 2010.

Q: It's a Friday and you are here in New York?

A: I am here as long and as hard as I need to be here—which this week is five days. And I participated in meetings in Washington by video, as I often do. We are working on stuff that requires me to be here. Most weeks on average I am here four days and in Washington one. But it is not always the same day. It varies.

Q: And your family and children?

A: I have a tremendous husband [the ABC News producer Ian Cameron] who has an important job of his own. And he also is a tremendous father. He works weekends. To be under the same roof, most weekends it would be in Washington.

Q: How does this administration differ from the George W. Bush administration at the UN?

A: I think we differ quite dramatically in many respects. In the first instance we view the United Nations as an important vehicle for advancing core U.S. national security interests. It is not the only vehicle we have but it is one that in many instances, whether it is dealing with issues like North Korea or Iran, is an important component of our foreign policy and our strategy. We view this as an institution, despite its imperfections, that allows for a degree of constructive burden-sharing on international peace and security that we think is valuable in hot spots in the world.

So the UN's role in peacekeeping, in preventive diplomacy, in post-conflict peacebuilding is valued and important and we are investing constructively in that. We are paying our bills in full and on time. We are dealing with all manner of nations large and small in a spirit of mutual respect and mutual interest. We are working to try to strengthen the institution and reform it from within rather than simply criticize from the outside or disparage. So I think in many different ways—how we perceive the institution and its value, how we approach the challenge of strengthening and reforming it and what we have gotten done—it's quite different.

You ask about policy. In development, this administration embraces the MDGs [Millennium Development Goals] and seeks to try to achieve them; in nonproliferation and disarmament we are working to make very concrete progress and have taken dramatic steps from Prague to now. [We differ] whether we are talking about human rights and women's rights and a whole range of things that come before the General Assembly that we opposed in the past.

Q: And on women's rights you have championed reproductive rights, which include birth control.

A: Sure . . . and there is climate change. I think there are few issues where there isn't some significant difference.

Q: Sudan? It seems your comments are more critical of the government than those of General [Scott] Gration [President Obama's special envoy to Sudan], who has been criticized quite a bit. Do you see daylight between the two of you?

A: First of all I have been working on issues related to Sudan for 15 years at least. And I have learned through hard experience that Khartoum responds to pressure more readily than to incentives. We have a policy that I think is a correct policy that employs both. And I was very much involved in crafting it and I think it is absolutely the right approach. I think that the emphasis that General Gration is putting on the situation in the south and the need to implement the CPA [Comprehensive Peace Agreement] and the referendum are absolutely correct. We are all in full agreement that that is necessary and the appropriate approach and we are working together towards that end. So, I think on both the substance and the policy and how it is implemented, the administration is fully on one page. My own comments reflect my experience. And my view [is] that the United States needs to continue to be clear in acknowledging the failings of all parties and I'll continue to do so.

Q: On Secretary Hillary Clinton. Do you consult regularly? How does it work?

A: We're both in the Cabinet. We sit around the same table. Usually if I am there we are next to each other. We have regular meetings. We talk on an ad hoc basis, if needed, so we are in quite regular communication. And of course our staffs are even more so.

Q: You have been criticized for not being here, available to diplomats or going to enough parties.

A: I am very much here. My kids will be the first to validate that. I am seeing my diplomatic colleagues very regularly. Not only in the council but meetings multiple times a week in a bilateral setting with various permanent representatives. And there are group settings as well, and lunches and dinners and receptions. I don't go to every reception that I am invited to. There is no question about that. I don't think any of us can. Monday nights I am here working quite late. I am here as I said most nights of the week. So frankly I don't know what you hear in the corridors. But what I detect is a good collegial relationship with my colleagues here, a very good working relationship with a broad swath of them, and friendly personal relationships with a good number of them. I very much enjoy working with my colleagues here and do some things socially just for fun. Occasionally I even manage to get my husband up here to join me. You know I am a human being and am only able to be at one place at a time. And if it is not in the office here, it is likely in the office in Washington. Eighty percent of my time is here on average and sometimes 100 percent is here, as demonstrated this week.

Q: Will you serve another four years?

A: I serve at the pleasure of the president [laughter]. We'll have to see what he thinks.

Q: Including yourself, three of your four top ambassadors are women. Did you choose that?

A: And my deputy in Washington is a woman, and my chief of staff. I selected these people. It wasn't a deliberate plot to ensure there were no men in the highest ranks of the US mission. I love my male colleagues and work very well with them. But I think it is exciting that we have strong women in important leadership roles in this mission. ■

UN Photo/Mark Garten

Secretary-General Ban Ki-moon, flanked by President Obama and the then British prime minister, Gordon Brown, addresses a Security Council summit on nuclear nonproliferation and disarmament in New York in September 2009. Obama chaired the meeting.

Haitians sweep dust and debris from the streets of their capital, Port-au-Prince, in January 2010 as part of a project run by the United Nations Development Program after a devastating earthquake left millions without homes and jobs.

Aid: Finding a Path for the Future

56 Development Aid: Is It Worth the Money?
Abigail Somma

62 Afghanistan: Rapid Changes that Presage More Difficulty
Robert P. Finn

67 From Farm to Market to Sustainable Development
Susan Blaustein

70 Iraqi Reconstruction: Behind a Veil of Violence
James Wurst

72 Primary School: Not Yet for Everyone
Dulcie Leimbach

74 Pursuing Peace in Nigeria's Troubled Delta
Musikilu Mojeed

Development Aid: Is It Worth the Money?

Abigail Somma

The international development community got a rude shock in 2009 with the appearance of "Dead Aid," a book by Dambisa Moyo of Zambia. The Harvard- and Oxford-educated Moyo added a dissenting female voice to a debate previously dominated by Western men. Her sharp criticisms of the "aid business" created controversy in the international development community while earning her a place on Time Magazine's list of the 100 most influential people of 2009.

According to Moyo, aid to Africa has not only failed to deliver on its promises, it has kept continent in poverty. By opening the door to corruption, creating aid dependency and adversely affecting exports by reducing competitiveness, she wrote, open-ended aid policies have been a large part of the problem. Her solution: end all aid to Africa within five years. In its place, let the private sector take over and focus national priorities on trade, investment, job creation, bond markets and microfinance.

While Moyo's five-year prescription sounds alarming, her argument resonates with an unhappy US public: Why haven't the billions of dollars sent to Africa over decades brought more progress? Why have some of the biggest advances come in such places as India and China, where development gains have been achieved largely through means other than aid? While more than 70 percent of Africans live in dire poverty today, that figure was 10 percent in 1970, she argues.

The debate over aid effectiveness is not a new one. Renowned economists such as Jeffrey D. Sachs, director of the Earth Institute at Columbia University, and William Easterly, co-director of New York University's Development Research Institute, have been fighting it out for years. But Moyo's media savvy and African roots pushed the rhetoric up a notch, catapulting the debate into the limelight.

After the book was published, some African leaders came to her defense while others went on the attack. President Paul Kagame of Rwanda wrote in the Financial Times that this was "the discussion we should be having: when to end aid and how best to end it."

On the Contrary, Sirleaf Says

But Liberia's president, Ellen Johnson Sirleaf, insisted that aid had been helping African countries grow, calling for more accountability and better targeting. "Reducing aid would slow private-sector growth, stall poverty reduction, and undermine peace and stability in countries that are struggling to become part of the global economy," she wrote in The Washington Post.

The usual contenders, Sachs and Easterly, took their opinions to the blogosphere. Sachs, a special adviser to Secretary-General Ban Ki-moon and author of a pro-aid book, "The End of Poverty," wrote in the Huffington Post that the debate had become "farcical." He said both Moyo and Easterly had accepted generous financial help for their educations while seeing "nothing wrong with denying $10 in aid to an African child for an anti-malaria bed net." As for Kagame, Sachs pointed out, Rwanda is now on its feet, largely thanks to large influxes of aid.

Easterly, in his own post, said he was asking for more accountability, not an end to aid. He believes that aid doesn't work because it ends up being funneled to corrupt governments. President Robert Mugabe was worse for Zimbabwe, he argues, than the Anopheles mosquito—the vector for malaria. "Corruption is more fatal for oil-rich Nigeria and Angola than latitude," he wrote in the Huffington Post.

Benchmarks of Global Progress

The Millennium Development Goals have given the world a common purpose to rally around in seeking improvement globally. In 2000, leaders from 189 nations endorsed the eight goals, which serve as global markers in the fight to eradicate poverty and achieve sustainable development. *[See "Millennium Development Goals and Targets," P. 188]*

In the 10 years since they were established, the goals have become the most popular reference point in the development lexicon. Now with only five years until the deadline for achieving them, the international development community is moving into high gear, planning to accelerate progress. Many of these ideas will be launched at the Millennium Development Goal midterm review this September, during which world leaders will gather to assess the situation and plan for the next five years. Everyone with a stake in the goals is expected to be involved: governments, international organizations, business leaders and interest groups.

To date, progress has been spotty and uneven, with countries showing varying degrees of success. On a global scale, there has been promising movement as well as disappointing setbacks.

Extreme poverty, as measured as the number of people living on less than a $1.25 a day, fell to 1.4 billion from 1.8 billion people globally between 1990 and 2005, decreasing to 26 percent of the population from 42 percent. The World Bank's Global Monitoring Report estimates that the goal of halving extreme poverty between 1990 and 2015 is within reach. Deaths of children under 5 years of age have also declined worldwide, from 12.6 million in 1990 to 9 million in 2007, even as the population has grown. Additionally, the estimated number of AIDS-related deaths appears to have peaked in 2005 at 2.2 million, decreasing to 2 million in 2008. That's all good news.

The bad news is that progress is uneven. The poverty rate in East Asia fell to 16 percent from 60 percent from 1990 to 2005, but remained above 50 percent in sub-Saharan Africa. Poverty levels in both sub-Saharan Africa and South Asia are notably high. Furthermore, the number of hungry people worldwide rose from 842 million in 1990-92 to 1.02 billion in 2009. In terms of maternal deaths, the global decline has been only marginal: from 480 deaths per 100,000 live births in 1990 to 450 per 100,000 live births in 2005.

As September nears, development agencies and private organizations are putting forward recommendations to speed things up. So far, there don't seem to be many novel ideas. The UN Development Program is emphasizing the need for developing nations to help assume responsibility for projects' success, manage aid effectively and cooperate with one another. The International Monetary Fund recommends increasing both aid and trade, sustaining growth, improving human development and integrating development and environmental sustainability. While these are sound ideas, the question is how to harness them to produce results.

It remains to be seen whether any fresh ideas or approaches come out of the September meeting. But with 2015 just around the corner, many people are already asking: what comes next? –*Abigail Somma*

"Health is determined more by public actions against disease than by species of parasite. Other factors that Sachs mentions such as illiteracy and poor infrastructure are also symptoms of bad government services."

While Moyo says her book focuses on aid provided by governments rather than humanitarian aid or charity work, some private organizations also jumped in. The One Campaign, started by the musicians Bono of U2 and Bob Geldof, said Moyo failed to differentiate between an earlier period when aid was widely misused, and more recently when it has been better targeted. As for corruption, it thrives because of poverty, not because of the availability of development assistance, the One Campaign said on its Web site. "Even if African countries relied solely on private investment, trade flows, and capital markets for economic growth, corruption would still be a factor. As we have all seen, corruption is no stranger to the private sector either."

Where Are the Spreadsheets?

For the average outsider, the conflicting opinions can be baffling. Why are there no conclusive data on whether aid works? On one hand, major aid recipients throughout Africa, as well as in countries like Haiti and Afghanistan, seem no better off with their lifeline of aid support. But on the other hand, statistics show that aid has made a dramatic difference in improving health and education. In Ethiopia, for example, death rates and cases of malaria were halved within three years after an anti-malaria campaign began in 2005. In Ghana, school enrollment rates increased more than 20 percent for both boys and girls in just a few years after the start in 2004 of a program for free compulsory universal basic education. Both of these campaigns were backed by aid.

Brenda Killen, head of aid effectiveness at the Organization for Economic Co-operation and Development, says part of the confusion stems from the difficulty of judging effectiveness. Do you look at growth, well-being or the outcome of a particular project? Measuring the effectiveness of aid is even more difficult because of the many factors that affect a country's overall development, such as weather, the global economy, various national policies and even a civil war nearby or failure to maintain roads, Killen says. "You'd have to have a parallel universe to see how these countries would be developed without the aid," she said.

Killen also faults the media for oversimplifying. "You can have quite complex discussions about the financial crisis in the banking sector in the newspapers," she said. "But when it comes to development, there is nothing about Africa. Then a relatively small amount of money is stolen, and that is what is featured, and it would be seen to apply to the whole continent."

There are efforts under way to clear the murky waters. At the local level, there is proof that aid works. And now, there are also experiments to figure out how to make it work best. Esther Duflo, a French economist at the Massachusetts Institute of Technology, conducts studies with control groups to determine which variables make aid more effective. While she acknowledges that measuring overall effectiveness of development aid remains elusive, individual interventions can be scientifically evaluated. And if they are well designed, better outcomes can be demonstrated, such as in a project coupling education with de-worming, or providing parents with a bowl of lentils when they bring children for vaccinations.

According to the development scholar Finn Tarp, aid is delivering results, albeit less than originally expected. Initial expectations were that aid flows equivalent to 10 percent of a country's gross domestic product would lead to 5 percent growth, he said at a recent event in New York. But that 10 percent investment actually leads to only 1 percent growth, he said. The British economist Paul Collier came to a similar conclusion in his book "The Bottom Billion," whose title refers to the world's poorest. Aid "over the last 30 years has added around one percentage point to the annual growth rate of the bottom billion," he wrote.

Donations Continue, Despite All

Whether that 1 percent growth rate can be improved remains to be seen. But in the meantime, donor nations seem willing to keep on giving, regardless of the results. Figures from the Organization for Economic Co-operation and Development show a 0.7 percent increase in 2009, despite the financial crisis.

Aid flows will most likely increase further when the global economy recovers. One reason is the international focus on the 2015 deadline for the Millennium Development Goals. In September, government leaders are gathering in New York to assess progress toward the goals and carve out a path for moving forward. A common sentiment before the meeting is that aid financing remains vital to meet the Millennium Development Goals.

One of the goals specifically presses donor countries to fulfill their commitments. In 2005, at a conference of the Group of Eight top industrialized nations in Gleneagles, Scotland, donors pledged to contribute 0.7 percent of their gross national product to aid by 2015. While only five countries have reached that target, others are under pressure to do better.

To entice donors to keep giving and to counter the critics, there is a movement to make aid "smarter" by, for example, testing the effectiveness of individual projects as advocated by the economist Duflo at M.I.T. "Smart aid" approaches are also enshrined in recent international covenants such as the Paris Declaration on Aid Effectiveness, which was endorsed in March 2005 by over 100 government ministers and others at a meeting. It was followed in September 2008 by a similar document, the Accra Agenda for Action, which built on the commitments made in Paris.

Free Online Resource to Learn How

These agreements promote transparency, accountability, national ownership, better governance and greater donor cooperation. Additional efforts to make aid more effective are popping up all the time. One is the free online tool, AidData, introduced earlier this year to help development practitioners, researchers and governments track information on aid activities around the world.

This will all be important going forward, especially if the opponents of aid increase in numbers and their voices grow louder. But regardless of how loud they shout, development aid still holds a very strong, even emotional, place in international policy. The intense global focus on the Millennium Development Goals is a case in point. As the development community gathers in September to review these benchmarks, it is clear we have not yet seen the end of the great aid debate. ■

Aid Gone Awry

Haiti

According to a 2006 report from the National Academy of Public Administration, Haiti received more than $4 billion in aid from 1990 to 2003. But even before the Jan. 12 earthquake, three-quarters of its population lived on less than $2 a day. After the earthquake, donors pledged another $5.3 billion for reconstruction. Will this aid fare better than past efforts, which fell victim to Haiti's notorious problems with governing?

Haitians have already taken to the streets to denounce corruption stemming from the influx of post-disaster aid. "It's what I'd call a perfect storm for high corruption risk," said Roslyn Hees of the corruption watchdog group, Transparency International, in a recent interview. "You have a seriously damaged institutional infrastructure, a country with endemic corruption, a weak or fragile state in the best of circumstances and sudden influxes of huge amounts of resources to a highly vulnerable population."

One hopeful sign is that donors are well aware of the problem and reconstruction efforts include an array of governance reforms. To try to keep an eye on the aid, Transparency International is recommending its guide, "Preventing Corruption in Humanitarian Operations," which was written after the 2004 tsunami relief efforts and is available on its Web site. The group is also setting up its own aid-monitoring project.

Somalia

At the very bottom of Transparency International's Corruption Perceptions Index is Somalia, a country that operates without a central government. Given its relative state of lawlessness, it's not a surprise that Somalia was also the site of a recent aid scandal.

In March, a UN Security Council report said that nearly half of World Food Program aid to Somalia ended up in the hands of corrupt contractors, radical anti-government Islamic militants and local UN staff. The report urged Secretary-General Ban Ki-moon to open an independent investigation into the World Food Program operations in Somalia.

The World Food Program, after initially denying the charges, said it would welcome such an inquiry and pledged not to give any new contracts to three Somali businesses accused of diverting food shipments to militants. While the agency is still delivering food in most of the country, operations across southern Somalia were suspended in January, largely for safety concerns.

Well before the scandal in Somalia, a 2008 Brookings Institution paper written by New York University's William Easterly and Tobias Pfutze questioned the reliability of the World Food Program itself, which asked donors for $6.7 billion in donations last year. The Brookings paper ranked 40 large aid donors on transparency, overhead costs, selectivity of aid spending and other criteria. The World Food Program tied for 27th place.

Afghanistan

Since the ouster of Afghanistan's Taliban leaders in 2001, the country has seen enormous inflows of aid, met with soaring levels of corruption. A UN Office on Drugs and Crime report in January concluded that Afghans over the past year paid $2.5 billion in bribes and kickbacks, about a quarter of the country's gross domestic product. Half of the 7,600 Afghans surveyed reported having paid a bribe to a public official. Moreover, in March, Pino Arlacchi, a member of the European Parliament and former UN official, estimated that 70 to 80 percent of the $34 billion in aid sent to Afghanistan over the last eight years through international organizations never reached the Afghan people. It hardly helps that the economy depends heavily on an illegal drug trade, particularly opium, which is estimated to bring in $3 billion annually.

The Afghan government admits there is a problem. "We are determined to put an end to the culture of impunity as we move along the path of rule of law and democracy," President Hamid Karzai said at a London conference on Afghanistan's future earlier this year. But government officials complain that they aren't included in aid disbursements and do not have enough say about the projects financed. Today, no more than 23 percent of aid is channeled through the Afghan government, but the amount should reach 50 percent in two years, if effective reforms are put in place, as promised. This pledge was agreed upon at the London conference, as were an independent High Office for Oversight, anti-corruption laws and civil service reforms. In theory, these initiatives should help, but the actual outcome is unclear. –Abigail Somma

Afghanistan: Rapid Changes That Presage More Difficulty

Robert P. Finn

Afghanistan is in a rapid state of change. Afghans want to be in charge and foreigners want to leave. President Hamid Karzai alienated Western leaders with the election—flawed by allegations of extensive ballot-box stuffing. He caused further alienation by announcing that he would hold a loya jirga—a grand council of tribal elders—that would include all of the Taliban leadership, to talk about national reconciliation. He has also been distancing himself from the international community with an eye to the endgame of intervention in Afghanistan in which he naturally wants to remain the leader. His visit to Washington in May ostensibly papered over differences, but the situation remains tense.

The seeds of disenchantment were planted when Karzai traveled to Bonn in 2001 for an international conference on his country's future following the US invasion. Karzai then, to international acclaim, presided over an unlikely assembly of adventurers, human-rights violators, returned exiles and monarchists. His pleas to get the foreigners to throw out the warlords he disliked fell on deaf ears, and his reluctance to get rid of the ones he liked meant he was eventually labeled as corrupt, inefficient and partisan. Karzai became increasingly mired in a situation he couldn't or wouldn't fix. His management style, more tribal than executive, relies on repetitive group discussions rather than an agenda for action follow-up.

What was a soothing and helpful methodology in 2002 became an impediment after the 2004 presidential and 2005 parliamentary elections and adoption of a constitution mandating a strong executive. A basic inability to govern remains a serious problem. The 2009 US civilian plan for support envisions working in cooperation with selected government ministries, but that has inherent problems.

The new US administration brought a new readiness to confront problems. There were testy meetings between US officials and a Karzai in denial. For many, the election scandal was the last straw. But Karzai was not solely to blame, and not just because the other side cheated too. The failure of US officials to wean themselves from the warlords, of the UN to take significant action against election fraud that began months in advance, and to deal with the Afghans as responsible equals meant that the Karzai government was constantly undermined and undercut with the Afghan people. Recent events have not much improved things.

Aid That Vanishes in a Pipeline

Insufficient financing from the start means that development has fallen far short of need and expectation. Because the government is bypassed for direct distribution meant that in 2009, the Afghan government managed at most 23 percent of assistance money while the UN and foreign governments handled the lion's share. Capable government cadres have not been trained, and much of the country's educated elite has been hired away by the international community. It is estimated that 40 percent of the money never makes it to its destination. For many Afghans, US regulations seem to benefit us at least as much as them.

The international community is dissatisfied with Karzai, whom they chose. Afghans are too. The Parliament twice rejected most of his cabinet nominees. The administration has still not dealt with basic issues of nepotism, corruption and ethnic favoritism. Karzai's unpersuasive commitment to weed out corruption should be turned into a real effort. This should not be hard to do. Simply ask politicians how they paid for their garish villas.

Sweetheart deals, such as that with First Vice President Marshal Fahim's brother to supply fuel for the US-financed Kabul electrical generator and deals with the CIA made by Karzai's brother Ahmad Wali Karzai, are patent evidence of wrongdoing for Afghans whose concept of justice omits expensive defense lawyers. The US and UN need to change the optics as well as the reality in Afghanistan.

There was perhaps less Afghan than international outrage over the election, partly because government interference in the election commission and UN support for the process led them to expect the outcome. When Peter Galbraith, the deputy UN special representative for Afghanistan, was dismissed after complaining of widespread voter fraud, Afghans took note. Karzai's attempt to take over the election commission afterward brought strong negative reaction globally, and he finally backed down.

Some Signs of Hopefulness

Nevertheless, Afghans are feeling better about their country. According to a BBC poll made public in January 2010, 70 percent of Afghans said things were heading in the right direction, up from 40 percent a year ago. Ninety percent want the current government to remain in power, and only 6 percent want the Taliban back. They gave Karzai a 72 percent approval rating, up from 52 percent a year earlier, and 60 percent viewed government's performance favorably. But 95 percent consider corruption a significant problem. Karzai recently allowed a law providing amnesty for war crimes before 2001 to go into effect, after initially pledging not to sign it. International law leaves the issue of human rights violations open for prosecution.

All of this drained support for a seemingly endless war. Less than half in the US think the war is worthwhile. Enthusiasm is lower elsewhere. Two-thirds of British voters want out, half of the Dutch, and most of the Germans. The Dutch government recently fell over the issue of its involvement. The German President resigned over Afghanistan-related remarks and support for involvement in Afghanistan is a major contributor to Chancellor Angela Merkel's waning popularity. Canada may withdraw its soldiers in 2011, Poland in 2012 and the Dutch will pull back 2,000 troops by the end of 2010. Efforts to increase allied contributions have met minimal success. A complex series of caveats restricting soldiers' operations continues to limit the usefulness of such contributions as are made. The US continues to shoulder most of the burden, although in terms of relative mortality, tiny Denmark takes the lead.

Most Afghans say that security is getting worse. Highly visible Taliban attacks reinforce a perception of deterioration, while the Taliban now claim shadow governments in 33 of Afghanistan's 34 provinces. A huge push into Marja, launched in February, has not succeeded. The plan was to enter with superior force and then to bring in Afghan police and administrators as a "government in a box." Afghan troops played a distinctly secondary role in the fighting and Afghan government officials have not shown they can govern. The Taliban are still active and threaten reprisal against any who cooperate with the government. Relying on Afghan police is questionable, since they are widely identified as part of the security problem. A similar operation planned for Kandahar in late summer has been put on hold. Taliban presence in and around the city seems only to increase, with deals between government officials on every level and the Taliban reported widely in the press. The abrupt replacement of Gen. Stanley A. McChrystal with Gen. David H. Petraeus in June raised questions about the leadership of the effort in Afghanistan, as did press stories about problems among senior US officials.

A Long and Expensive Road

The US plan for Afghanistan is designed to produce a military victory and a space for Afghan governance. The plan's civilian side, announced late in January, commits $10 billion and more than 1,000 US embassy civilians, with a further 20 to 30 percent increase in civilian staff planned before the end of the year. The embassy is now taking the lead in development and reconstruction work, including the tasks of Provincial Reconstruction Teams, an important optical change. The plan envisions training Afghan military and police officers, as many as 400,000. What remains unclear is who is going to pay. It will take years to train, and many more years before Afghanistan can possibly expect to finance them. In all the discussion, no one seems to deal with this critical question of cost. The announcement of the "discovery" of extensive mineral wealth in Afghanistan in late spring of this year provides one answer to the question. The development of the resources will take many years and, in any event, was no secret. I pushed for a US geological team to do a survey of Afghanistan before I even went out to Afghanistan in early 2002 [as its first US ambassador in more than 20 years].

The problems that led to the Taliban takeover are strongly economic. Former Finance Minister Ashraf Ghani once said Afghanistan could be a self-respecting poor nation, but that did not include security costs. If, down the road, there is peace, a reappraisal can take place. But that should be thought about now.

Afghanistan's economy simply cannot support what is currently planned. Afghanistan has the potential to become a self-sustaining country, with oil and gas deposits, its already-mentioned mineral wealth, transport, gemstones and agriculture. Pipelines and transport networks would benefit the whole region. Investment is needed. Afghanistan used to feed itself; it can do so again. The Russians destroyed the backbone of Afghan agriculture. The rise in opium production was one response. Farmers say they would prefer to grow a different crop, and need price supports, alternative crops and a multi-year program. Opium production, down this year, is centered in Taliban-thick Helmand Province. The production supports them and places producers in a confrontational relationship with the government. The money is made mainly by the traffickers and transporters. They must be targeted first. One of the most visible failures of the Kabul government is its inability and/or unwillingness to move on this with regard to government officials and, it is said, relatives of President Karzai.

Afghanistan remains one of the poorest countries in the world on virtually every human indicator. Although income has trebled since the days the Taliban was in control, and 80 percent of Afghans now have access to some kind of health care, one of four children still dies before the age of 5. Fifty-two percent of the population now has access to a cell phone and 41 percent to a television. There are now six million children in school, about half of the country's children of school age. In primary school about 40 percent of the students are girls; in secondary schools, that falls to 5 percent, according to an assessment conducted in 2007 by the Afghan Ministry of Education.

More could have been done. Some 95 percent of US financial aid for Afghanistan has gone into military expenditures, and overall aid has remained woefully low, even in comparison with other situations in more advanced countries. Pledges have not been realized. The US has actually given Afghanistan about 83 percent of the money pledged, much better than many others.

Pashtuns on Two Sides of Border

There are more Pashtuns in Pakistan than in Afghanistan, and the tribes on either side of the Durand line separating Afghanistan and Pakistan do not recognize the international border. Both Afghanistan and Pakistan have toyed with the border. For Kabul, the Pashtun areas of Pakistan are not a foreign country. For Pakistan, the border is a line that foreign troops should not cross, but one the Taliban can happily ignore.

Pakistan has its own problems with Pashtuns. Long in denial about the Taliban danger to Pakistan, the Islamabad government, including the army, had a rough wakeup call with last year's attacks. Since then, the Pakistani military has launched vigorous campaigns, but still draws the line at entering some critical areas.

Pakistani popular opinion is on their side; 83 percent of Pakistanis think the US is an occupying power in Afghanistan and 58 percent think the Taliban were better than the Karzai administration. Arrests of Taliban leaders in Pakistan in 2010 raised questions whether the Pakistanis are trying to root out the Taliban leadership or just setting themselves up for peace negotiations. Meanwhile, terrorist attacks in Pakistan are bringing the problem home to Pakistanis, whose reaction is to blame others for getting them involved.

Drone attacks, highly unpopular in Pakistan, are taking their toll on the Taliban and Al Qaeda leadership. Elimination of the Al Qaeda presence in the region will be one non-negotiable part of any peace plan. If Al Qaeda leaves, Central Asia will be on the alert as Islamic fundamentalism is a primary threat. The specter may be greater than the reality, but Tajikistan and Uzbekistan have past experiences and indications for the future that make them wary.

Both India and Pakistan are guilty of using Afghanistan as a playing field, and both must find reasons to support a peace agreement if it is to work. Economic benefits are obvious, but security concerns and regional political relations may overshadow them. The UN could play an important role in moving India and Pakistan from their current antagonistic positions.

Impact on the Neighbors

Much of what has happened in Central Asia has been informed by what has happened in Afghanistan. Tajikistan ended its civil war in the 1990s because the people felt they were turning into another Afghanistan. Uzbekistan's president, Islam Karimov, has used the threat of Islamic fundamentalism to crush political opposition. All of the countries in Central Asia, together with China and Russia, are supportive of the war against Al Qaeda and at the same time concerned about future US plans for Central Asia. One contributing reason to the fall of the Kurmanbek S. Bakiyev regime in Kyrgyzstan last April was the relationship between Bakiyev and the US government. Russia uses Afghanistan to maintain strong ties with Central Asia. The lack of clarity in US intentions makes the northern neighbors anxious. The US has recently worked to bring these countries more closely into the effort, through the Northern Distribution Network, providing new northern supply routes into Afghanistan.

Iran is still smarting over being placed by George W. Bush in the "axis of evil." Iran has been accused of helping some Taliban groups while at the same time supporting the Karzai government. Iran regards Afghanistan as part of its relations with the West and in particular the US. Any trouble with Iran would find expression in Afghanistan. A Persian sword is one that cuts both ways.

The future remains clouded for Afghanistan. President Obama's announcement of a troop withdrawal date signaled a major change. The Bonn conference set up a government to bring Afghanistan back into the world community, but did not plan for the difficulty of doing that in a country at the bottom of world indicators, destroyed by 30 years of war. The initial military successes led to mistakes of planning and perception that all can see. The future of Afghanistan is likely to be less clear, less democratic and less in line with Western standards than we would like. The effort will involve enormous problems, which will require years of expensive commitment to help Afghanistan become master in its own house. The question now is whether that commitment will be there. ∎

From Farm to Market to Sustainable Development

Susan Blaustein

After the United Nations General Assembly embraced the Millennium Development Goals in 2000, then-Secretary-General Kofi Annan enlisted a development economist, Jeffrey D. Sachs, to map out how to transform these noble declarations into a detailed plan to help the world's "bottom billion" escape extreme poverty.

To help him, Sachs convened a team of 250 scientists, economists and development experts. In 2005, Annan was handed 13 fat volumes, laying out, step by step, how to bring the goals to life.

To put the plan into action, Sachs, working with then-UN Millennium Project Director John McArthur, the renowned agro-forestry expert Pedro Sanchez and others, first considered how best to show that the goals could be achieved within the levels of aid that the world's wealthy nations were willing to provide. Among the ideas they came up with was the Millennium Villages Project, a multinational public-private nonprofit partnership that is now striving to achieve the Millennium Development Goals in 80 impoverished sub-Saharan villages, with hundreds more on the way.

The project began as a single village, a pilot project of Columbia University's Earth Institute, which Sachs leads, with help from specialists in fields as diverse as tropical agriculture, energy, transportation, public health and economics. The first village, in western Kenya, quickly became two, expanding to northern Ethiopia. With the support of Raymond Chambers, now a special envoy of the secretary-general for malaria, and the nonprofit Millennium Promise, the project has expanded to 14 clusters of villages across Africa, each a "hunger hot spot" representing a different agro-ecological zone.

With the project now entering its fifth year, some things are already clear: food security is within reach for all hunger hot spots, although these still-fragile sites remain vulnerable to drought, floods, agricultural pests and the as-yet unpredictable effects of climate change. With a lean health system based on simple mobile technologies, rapid diagnostic testing, well-trained community health workers and clinics equipped with trained medical practitioners, refrigeration and emergency vehicles, maternal and child mortality can be brought down significantly and infectious diseases can quickly be treated. School meals, made whenever possible from local farmers' surplus commodities, can make it more likely that the farmers' daughters will be allowed to go to school. Putting computers in the schools links those farm girls to whole worlds of information and hope. And building eighth-grade classrooms can often mean the difference between those same girls' reaching the end of their education, or continuing to secondary school and beyond.

Having demonstrated some successes, the project has attracted many corporate, private-sector and multilateral partners, including a number of UN agencies. Twenty countries in Africa alone have lined up to have their own Millennium Villages; Nigeria is using money from international debt relief measures to scale up the project across the country, and Mali is preparing to raise funds to expand the project's reach to 166 villages from 12. Also, Kenya is planning to scale up to 96 Millennium Villages in an effort to create a Millennium District.

Adding Value

But there is more to be done. Once the farmers have a surplus and can diversify their crops, they are eager to add value to their agricultural production and get that production out to regional and international markets. When a mother going through a complicated labor is referred to the care center in a nearby city, the center needs to be ready to receive her, with skilled medical practitioners, safe blood and a functioning operating room. And when that bright eighth-grader from the Millennium Village is accepted into secondary school in the city, she and her parents need to know the school will be challenging and that she'll be living in a safe and healthy urban environment.

Enter the Millennium Cities Initiative, the integrated urban complement to the Millennium Villages Project and also a program of the Earth Institute. With help from policy analysts, expert field staff and local and international partners, this helps under-resourced urban centers become viable and sustainable "Millennium Cities"—with distinct job opportunities, improved access to public services and links to the countryside and international markets. Founded by Sachs in early 2006, the initiative now includes two national capitals—Accra, Ghana, and Bamako, Mali—and an economic capital—Blantyre, Malawi—as well as eight secondary sub-Saharan cities.

To gain insight into participating cities, the initiative assesses needs in public health, education, gender equality and water and sanitation. The assessment tools, developed by the UN Millennium Project and applied for the first time at the municipal level, are designed to determine each jurisdiction's degree of progress toward the various Millennium Development Goals and what it will cost to attain each target. This helps local, regional and national governments and their development partners understand just what resources are required to meet each goal.

The initiative also seeks out and investigates potential investment opportunities and promotes those it finds promising. It has commissioned reviews, carried out at no cost by partner law firms, of the regulatory environment and business and investment climate in the countries and cities where it is active. The global accounting giant KPMG has conducted its own studies of investment opportunities in numerous Millennium Cities and published an investment guide to Kisumu, Kenya, and Kumasi, Ghana. And the UN Industrial Development Organization has profiled small-to-medium-sized enterprises in five Millennium Cities and posted its findings on the Internet.

The Millennium Cities Initiative also helps the Villages Project promote business development by, for example, helping to link producers of such commodities as palm oil, honey, sunflowers and shea butter to processing facilities and regional and international markets. The initiative's familiarity with each Millennium City's needs also enables it to line up external partners to help address needs in such crucial areas as maternal and newborn health, early childhood education, water and sanitation and connecting schools to the Internet.

Once the initiative has completed its research on a given Millennium City, area leaders—both public and private, rich and poor—will sit down with a list of recommended interventions and their estimated cost and draft a detailed urban strategy. The initiative can then help the city promote its plan to potential investors and development partners.

If all goes according to plan, the resulting economic development and improved quality of life will demonstrate that the Millennium Cities Initiative and its companion Millennium Villages Project can serve as models for larger-scale projects, enabling under-resourced towns and villages across Africa and beyond to chart their own progress toward the Millennium Development Goals. ■

UN Photo/Eskinder Debebe

Herders drive their horses in Must, Khovd Province, Mongolia, in July 2009. The United Nations Development Program is helping herder groups in Must to manage their water resources, pastures and forest lands better, improving their livelihoods while protecting the region's biodiversity.

Iraqi Reconstruction: Behind a Veil of Violence

James Wurst

The reconstruction of Iraq after two wars and a decade of sanctions continues—largely out of sight—as the government of Iraq and the United Nations grapple with the issues of reconstruction in an environment in which only the horrific killing of civilians still draws international attention.

National elections in March, which the UN helped run, were the latest step to stabilizing Iraq's government and society, and the most visible to the world at large. But in yet another sign of obstacles to stability, continuing street violence, political disputes and the simmering distrust among Iraqi parties combined to slow negotiations to a crawl on the makeup of a new government. Adding to the uncertainty are US plans for a full military withdrawal by the end of 2011.

The UN Assistance Mission for Iraq got a start in August 2003, shortly after the US-led invasion that overthrew Saddam Hussein. In June of the next year, the Security Council gave the mission an ambitious mandate, anticipating the end of the occupation of Iraq by the US-led Coalition Provisional Authority. The new responsibilities included assisting Iraq in writing a constitution, laying the groundwork for elections and helping run the elections. The UN mission was also authorized to advise Baghdad on the development of a civil service, to help coordinate and deliver reconstruction, development and humanitarian assistance, to promote and protect human rights and strengthen the rule of law.

The UN mission in Iraq is considered a "special political mission" as opposed to a peacekeeping or peace-building mission. It is the second largest mission of its kind under UN authority (Afghanistan hosts the largest). It has 600 staffers (half involved in security) with an annual budget of $160 million and offices in Baghdad and Erbil, in Iraq's Kurdish region, as well as in Jordan and Kuwait. Ad Melkert, the special representative appointed by Secretary-General Ban Ki-moon in July 2009, previously held top positions in the UN Development Program and the World Bank, which underlines the emphasis the UN role places on development.

Ban Assesses the Hurdles

In his latest quarterly report, issued two months after the March elections, Ban wrote: "Once the new government is formed, it will have to deal with major challenges including national reconciliation, resolving outstanding Arab-Kurdish issues, the sharing of natural resources, constitutional issues, effective public administration, human rights, IDPs and refugees, and reconstruction and development." IDPs are people who have been driven from their homes but are still within Iraq's borders.

While the UN mission and the UN country team "continue to assist in all these areas, ultimately, it will be the Iraqi people themselves who need to resolve these issues," Ban's report said. "The challenge is to consolidate the gains that have been made in recent years and not allow armed groups and other spoilers to exploit the situation."

Just before the elections, Melkert wrote in The Washington Post: "Formidable obstacles, including social disparities and the reconciliation 'gap,' remain sources of instability. But these cannot be good reasons to continue to perceive Iraq as if it would still need some form of supervision. Letting the people of Iraq make their own decisions requires a change of mind and habit of many regional and international stakeholders. All stand to gain if we take the right course."

In May, the UN and Iraq launched the 2011-2014 UN Development Assistance Framework, designed to improve the country's governance and services for the next five years. According to the UN, there are five priority fields: ensuring inclusive economic growth; environmental management; promoting good governance and protecting human rights; boosting access to basic services for all; and stepping up investment in women, youth and children. The framework was designed to dovetail with the Iraqi National Development Plan, a five-year program drawn up in 2009 between the Iraqi government and the US Agency for International Development; it focuses on promoting economic and agricultural growth and improving local governance.

'Donor Fatigue' Is the Challenge

In an e-mail interview, Christine McNab, the UN resident coordinator in Iraq, called the framework one of the UN's "greatest achievements" in the country. "The challenge now, is to ensure [it] is properly funded by the UN, international donor community and most importantly by the government of Iraq." The combination of other crises such as Haiti, the global economic crisis and traditional "donor fatigue" diverts attention from Iraq, McNab conceded, but she said, "There is still a great deal of interest in Iraq, not just from the United States but from a wide range of member states, all of which want to see a sovereign and successful Iraq capable of meeting its tremendous development challenges."

Besides concerns over donor fatigue, some argue that Iraq—as an oil-producing country—should be paying for its own reconstruction. Iraq produces nearly 2.5 million barrels a day. "While Iraq may be considered a 'middle income' country, it will be several years before Iraq has sufficient revenues to tackle the country's development needs head-on," McNab wrote. "Iraq still needs the assistance of the UN and its donors to consolidate the peace through tangible development, both physical and human."

Security is always a priority in Iraq, for the UN even more so since the Canal Hotel bombing in August 2003. Occurring so early in the UN's involvement in the country, the incident helped to define the mission. The Canal Hotel served at the time as the UN mission's headquarters and the attack by a suicide truck bomber killed at least 22 people, including the UN special representative in Iraq, Sergio Vieira de Mello, and wounded more than 100.

When the US ends its military presence in Iraq, withdrawing its forces by the end of 2011 under an agreement with the Iraqi government, the UN will rely on increased UN security and Iraqi forces to keep safe. Financially, this translates into $30 million to $50 million additional for both general security and the construction of a new UN compound. The compound is still being designed. ▪

Primary School: Not Yet for Everyone

Dulcie Leimbach

In the last 10 years, the number of children who did not attend school was reduced by 33 million, marking a golden era in which the number of young people enrolled in elementary school reached a historic high point.

But the odds remain daunting for the Millennium Development Goal of universal primary education by 2015, the United Nations acknowledges. "We are still very far from Education for All in many parts of the world," Secretary-General Ban Ki-moon said in early 2010. Achieving that goal by the deadline will be "difficult but not impossible," Ban said.

Real progress is being made. Sub-Saharan Africa, traditionally a laggard in education, increased enrollment fivefold, while South and West Asia reduced by half the number of children not attending school—an incredible reduction of 21 million—leaving 18 million to go.

In India alone, the number of children who did not go to class fell by nearly 15 million from 2001 through the end of 2002. This was a result of a new universal primary-education program.

Although enrollment rates vary drastically among countries in the sub-Saharan region, between 1999 and 2007 the average increased to 73 percent of the child population from 56 percent. Benin, which had one of the world's lowest ratios in 1999, is now on track for universal enrollment by 2015.

Unesco's annual Global Monitoring Report, part of the agency's Education for All program, which set six achievement goals embraced by 160 countries in 2000, found rosy pictures in parts of the world where childhood education at one time was barely an afterthought. But the global financial crisis threatens to roll back progress in the poorest countries, as their economies falter behind the West in recovery and the West continues to offer its own children superior education.

Poverty a Major Barrier

Unesco's 2010 report, "Reaching the Marginalized," says that 72 million children worldwide did not attend school in 2007, 54 percent of them girls. It says current projections suggest that 56 million primary school-age children will be missing from the classroom in 2015, the finish line for the Millennium Development Goals.

Gender disparities, despite some successes (Senegal, for example, has attained parity in primary school), remain ingrained in some regions, with 28 countries having 9 or fewer girls in school for every 10 boys. Malnutrition is also a persistent barrier to gains in education.

Even more dispiriting is that children who do get to school might not emerge with adequate reading or writing skills, the report says. In sub-Saharan Africa, 40 percent of young adults with five years of primary school are illiterate. Moreover, 59 percent of the children not in school in the region are most likely never to attend, the highest percentage of nonattendance in any Education for All region. West

Africa's statistics are particularly numbing: In Burkina Faso, Mali, Niger and Senegal, more than 70 percent of children out of school are expected never to enroll.

Meanwhile, numbers in South and West Asia (which include India, Pakistan, Nepal, Bangladesh and Afghanistan) are not rising fast enough.

New setbacks in education in the developing world reverberate far beyond the classroom, often precipitating a slowdown in a country's development, since they dampen economic growth, poverty reduction and health improvements.

The collective will of donors has lapsed and needs major reform, the report said. Aid to education has been increasing, but commitments have recently stalled, and nearly $16 billion is still needed to reach the Education for All goals.

Rich countries, the report says, exaggerate the money they have sent to poor countries. A project for a fast-track global education and coordinating body has failed. The report suggested that developing countries could make a difference by raising their spending for education by less than 1 percent of their gross domestic product. Most often, however, the political will and effective national policies are missing.

Tremendous Disparities

A new measurement tool used in the report reveals stark disparities based on family wealth, gender, ethnicity and language. If you're born into a poor family, your chances of lifelong deprivation are great. In India, for example, the report finds a seven-year education gap between the richest and poorest households. In more prosperous Turkey, Kurdish-speaking females from poor families average three years in school, about the same as the national average in Chad, one of the world's poorest nations.

Despite great strides in Benin and Mozambique, 50 percent of young adults in 11 countries elsewhere in sub-Saharan Africa have less than four years of schooling.

Recommendations from the report include increasing access to schools by lowering the cost of tuition, creating schools closer to poor areas, assigning teachers more equitably among countries and regions, offering more bilingual instruction and enforcing laws to prevent discrimination against girls.

"Hire females to teach girls," Unesco Director-General Irina Bokova recommended. ■

Pursuing Peace in Nigeria's Troubled Delta

Musikilu Mojeed

For years, the United Nations watched Nigeria struggle on its own with the protracted turbulence in its oil-rich Niger Delta region. But with the crisis spinning out of control, the UN has recently changed course and joined government efforts to turn the region around.

Nigeria is Africa's most populous country and the world's most populous black nation. Oil is the mainstay of its economy, and the delta produces more than 90 percent of the country's oil exports.

But the delta is also a hot spot, torn for years by killings, hostage-takings, attacks on oil facilities and other forms of violence. Insurgents in the delta pursuing an armed campaign accuse the government, one of the world's most corrupt, of taking much from the area while giving back little.

In an effort toward peace in the area, the UN has now launched a program to rehabilitate insurgents who renounce violence, to help them re-enter civilian life.

The success of such efforts is crucial to Nigeria's future as years of unrest have prevented the country's oil industry from producing much more than two million barrels of oil per day, two-thirds of its capacity. That is estimated to have cost the country $1 billion a month in lost revenues, robbing it of vital development funds and depriving its people of desperately needed help in climbing out of poverty.

While Nigeria earns about $25 billion a year from oil and gas sales, according to the Revenue Watch Institute, the country remains among the most poverty-stricken in the world, ranking 158th out of the 182 countries rated in the UN's most recent Human Development Index.

Staff Evacuations Are Frequent

The Niger Delta, comprising 6 of Nigeria's 36 states, has become so lawless and dangerous that bombs and kidnappings are constant. Multinationals and other oil companies in the area must frequently evacuate their staffs and shut down their operations. The United States and other countries regularly issue travel advisories warning citizens against venturing into the area.

Successive governments have tried to stem the violence, but militant groups have refused to give up their armed resistance. Experts consider the reintegration of former fighters and vulnerable youth into the community as necessary for sustainable peace and development. About 20,000 militants last year heeded a government call to lay down their arms in exchange for amnesty. But the local economy offered them few good options, and many are believed to have resumed fighting.

With that in mind, the United Nations Development Program is helping underwrite a nearly $11 million project in the delta to create jobs for former militants, in partnership with the Shell Petroleum Development Company and the governments of three Nigerian states, Bayelsa, Delta and Rivers.

The money is being used to build youth centers offering vocational training in each of the states. Those accepted into the program are taught how to start up a business, analyze a market and draft a business plan. They are also able to learn such vital skills as welding and metalworking, automobile mechanics, information technology, marine engineering, carpentry and cabinetmaking.

After they have completed the program, the centers help them find jobs, scholarships for further study, or loans to start businesses.

Selected from the initial group of 748 applicants, 150 former combatants have already undergone a three-month program called "mindset-change orientation" before beginning vocational training.

Wirba Alidu of the UN Office for Project Services in Nigeria said the initiative was based on research into the region's needs and how to fulfill them. "The project has raised a lot of hope among the youth and the population, and it is now clear that its success is critical to peace in the region," he said. "It is bringing about social cohesion and the communities are happy."

But the new UN program does not begin to address other grave regional problems including a paucity of development initiatives and wide environmental degradation left in the wake of oil exploration.

Nigerians hope UN involvement will bring more credibility to the peace effort. "When the UN is involved in a process," said Omoyele Sowore, a Nigerian activist based in New York, "concerned parties tend to have more confidence in it. We hope the UN will do more than a token intervention and make an impact by engaging with the militants at a higher level." ▪

Wikimedia Commons/Utibe4you

A busy street in Port Harcourt, Nigeria's oil capital. The city is in the heart of the Niger Delta region, which has been torn for years by killings, hostage-takings and attacks on oil facilities.

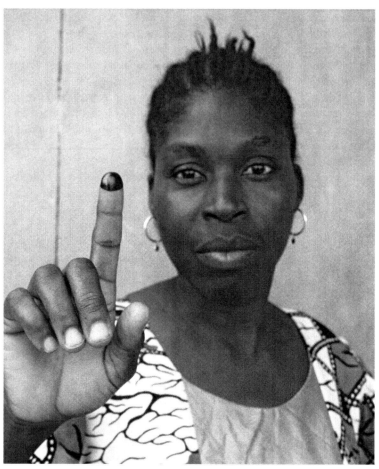

Joe Penney

A voter shows her inked
finger after voting in the
2009 presidential elec-
tions in Guinea-Bissau in
West Africa. Malam Bacai
Sanhá won the vote and
now has the task of rein-
ing in the army, which is
accused of human rights
violations, including
the assassination of the
previous president, João
Bernardo Vieira.

Fresh Start on Human Rights?

78 The Human Rights Council: Smoke and Mirrors
Jacques Fomerand

86 Washington's First Rights Review
Edward R. McMahon

88 A Mandate to Protect
Tendai Musakwa

92 Coaxing Europe to Welcome Two-Time Refugees
Indra Baatarkhuu

The Human Rights Council: Smoke and Mirrors

Jacques Fomerand

After two years as a work in progress, the United Nations Human Rights Council got down to business in 2009, with substantive human rights questions at the top of its agenda. Sharing the rights spotlight was a new High Commissioner for Human Rights, Navanethem Pillay of South Africa, who succeeded Louise Arbour of Canada in September 2008.

Following a halting take-off, the council now appears to be climbing toward its cruising altitude. But it is still buffeted by strong crosswinds. Indeed, it is becoming increasingly clear that the critics and would-be reformers of the now defunct Commission on Human Rights, abolished in 2006, seriously erred in thinking that a political body like the council could ever shed the "politicization" of its predecessor body.

That politics would shape the commission's work was a foregone conclusion the moment it was determined in the 1940s that it would be a body of governments rather than experts, as had been entertained at one time. In odd if not perverse ways, the politics of the cold war, decolonization and apartheid all constrained the commission's work and led to the slow emergence of a disjointed human rights architecture that would have dumbfounded the drafters of the UN Charter. These issues have now receded but enduring and no less divisive and polarizing problems have gained prominence: North against South, industrialized countries versus less industrialized countries and universalists against cultural relativists.

The new council is, accordingly, no less "politicized" than the commission. While then-Secretary-General Kofi Annan concluded in 2005 that the commission had to be ended because of its "declining credibility," it had by that time achieved much, having played a central role in the development of international human rights law and procedures for the investigation of rights abuses. But since human rights is inherently a political matter, it is not surprising that a significant number of countries saw in the establishment of the council an opportunity to roll back the commission's achievements rather than to hatch a more effective human rights body.

Shifting Grounds

At the time of its abolition, the commission consisted of representatives of 53 nations, elected by the Economic and Social Council for three-year terms. Countries seeking one of the new council's 47 seats are chosen by secret ballot of the General Assembly. Under the terms of its 2006 founding assembly resolution, council candidates must uphold the highest standards in the promotion and protection of human rights, agree to a review of their records and pledge cooperation with the council. But these requirements are purely voluntary. Candidates continue to be put forward by regional groups. Countries with dubious rights credentials may with relative ease circumvent the modest obstacles erected by the new system.

More disquieting, the balance of power among regional groups has shifted in favor of Africa and Asia at the expense of other regions. Africa lost 2 seats but Asia gained 2, leaving each with 13. While Eastern Europe gained a seat, bringing its total to 6, Latin America and Western Europe each lost 3, leaving them with 8 and 7 seats, respectively. That leaves Africa and Asia with a majority of the council's seats. In effect, the council's center of gravity has shifted in favor of a group of countries more focused on economic and social rights, which tend to view human rights accountability as a form of Western imperialism.

The US presence in the council adds complexity. In March 2009, the Obama administration reversed the previous administration's decision to shun a body it considered hopelessly flawed. After a robust campaign, the US won a seat in May. Since then, it has been actively involved in the council's work and consistently supported the UN High Commissioner for Human Rights. At the same time, it has taken a strong stand on some of its long-standing concerns, for example, repeatedly voicing its reservations about the use of the council to condemn Israel.

Tensions with High Commissioner

In creating the Office of the High Commissioner for Human Rights in 1994, the General Assembly kept it independent from the Human Rights Commission. That situation remained unchanged with the council's creation, but the commissioner and the council work closely together and the council relies on the commissioner's staff. Their differences on rights issues and procedures have often led to tensions.

Mary Robinson of Ireland, the second rights commissioner, was appointed by Kofi Annan in 1997 to be a rights activist rather than an administrator. But she found herself crippled after accusing Washington of rights violations in its war against terrorism. Canada's Arbour, who took the job in 2004, was mired in controversy from the start. Credited by some for increasing the number of global rights monitors around the world and for criticizing the US-led invasion of Iraq and counterterrorism strategies, she was accused by others of being soft on the rights records of Cuba, Zimbabwe, China, Sudan, Belarus and Russia. In March 2008, Arbour announced that she would leave the commission rather than seek a new term.

Pillay's appointment appears to have done little to quiet the critics, who bristled at her early statements touting the independence of her office and criticizing "huge gaps between lofty pledges and national realities" on human rights. In a special session in May 2009, the council snubbed her plea to set up an independent investigation of possible human rights violations in Sri Lanka. Her blunt support of efforts to address rights violations based on sexual orientation drew a stern warning from Pakistan and Algeria that "this issue does not enjoy universal agreement." Cuba, Egypt and Russia hinted they could use a 2011 review of the council's first five years to discuss ways to tighten the council's oversight over the commissioner's office.

Tensions surfaced again when the commissioner appeared before a General Assembly committee in October 2009. Sudan criticized the "multitude" of human rights mechanisms dealing with developing countries while China suggested the council should exert greater control over the commissioner. In a polite but blunt response, Pillay voiced a commitment to "truth, impartiality and integrity, with no toleration for double standards" and recalled that the independence of her office was enshrined in a resolution of the General Assembly. The swords appear to have been crossed.

Searching for an Elusive Consensus

Governments have long quarreled over whether human rights are universal, interdependent and indivisible. Among the UN's 192 members, such nagging questions have been resolved through uneasy ad-hoc political compromises among competing interests. In the 47-nation council, the large number of resolutions adopted in 2009 without a formal vote, on a wide range of subjects, hints that compromise is generally the order of the day. But the political consensus supporting these resolutions can be very thin. For example, in debate on a resolution put forward by the US and Egypt on freedom of opinion and expression, Egypt, the US, France, Pakistan and Cuba offered widely varying views of the meaning of these rights.

Divisions also often surfaced in the form of disputes over the council's jurisdiction. When Brazil offered a resolution asserting that access to medicine was part of an individual's right to health and could not be compromised by patent or trademark issues, developing nations praised the measure while wealthy nations argued that it was better left to the World Health Organization or the World Trade Organization.

Putting resolutions to a vote meant that political differences could not be bridged by compromise or ambiguous language. In these cases, the gloves came off and outright rejections were the rule. Such was the fate of a Cuban resolution that would have enshrined a "right to peace." Developed nations dismissed the matter as a misinterpretation of international law unrelated to human rights.

Inevitably, in this charged atmosphere, the ever-looming issue of the universality of human rights came up when Russia in June 2009 proposed a workshop on how a better understanding of "traditional values" could help promote and protect human rights. China, Indonesia and Senegal reasoned that traditional values predated human rights standards. Western countries countered that in some instances, traditional values could be used to justify harmful practices such as female genital mutilation. Mexico and Chile then expressed concern that the Russian proposal could give an unwelcome boost to the concept of cultural relativism. The Russian draft was eventually adopted, 26-25 with 6 abstentions.

Stalemate in Special Sessions

The council was created with the power to convene special sessions to convey the idea that it is a standing body, like the Security Council, prepared at any time to address crisis situations on short notice. So far, the council has held 13 special sessions, four of them in 2009. By and large, these sessions were driven primarily by political considerations—legitimizing or de-legitimizing, blaming, justifying policy demands and the like. None of the 2009 sessions had much of a practical impact on the ground or tangibly improved human rights conditions. In fact, the two special sessions devoted to the Gaza War, which began in December 2008, heightened tensions in the region.

It was Germany on behalf of 17 council members that called for a special session on the Sri Lanka civil war a week after the defeat of the Liberation Tigers of Tamil Eelam by government forces. According to unofficial UN estimates, 7,000 civilians were killed in the fighting from January to April 2009 and 300,000 were driven from their homes and detained in camps in the final stages of the war. Debate during the ensuing session seesawed between concern for innocent civilians caught up in the fighting and Sri Lanka's sovereign right to manage its own affairs. Council members ignored a plea from the commissioner for an independent investigation of possible rights violations, and Brazil, Cuba, India and Pakistan blocked a draft resolution deploring human rights abuses by both government forces and the insurgents. The session ended up adopting a resolution commending the government and reaffirming Sri Lanka's sovereignty, territorial integrity and independence, including its sovereign rights to protect its citizens and combat terrorism.

A special session dedicated to the global economic crisis, convened at the request of Brazil and African nations, split along North-South lines. Developing nations focused on the disproportionate impact of the crisis on poor countries and the need for developed countries to honor, if not strengthen, their commitments to development assistance. Since the turmoil began in wealthy nations, they argued, global financial institutions should be reformed to give the developing world a bigger say in policymaking. The European Union, Canada and Switzerland retorted that the crisis did not excuse governments from protecting and promoting rights and that, in any case, the council was not the proper setting for questions of development policy. In the end, a large majority backed a resolution calling for greater participation of developing countries in economic decision-making. A polarized council urged all nations to avoid cutting development aid and to avoid protectionist measures, even as Germany argued that Europe could not accept the idea that the crisis posed a direct threat to human rights.

War in Gaza

Saying it wanted to put an end to Palestinian rocket attacks, Israel launched air strikes on Gaza on Dec. 27, 2008, followed by a full-scale ground offensive. Military operations came to an end on Jan. 18, 2009, and Israel completed its withdrawal three days later. At the prodding of the Organization of Islamic Conference, Arab and Muslim states called for a special session to address the "grave violations of human rights committed in the Gaza Strip." Capping a three-day meeting, the council on Jan. 12 voted 33-1 with 13 abstentions to dispatch an urgent independent fact-finding mission to the region to investigate violations of international human rights law and international humanitarian law by Israel.

Because the resolution singled out Israel, Mary Robinson, the former rights commissioner, turned down an offer to head the mission. Richard Goldstone, a widely respected South African jurist and former chief prosecutor for the UN international tribunals for the former Yugoslavia and Rwanda, also initially declined the offer. He accepted it only after the mission's mandate was informally broadened to investigate violations "committed in Gaza."

The key conclusion of the mission's 575-page final report, released in September 2009, was that both Israel and Hamas, the militant Palestinian group that controls Gaza, were responsible for serious violations of international human rights and humanitarian law, possibly amounting to war crimes and crimes against humanity. The report portrayed the Israeli military campaign as part of a governmental policy of "massive and deliberate destruction… aimed at punishing the Gaza population." It called on Israel and Hamas to conduct independent, impartial investigations within six months. Should they fail to do so, the report said the Security Council should refer the matter to the International Criminal Court.

The report ignited a powder keg. While it was praised by many international legal experts and human rights organizations, the Israeli government issued a 32-point analysis calling it one-sided and replete with double standards and misstatement of law and facts. Torn between its long-standing support of Israel and its self-assigned role of mediator committed to a two-state solution to the Middle East conflict, the US initially remained silent but eventually inched closer to the Israeli position, in effect rejecting the report's conclusions and recommendations.

Washington then pressed the Palestinians to seek a delay in the council's consideration of a resolution seeking a second special session, to consider the report. The Palestinian leadership initially agreed to a postponement, then reversed itself after a domestic outcry, and the new session was set for Oct. 15. A resolution condemning Israeli human rights violations in East Jerusalem, the West Bank and Gaza was adopted the next day, by a vote of 25-6 with 11 abstentions. Among the Security Council's five permanent members, China and Russia supported the measure, the US voted "no" and France and Britain were among four nations abstaining.

A subsequent Libyan plea for an emergency session of the Security Council fizzled out when its permanent members showed no interest. The General Assembly on Nov. 5 then adopted a resolution, by a vote of 114-18 with 44 abstentions, giving Israel and the Palestinians three months to undertake "independent, credible investigations" into the Goldstone mission's findings. While maneuvering over the report continues, council actions appeared to have little if any impact on the situation in Gaza.

Experts on a Short Leash

The number of UN rights experts and investigators has expanded considerably since the Human Rights Commission set up its first expert group to investigate Apartheid in South Africa in 1967. These experts, variously known as special rapporteurs, independent experts, working groups and special representatives of the secretary-general, have evolved into one of the most effective rights protection mechanisms. They prepare studies and reports on individual countries or rights issues, carry out fact-finding missions, issue urgent appeals, develop rights standards, act as intermediaries on behalf of victims of rights abuses and generally raise public awareness.

At the end of 2009, the Office of the High Commissioner for Human Rights supported 39 special rights missions involving 55 individual experts or investigators. The missions cover countries—Burundi, Cambodia, North Korea, Haiti, Myanmar, the Palestinian Territories, Somalia and Sudan—as well as an array of issues ranging from adequate housing to cultural rights, foreign debt, freedom of religion, terrorism, torture and violence against women.

In 2009, these independent experts submitted 136 reports to the Human Rights Council and 24 reports to the General Assembly, carrying out 73 investigative missions to 51 countries and territories. Half of these missions were conducted with the approval of the government involved.

On one typical fact-finding mission, Raquel Rolnik, an expert on housing rights, investigated US housing practices in the fall of 2009. In the course of her 18-day inquiry, she met with local, state and federal officials, held public meetings in Washington, New York, Chicago, New Orleans, Los Angeles and the Pine Ridge Indian Reservation in South Dakota, and met with activists and ordinary citizens including homeless people. Her official report, reviewed by the council in March 2010, blamed flawed lending practices, a shortage of public housing and holes in the social safety net for a lack of adequate housing.

It is not unusual for these UN experts to publicly criticize government policies and practices, and some have come close to acting as national prosecutors, making them a crucial element in the UN human rights machinery. But their success depends to a significant extent on a government's cooperation and support. Some countries have tried to rein in or abolish this institution. While most of the special rights missions have been extended and some new mandates added (on contemporary forms of slavery in 2007, access to safe drinking water and sanitation in 2008 and cultural rights in 2009), there was a political price to pay: Missions dealing with Belarus, Cuba and Liberia were discontinued. The controversy provides yet another reminder of the fragility of an independent UN human rights apparatus.

In one case, a June 2009 debate over the appointment of a new independent expert for Sudan pitted the European Union against Sudan and left the council deeply divided. A new expert was approved by a narrow margin, but with a more limited mandate. The reappointment of an expert on freedom of expression was another bone of contention, with Egypt, Pakistan and Cuba intensely criticizing statements he had made on the role of religion. Cuba proposed a resolution binding UN rights experts to a code of conduct, a move denounced by Canada as "a deeply regrettable and inappropriate attempt to stifle and intimidate the system."

Universal Reviews

Among the new council's most innovative features is its periodic review of the human rights performance of each of the UN's 192 members. The process was launched in April 2008 after considerable haggling over how it would work. Early experience suggests that the reviews are evolving into a nonadversarial exercise, not meant to make deep wounds in their targets.

Under the system set up by the council, 48 countries are to be reviewed every year, and each of the council's 47 members are to come up for review at some point in their term. The US, an outspoken critic of the council just two years ago, is due to undergo its first rights review in November *[See "Washington's First Rights Review," P. 86]*.

Each review is led by a group of three countries, known as a "troika," and is based in part on a national report submitted in advance by the country under review. Any UN member can ask questions and make recommendations during the reviews, and outside groups such as local and global human rights organizations can submit information in advance and also address the council as it considers the "outcome reports" prepared by the troikas to wrap up each review.

The reports summarize the discussions and recommendations made during the reviews as well as the target nations' responses. The 2009 reviews confirmed that the countries in the hot seat are taking them seriously by sending large delegations of senior officials to participate. Council members and other countries observing the reviews also indicated their commitment, making nearly 2,300 statements and issuing 5,500 recommendations. Outside organizations spoke 284 times in the 2009 reviews, often making refreshingly candid and informative statements.

This said, the process has not taken the world to a human rights nirvana. The code governing the reviews appeared to be based on consensus building, deference and cooperation. National reports were rarely self-critical. A bloc mentality prevailed as friendly countries, often from the same region, took the floor to praise the target country's record or blame lapses on the burdens of foreign debt, poverty and other factors beyond the reach of a national government. On the whole, this meant that many sensitive questions were left hanging. Saudi Arabia shrugged off criticisms focusing on the independence of its judiciary, discrimination against women, its high rate of executions, arbitrary detentions and restrictions on religious freedom and free speech. China denied the existence of any state censorship and regretted "the ill-founded politicization" of its review, which looked at Tibet and Beijing's treatment of its Uighur minority. Pakistan, Nigeria and Egypt sought to limit critical statements by outside groups or interrupt them with points of order.

While Cambodia and Uruguay accepted each of the recommendations made during their reviews, North Korea and Russia rejected or failed to address all. China rejected about half, and Vietnam and Brunei Darussalam about a third of them. The Cuban delegation seemed to sum it all up, stating that "no people can accept that its right to self-determination and its sovereign right to choose its political, economic, juridical, cultural and social system is questioned."

Taking Stock

Three years in the life of a new institution is hardly enough for confident assessments. On balance, 2009 displayed more continuity than change. The council is as "politicized" as the commission. Its response to crises is just as sluggish and ineffective. Its decisions are just as inconsistent and selective, overshadowed by bloc voting and the influence of regional groups which act as a kind of group insurance against criticism. True, the universal review process subjects powerful countries to scrutiny, a scenario barely imaginable a few years ago. But a more realistic evaluation will have to wait until the second round of reviews, which begins in 2011 and will look at what governments have done to carry out the recommendations of the first round.

In the meantime, problems of reform and standard-setting are neglected. The African-Asian bloc of developing countries, routinely supported by China, Cuba and Russia, enjoys a numerical majority, even though its sway over the council is at times loosened—by its own divisions rather than US or European Union leadership.

It also will take time to see whether the US can restore its moral authority after eight years of the George W. Bush administration's reliance on exceptionalism and unilateralism. Washington is also constrained by its own ideas on human rights, which are at odds with the developing world, which has embraced "solidarity" as a central focus in its pursuit of economic and social rights. No doubt these political battles will flare up again in 2011 when the General Assembly is scheduled to convene a conference to take stock of the council's work in its first few years. Will the council end up an improvement over the commission? No one can foretell. But those countries that sought to defang the core UN human rights apparatus back in 2006 are likely to try once again to undo the laboriously crafted achievements of the commission, whose passing may soon be regretted. ■

Washington's First Rights Review

Edward R. McMahon

The new United Nations Human Rights Council gets its first chance this fall to review the United States on its performance in promoting and protecting human rights.

The evaluation, beginning in November, is part of an assessment of all 192 UN members intended to take place over four years. Begun in April 2008, this is the initial Universal Periodic Review since the council's creation in 2006. It will be closely watched both by the US and the international community as a test of the new rights body, which was created by the General Assembly to replace the discredited UN Commission on Human Rights.

The United States has long used the main UN rights body as a platform to press other nations on their records. The George W. Bush administration led the push to abolish the rights commission after accusing it of becoming captive of a bloc of violators and of ganging up on Israel. Even after the General Assembly replaced it with the 47-seat council, the Bush administration refused to seek a seat, saying the new body fell short of Washington's hopes for reform. The Obama administration, however, reversed that decision shortly after taking office in 2009, arguing that participating in the council's work was the most effective way to improve it.

At the same time, many UN members will be watching the US to ensure it provides a full airing of its own record, warts and all, in this initial review. Seeking to address these concerns, US Secretary of State Hillary Clinton has pledged to prepare a report on compliance with rights obligations that will be as tough on Washington as it has been on other countries. "Human rights are universal, but their experience is local," Secretary Clinton said to reporters in March. "This is why we are committed to holding everyone to the same standard, including ourselves."

"My goal is to be able to complete the report and after that come out even more aggressive on countries like Cuba, North Korea, Burma [Myanmar] and Russia," said Michael Posner, assistant secretary of state for democracy, human rights and labor, in an interview with The Cable blog. "We'll be in a stronger position if we do a good report, and we will."

As set out in the resolution creating the new council, the Universal Periodic Review is to be "based on objective and reliable information" and is intended to gauge, over a four-year cycle, "the fulfillment by each state of its human rights obligations and commitments." Its creation was an integral part of 2005 reforms championed by Kofi Annan, when he was secretary-general. How well the council has performed in its first five years is to be evaluated by a UN conference in 2011.

The first cycle of the universal periodic review was launched in 2008; 48 countries are reviewed every year in three sessions examining 16 states each. Each nation under review presents a report, drafted with input from local rights groups and other nongovernmental organizations, on the status of its human rights. All UN members, including the 47 chosen by the General Assembly for a seat on the Human Rights Council, then have the opportunity to participate in an "interactive dialogue" with representatives of the government under review and to make recommendations, which the government is free to accept, reject or ignore.

How Will Washington Fare?

In preparation for its review, the US has actively sought input from groups across the country, giving ordinary Americans an unusual opportunity to participate in an important UN activity. It is unclear at this point how self-critical the Obama administration's report to the UN will be, but recommendations issued during the review process are expected to focus on the rights of minorities and other disadvantaged citizens, including native Americans, abuses linked to the war on terror, abolition of the death penalty, and the US failure to ratify several key UN international agreements including the Convention on the Rights of the Child, the Convention on the Elimination of All Forms of Discrimination Against Women and the treaty establishing the International Criminal Court.

Over all, however, it is quite possible that Washington will fare well in the review, due at least in part to the US administration's decision to participate fully in the Human Rights Council. In addition, so far the council's practice has generally been to phrase recommendations in a diplomatic, constructive and forward-looking manner, although some nations, including Eritrea, Israel and North Korea, have undergone more pointed critiques.

The Universal Periodic Review itself has so far gotten mixed grades. Supporters view it as one of the council's most innovative and potentially valuable elements. They say that providing a regular platform for countries to raise a wide range of human rights concerns with one another makes promoting universal human rights a regular and accepted UN function.

Critics, however, including a number of Western human rights organizations, complain that the process is voluntary and lacks enforcement, creating a futile exercise that is long on rhetoric and short on results. In the council's review of China, for example, some rights groups accused African and Asian nations of pulling their punches. Some critics from developing nations, on the other hand, have emphasized the importance of national sovereignty and criticized Western states for using the reviews to promote values that they consider alien to their societies.

The first 112 countries to be scrutinized by the Human Rights Council were the target of about 10,000 recommendations, about two-thirds of which were accepted by the states in question. Some of the most frequent recommendations centered on women's and children's rights, torture, abolition of the death penalty, the ratification of UN human rights treaties and conventions, the rights of indigenous peoples, and permission for country visits by UN human rights investigators. Analysis of the recommendations so far shows that Asian and African states have generally tended to issue softer recommendations to one another than to Western states, while Western nations have made more action-oriented and apolitical recommendations, regardless of the target government's region. ■

A Mandate to Protect

Tendai Musakwa

Walter Kälin, the secretary-general's representative on the human rights of internally displaced persons, is charged with protecting the rights of people left homeless within their own countries by violence or natural disaster.

Kälin, a Harvard-educated Swiss legal scholar who has written many books on human rights, has served in the United Nations post since 2004; and his term expires in October 2010. The job is part-time and voluntary. In his regular work, he is professor of constitutional and international law at the University of Bern.

The UN makes a distinction between refugees—people who have left their country for fear of persecution—and internally displaced persons, who have fled their homes but remain in the same country.

UN Photo/Jean-Marc Ferre

Walter Kälin, the secretary-general's representative on human rights for internally displaced persons, addresses a special session of the Human Rights Council in January 2010 on the work in Haiti since a devastating earthquake.

The UN's guiding principles give national authorities the primary responsibility for protecting and providing humanitarian assistance to the displaced, but governments often fail to exercise this responsibility, leading to widespread human rights abuses.

The biggest challenge faced by Kälin is to ensure the basic welfare of a steadily growing number of people despite a shortage of funds. According to the UN and the Norwegian Refugee Council, 64 million people were homeless in their own countries in 2008, and monitoring agencies say that figure is increasing every year. The 2008 total includes 36 million displaced by natural disasters and 26 million displaced by conflicts.

"Nevertheless, the international community must not abandon Somalia."

One of Kälin's top priorities has been to try to focus international attention on Somalia, a northeast African nation torn by decades of anarchy, including most recently, years of fighting between a weak but internationally recognized transitional government and Islamist groups. Many of the 1.5 million Somalis displaced in the current struggle suffer from starvation, a lack of drinkable water and violence, including rape.

In his UN work, he has helped the governments of Georgia and Sudan adopt laws to protect their internal refugees. Working with the African Union, he helped develop the first regional agreement securing the rights of internally displaced people, the 2009 Convention for the Protection and Assistance of Internally Displaced Persons in Africa, also known as the Kampala Convention.

Kälin also helped the Sri Lankan government find shelter for those forced from their homes by a lengthy conflict pitting the country's army against the separatist Tamil Tigers, which ended in the Tigers' defeat in May 2009. His mediation in Nepal enabled many Nepalese to return to their homes after being caught in the fighting between Maoist rebels and government forces, which ended in 2006.

Kälin discussed the challenges he faces in an e-mail interview with UNA-USA in May 2010.

Q: What are the main challenges the international community faces in protecting the rights of the internally displaced?

A: First, the size of the problem is increasing. At the end of 2009, conflicts around the world displaced 27 million persons. This is the highest number recorded since systematic monitoring began in 1997 and represents more than twice the number of refugees worldwide.

The capacity of governments and international organizations to protect the human rights of internally displaced persons also needs to be improved. Some countries are not willing, or lack the capacity, to provide sufficient protection and assistance to internally displaced persons. Meanwhile, humanitarian and human rights organizations lack the resources to do everything that they need to protect the human rights of internally displaced persons. The overall humanitarian needs for the internally displaced in 2010, which were compiled in a consolidated appeal to donors, are at present only 40 percent funded.

Coordination of the different actors on the ground is another key challenge. Unlike the case of refugees, there is no single UN agency mandated to protect the human rights of internally displaced persons, and there are unclear responsibilities when it comes to the protection of their human rights.

Q: What is the scope of the problem of countries that deny the existence of internally displaced people?

A: I must emphasize that over the past 10 years, most countries have recognized the phenomenon and complexity of the problem of internal displacement. The few countries that continue to deny the existence of internally displaced persons may want to avoid the involvement of the international community in what they consider an internal affair, may not wish to assume their responsibilities under international law, or may not want to be held accountable for having failed to assume these responsibilities.

The UN advocates with these governments privately and publicly for the protection of persons displaced within their countries.

Q: What has the UN done to solve the humanitarian crisis in Somalia?

A: I visited Somalia last October and was appalled by the degree of violence, including sexual violence, which was committed with total impunity by all parties in the conflict.

The situation for humanitarian actors is extremely difficult. First, there is a sense of hopelessness and fatigue among donors, which has resulted in largely underfunded humanitarian activities. Second, the security situation in central and south Somalia is so severe that humanitarian workers cannot operate.

Nevertheless, the international community must not abandon Somalia. The humanitarian needs are enormous and the international community must step up its efforts. In [the Somali regions of] Puntland and Somaliland, humanitarian and development organizations must help strengthen local authorities' capacities for receiving new aid, and work to enhance and expand basic services for communities affected by displacement. In central and south Sudan, the main challenges are ensuring the safety and security of humanitarian workers and improving their access to internally displaced persons.

Q: How is the UN working to protect the rights of people displaced by natural disasters?

A: Human rights violations of persons displaced by natural disasters do not usually occur because of deliberate strategies. More often, they are a result of inappropriate policies, oversight or neglect. Governments can therefore prevent human rights violations if they apply appropriate policies.

I led a process within the Inter-Agency Standing Committee, which brings together humanitarian actors from the UN, the Red Cross/Red Crescent movement and other nongovernmental organizations, to develop operational guidelines for the protection of persons affected by natural disasters. These guidelines give easy-to-use recommendations to ensure that governments and international actors integrate human rights protection standards into all disaster response, recovery and reconstruction efforts from the earliest stage possible. I have been promoting these guidelines in workshops all over the world. ■

Coaxing Europe to Welcome Two-Time Refugees

Indra Baatarkhuu

Unable to find enough new homes for people forced to flee an adoptive homeland after earlier leaving their own countries, the United Nations is pressing Europe to be more welcoming to such two-time refugees.

The UN High Commissioner for Refugees is encouraging Europe to take on a larger share of the burden as the number of refugees in need of a second new home remains high and available spots remain scarce. The UN refugee agency has set a goal of resettling 203,000 refugees in 2010, even though it expects to find only 79,000 spots for them.

Refugees in need of a second resettlement have typically been living in exile in the country that initially granted them asylum when they fled their homelands. But things don't always work out on the first try. In 2009, the agency helped 84,000 people resettle in a third country after their initial choice brought a risk of fresh persecution or detention, a threat to be forcibly returned to their original home, or because they simply could not fit in, possibly for lack of housing or jobs. By country, the greatest numbers of refugees requiring resettlement last year came originally from Afghanistan (260,662), Iraq (89,125) and Somalia (49,115).

"Resettlement is an important tool of refugee protection," Andrej Mahecic, a spokesman for the agency, said in February. "It provides a durable solution every year for tens of thousands of refugees who cannot safely remain in their first countries of asylum and for whom return to their countries of origin is not possible."

Because of the scarcity of choices, those who can't find a place to go "stay where they are," Mahecic said. "They wait for another solution—next year. Some people stay for years."

Given the gap between supply and demand, High Commissioner António Guterres, a former Portuguese prime minister, hopes to encourage more resettlement in Europe, where many governments are not eager to allow in additional foreigners. Europe provided spots to only 6.6 percent of the 65,859 people successfully resettled around the world in 2008. By contrast, about 90 percent ended up in the United States, Canada or Australia.

"Europe needs to take its responsibility and show international solidarity with countries of first asylum that are often among the poorest in the world," said Berend Jonker of the Foundation for Refugee Students UAF in the Netherlands.

Europeans Were Once Beneficiaries

A 1951 international treaty defines refugees as those who have left their country because of "a well-founded fear of being persecuted on account of race, religion, nationality, membership of a particular social group, or political opinion." The definition excludes the "internally displaced," people who have been driven from their homes but are still in their home countries. While refugees come under the care of the refugee agency, the internally displaced are the responsibility of other UN agencies, national and nongovernmental programs.

Some 80 percent of all refugees end up living in developing nations, many of them poverty-stricken.

According to the UN's 2008 Global Trends report, 42 million people were forcibly uprooted worldwide in 2008, a drop of 700,000 from 2007. That figure includes 16 million refugees and asylum-seekers hoping to gain refugee status, as well as 26 million internally displaced people.

The UN refugee agency has had an international mandate to assist refugees since its inception after World War II; its initial task was to help millions of Europeans driven from their homes by war. With an annual budget of $3 billion and 6,600 staff members, it works now to assist 34.4 million people in more than 110 countries.

Refugees and asylum-seekers have always been part of the European landscape, although their numbers and the receptions they have received have fluctuated wildly. But the need to accept refugees seeking resettlement is a relatively new and growing phenomenon there.

One of the problems is that most refugees these days come from poor nations, and Europe is also suffering rising unemployment and economic hardship. That makes many European governments nervous about letting in more refugees, however great their need.

One way the UN is encouraging European nations to open their doors a little is by helping them to adopt international standards in judging individual cases that are fair, democratic and transparent. ■

Secretary-General Ban Ki-moon and Erik Solheim, Norway's environment minister, visit the polar ice rim in September 2009 to witness the impact of climate change on icebergs and glaciers. Ban led a campaign to urge UN members to negotiate an effective agreement at climate change talks in Copenhagen later that year.

Seeking Common Ground on Climate Change

96   **After Copenhagen, Climate Dealers Shuffle the Cards**
Karen Freeman

104   **The Secretary-General's Point Man on Climate Policy**
Karen Freeman

107   **Help, My Island Is Sinking!**
Mirva Lempiainen

After Copenhagen, Climate Dealers Shuffle the Cards

Karen Freeman

A comma inserted at the insistence of the United States turned one paragraph of a climate-change plan debated in 2007 into a Rorschach test of sorts for diplomats: Look at it the way the US sees it, and developed and developing nations must all reduce greenhouse gas emissions through actions that are "measurable, reportable and verifiable." Look at it another way, and developing countries are essentially off the hook.

Two years later, when diplomats gathered in Copenhagen for the crucial next round of negotiations called for by the 2007 document, known as the Bali Action Plan, the argument was still on the boil. It may look like a kerfuffle over a lowly comma, but it marks the sore spot of climate negotiations: the chasm between developed nations and developing nations.

The contentious comma comes after the phrase "capacity-building" in the plan's call for "national/international action" on nationally appropriate "mitigation actions by developing country parties in the context of sustainable development, supported and enabled by technology, financing and capacity-building, in a measurable, reportable and verifiable manner."

The US says it intended the comma to make it clear that developing nations' anti-warming steps would be open to outside scrutiny, just like the steps taken by developed countries. But developing countries say the comma does not alter their view that such scrutiny is solely confined to the technology, financing and capacity-building that comes from the industrialized world.

Once Again: Whose Responsibility?

The issue of scrutiny is not the only point of disagreement between the developed and developing nations. Their biggest clash is over the question of whether relatively well-off developing nations such as China and India, which compete with the major industrial powers in global trade, should share the financial burden of halting global warming.

That divide goes a long way toward explaining why the Copenhagen talks did not follow the lead of the 2007 plan and culminate in an agreement to extend the Kyoto Protocol beyond 2012, the year marking the end of the initial commitments of industrialized nations to cut greenhouse gas emissions. Nations could not agree on a new treaty, so they instead produced a political agreement, the Copenhagen Accord.

The accord declares itself to be "operational immediately," but since it is a political agreement, it's only the political will of the nations signing up for it that will determine whether it works.

Such voluntary approaches are not new to UN climate-change diplomacy. Countries are free to participate as they wish in the work of the Intergovernmental

Panel on Climate Change, the agency set up by two UN organizations in 1988 to assess scientific evidence in the field. And countries took voluntary steps to get their greenhouse gas emissions below 1990 levels under the UN Framework Convention on Climate Change, a treaty negotiated in 1992, until dissatisfaction grew over the convention's lack of bite. The step away from voluntary targets came with a protocol to the convention that went into effect in 2005: the Kyoto Protocol, a treaty that set mandatory emissions reductions for the industrialized nations that had ratified it.

US Wants a Division of Group

The US was not one of them because no American president has asked the Senate to ratify Kyoto. The sticking point, quite simply, is this: the US rejects any process that treats developing nations as a homogeneous group that should not be expected to sign up for concrete, verifiable steps to combat climate change. While it supports the idea that poor nations should get lots of aid from rich countries, it contends that China, India and other rapidly growing developing nations should share the financial burden in reducing their own emissions. The Copenhagen Accord deals with both issues: It makes generous aid promises to the developing world, and it nudges the most prosperous members of that group toward greater responsibility.

But the agreement that emerged in Copenhagen did not result from the expected process. The problem was that UN treaties are traditionally negotiated by consensus, with final approval conditioned on unanimous support. For this text to become a legally binding treaty would have required the backing of each of the 193 parties there, but a handful adamantly opposed the US position. With a treaty out of reach, negotiators whipped up the diplomatic soufflé called the Copenhagen Accord.

As a political agreement, it lacks the heft of a legally binding treaty, but that is still the goal as negotiations lead up to Framework Convention meetings in Cancún, Mexico, at the end of this year, and in South Africa next year. If a binding deal is reached, however, it may not come together at one time and in one place.

"It takes a little bit of the high drama away to not have an agreement on one treaty at one time with a big press conference at the end," said Robert C. Orr, the UN assistant secretary-general for policy coordination and strategic planning. "But it's more likely to be an iterative set of agreements."

Objections to Action as Atonement

The issues of guilt and redemption will keep popping up during this process. Developing nations contend that the industrialized nations responsible for most of the greenhouse gases in the atmosphere today have a historical responsibility— even a moral obligation—to bear the burden. But the US rejects any approach that smacks of atonement for past sins. It notes that China surpassed the US as the leading emitter of greenhouse gases in 2006 and that the emissions of industrialized nations will soon be dwarfed by such nations as China and India.

"I actually completely reject the notion of a debt or reparations or anything of the like," said Todd Stern, the US special envoy on climate change, in Copenhagen.

"For most of the 200 years since the Industrial Revolution, people were blissfully ignorant of the fact that emissions caused a greenhouse effect. It's a relatively recent phenomenon."

In a speech in May, Stern explored that idea further: "Most fundamentally, you cannot address the climate challenge by focusing only on developed countries; they account for around 45 percent of global emissions now and will account for some 35 percent by 2030. Instead, you need to start with the 85 percent of emissions represented by the major economies and build out from there. Moreover, as a matter of political reality, we could get no support in the United States for a climate agreement that required action of us but not from China and the other emerging markets."

The US stance was at center stage at Copenhagen, and it left many observers cold. The European Union, in particular, was reported to feel shut out of a leading role at the talks despite its exemplary efforts in Kyoto. Early assessments of the accord ranged from "better than nothing" to "disaster." And most conference participants were also unhappy about the process used to push it through.

Obama Enlisted Rapid-Growth Group

Washington made its diplomatic move after the expected negotiating process imploded and delegates started heading for the exits. That's when President Obama cornered the leaders of Brazil, South Africa, India and China—known as the BASIC group of rapidly growing developing countries—and enlisted them in writing the accord. Then it was handed off for consideration by 28 nations, many of them representing other groups of countries. Finally, it went before all conference participants.

Adoption required unanimous consent, however, and a few nations raised objections, including Bolivia, Cuba, Sudan and Venezuela. So the conference merely "noted" the Copenhagen Accord, reducing it to the status of a political document rather than a treaty. Countries were then asked to sign on voluntarily in the ensuing weeks and months and to list the steps they intended to take to tackle climate change.

Many groups were unhappy with the result. Nnimmo Bassey, chair of Friends of the Earth International, called the conference "an abject failure," adding, "By delaying action, rich countries have condemned millions of the world's poorest people to hunger, suffering and loss of life as climate change accelerates."

Even José Manuel Barosso, president of the European Commission, said the accord was "clearly below our ambitions." He offered faint praise: "This accord is better than no accord."

Orr, the assistant secretary-general, acknowledges that the Copenhagen Accord has been a messy process with few fans. "Governments got the accord only hours before they were supposed to agree, so it left a bad taste," he said in a telephone interview in April.

Wide Range of Possibilities

"The debate is now over how to incorporate the Copenhagen Accord into a formal legal negotiating track," Orr said. "Does it get incorporated in as a whole? In pieces? Who gets to decide? Do we get a new treaty that supersedes Kyoto, or do we get a second commitment period? Or allow another treaty that wouldn't supersede Kyoto?"

If the Copenhagen Accord has a good track record among the Framework Convention's 194 parties, that could presumably make it a more attractive model for further negotiations. As of early July, 138 countries accounting for more than 85 percent of global emissions have in some way embraced the accord, while eight countries, representing about 2 percent of global emissions, have expressed opposition, according to the US Climate Action Network, a group of organizations. The rest have not announced a decision.

While that is positive, the steps countries have promised to make so far will fail to meet the modest target of keeping the average global temperature from rising more than 2 degrees Celsius (3.6 degrees Fahrenheit), compared with preindustrial temperatures. But the Copenhagen Accord is seen as just one step of many. When the process is described as "iterative," as Orr did, it means that practical targets will be set, then modified as needed in later deals.

The US intends to stay in front in the negotiations, Obama said in Copenhagen. "Going forward, we're going to have to build on the momentum that we established in Copenhagen to ensure that international action to significantly reduce emissions is sustained and sufficient over time," he said. "I want America to continue to lead on this journey."

Looking on Toward South Africa

While Secretary-General Ban Ki-moon wants the Cancún conference to produce an overall treaty, most experts are predicting it will not. Such a result may not be possible until South Africa in 2011, or even afterward.

"The betting for Cancún," Orr said, "is not that we're going to be able to get a formal, legally binding agreement that is a top-to-bottom agreement—while that is the goal—but agreement on significant chunks of substance, some of which come out of the Copenhagen Accord and some that come out of a formal negotiating track."

He added: "But if a large set of the chunks happen in Cancún and/or in South Africa, you might get over a threshold where you'd say, 'Yes, there is now a comprehensive, or relatively comprehensive, treaty.' And then all the subsequent negotiations become additions or tweaks to that."

Now that the vehicle of a political agreement has been used to get around the traditional requirement that UN treaties be adopted by consensus, it will be interesting to see whether political mechanisms will be used at other points in these negotiations. But it should be kept in mind that the Copenhagen Accord has certainly not shoved aside the Kyoto Protocol. Because Kyoto counts on the industrialized countries to finance the work to stop global warming, developing nations are especially loyal to it.

Outflow from Copenhagen Accord

Even though Brazil helped negotiate the Copenhagen Accord and then signed it, President Luiz Inácio Lula da Silva warned in April of a "negotiating impasse" on climate change, saying that the large traditional polluters have "a special charge." "The balance established by the Kyoto Protocol," he said, "is essential for us to move forward together." Any future negotiations based on Kyoto could proceed with or without parallel talks based on Copenhagen, but the US, of course, would be outside any Kyoto track.

Whatever happens, the Copenhagen Accord has injected new elements into the process. One is the bottom-up strategy used to put it together, an idea the US says came from Australia. In bottom-up negotiations, countries have maximum flexibility in making pledges, and that helped the US and China reach agreement in the nonbinding Copenhagen Accord. A top-down approach, as in the Kyoto Protocol, means setting overall goals that can be enforced.

"What we need is something in between," said Elliot Diringer, a vice president at the Pew Center on Global Climate Change, "an international framework that is flexible enough to ensure broad participation, and binding enough so that parties can be reasonably confident that others will fulfill their commitments."

The commitments that are made by countries fall under the headings of adaptation and mitigation. Adaptation means helping countries cope with the problems that will be caused by global warming, such as flooding or hazardous weather. Sea walls may be built, for example, or people moved to safer sites. Mitigation efforts limit the amount of warming by cutting greenhouse gas emissions and expanding carbon "sinks" such as forests, which store carbon. The Copenhagen Accord pays particular attention to a UN program to protect and plant more forests, which is one of the most economical ways to sequester carbon and keep it out of the atmosphere.

Poor and Small Head the List

The Copenhagen Accord says the least developed nations and the small island countries will be at the head of the line when financial support is parceled out for the climate projects such nations take on voluntarily. The accord sets up a Copenhagen Green Climate Fund, which will have a lot of money to hand out if the fund meets its goal: $30 billion for the 2010-2012 period, which then increases until the kitty reaches $100 billion per year by 2020. Developing nations have recently expressed concern that some of this aid may be money recycled from established projects instead of new assistance, so this will be an issue as the work progresses. And some of them are unhappy about the US policy to deny climate-change aid money to nations opposing the accord.

The secretary-general has convened the high-level Advisory Group on Climate Change Financing to find ways to underwrite the Copenhagen Green Climate Fund, and by doing that has made it clear that the Copenhagen Accord is part of the UN process despite its status as a political agreement rather than a treaty. The advisory group is made up of private experts such as the financier George Soros as well as public officials.

What Will UN's Status Be?

But the challenges facing the UN go beyond the Copenhagen Accord. For one, global warming is being discussed in several prominent global forums now, raising the question of whether the UN will continue to be the pre-eminent place for such diplomacy.

Among these are the Group of 20 and the Major Economies Forum, which bring together major developed and developing nations, and, for developing nations, the Group of 77 and China; the BASIC group, Brazil, South Africa, India and China; and the BRIC coalition, Brazil, Russia, India and China. But Orr insists that governments continue to believe that the UN Framework Convention on Climate Change is the only forum where a major agreement could be reached.

"Obviously if the G20 had some kind of an understanding on financing, that would be very helpful, given that they account for over 80 percent of the world's economy," Orr said. "But I think it's safe to say at this point the bitter taste of Copenhagen is fading in a lot of mouths, that the idea that everyone was hearing about right after Copenhagen, that this could somehow be done outside the UN … you just don't hear that these days."

The UN also faces challenges from climate-change skeptics who appear to be newly emboldened by errors in the work of the Intergovernmental Panel on Climate Change.

It seems like a long time ago that the panel drew world attention for a simple statement in its Fourth Assessment Report—that most of the recent increase seen in global average temperatures was "very likely" due to human activities.

What Errors and How Many at Issue

That came out in 2007, the year the Nobel Peace Prize was awarded to the panel and to former Vice President Al Gore for their separate efforts on global warming. But since then, climate skeptics have pointed out flaws in that report, as well as in communications and work by climate scientists outside the UN. Most of the flaws have since been declared to be inadvertent. The most publicized error in the Fourth Assessment Report exaggerated the effects of global warming on Himalayan glaciers.

Some skeptics doubt the extent of the average global temperature rise or the danger it presents. Some doubt that today's warming is unusual or primarily due to human activities. Others doubt the competence and even the motives of UN leaders and scientists involved. But at a UN forum in February, Ban reassured his audience that the climate experts' findings remain solid. "I urge you to reject the last-ditch attempts by climate skeptics to derail your negotiations by exaggerating shortcomings," he said. "Tell the world that you unanimously agree that climate change is a clear and present danger."

Ban and the panel's chairman, Rajendra Pachauri, have asked the InterAcademy Council, an organization of national science academies, to review the panel's working methods. (Most of the material analyzed by panel scientists has been published in scientific journals after being cleared by experts in the field.) The InterAcademy Council says it will try to complete its work by fall 2010 because the panel is already working on its Fifth Assessment Report.

Pachauri himself has drawn criticism. In March, the accounting giant KPMG cleared him of allegations of personal financial improprieties. Critics also say he has been too dismissive of dissent. When the Indian environment ministry challenged the panel's conclusions on glaciers, Pachauri initially accused it of "arrogance." In February, he was quoted as saying of climate-change skeptics, "They are people who say that asbestos is as good as talcum powder—and I hope they put it on their faces every day."

Recently, however, Pachauri has been more tactful. "I am not deaf to those who do not agree with the scientific consensus on manmade climate change," he wrote in an article in June. But elsewhere in the article, he acknowledged only "a mistake" in the panel's Fourth Assessment Report, even though Ban has referred to "a few errors" in that report and 250 scientists who support the panel's work issued a letter in March mentioning "a handful of misstatements."

Shift in Leadership Also a Factor

Uncertainty has also been injected into the quest for a new global climate-change deal by a recent shift in leadership at the UN Framework Convention on Climate Change. Christiana Figueres of Costa Rica became executive secretary of the convention's secretariat in July, following the departure of Yvo de Boer of the Netherlands, who left after four years in the post to work for KPMG.

De Boer also had his critics; some accused him of being too much of an advocate. "I try to make a distinction between the secretariat—which is, and should be, neutral—and my own personal role," he was quoted by Agence France-Presse as saying in June. "So if you don't like it, shoot at me—don't shoot at the secretariat." A less than diplomatic confidential memo he wrote after the Copenhagen conference, which was later leaked, accused the Danish Prime Minister, Lars Løkke Rasmussen, of undermining the negotiations by circulating a compromise draft text at the wrong time. The prime minister's move, de Boer wrote, "destroyed two years of effort in one fell swoop."

Figueres brings many years' experience with Framework Convention negotiations to her new post and appears well-prepared to put her own stamp on the process. In 2003, as executive director of the Center for Sustainable Development in the Americas, which she founded, she wrote an analysis with Kevin A. Baumert of the World Resources Institute on the options for Kyoto beyond 2012. This analysis addressed the question of who should get the bill for stopping global warming. While supporting Kyoto's distinction between the obligations of developed and developing nations, she was open even then to the idea of looking to parameters like per-capita gross domestic product as a "useful complement" in determining countries' responsibilities.

In holding onto ownership of the post-Copenhagen process, the UN faces a gargantuan task. But Obama and his administration face some heavy lifting as well. Above all, they must sell their vision of the best direction for climate negotiations to take. Even though the fastest-growing developing nations signed on to the Copenhagen Accord, they are not eager to assume substantial financial responsibility or subject themselves to outside oversight in future deals.

Pondering Life After Kyoto

So it may be only a subtle clue, but Washington must have been heartened a bit by a Reuters report on April 21 about the agenda for a meeting of Brazil, South

Africa, India and China, showing that they were at least thinking about life without the Kyoto Protocol. The agenda included these questions: "How long will the Kyoto Protocol survive? … If no second commitment period, what would replace Kyoto?"

Obama needs to win backing at home as well as abroad for his new approach. America's standing in the negotiations depends on getting his own energy legislation through a deeply divided Congress. While the administration hopes the catastrophic oil spill in the Gulf of Mexico will help build support for Obama's proposals, the Senate appears unlikely to pass a strong energy measure, if it passes one at all.

Nonetheless, the US administration sounds optimistic. It sees the Copenhagen Accord as the beginning of "a new climate architecture," according to Stern, the special envoy for climate change, and it's pushing that vision hard. And certainly the US considers the obligations of fast-growing developing countries to be an important part of that architecture. That's a long way from the consensus of 1992, the year the UN Framework Convention on Climate Change began. The convention treaty told all developing nations they had no obligation to try to reduce emissions unless developed countries furnished the necessary money and technology.

In his May speech, Stern explained the new American approach this way:

"It is grounded in the need to take action that can actually address the problem. It pushes countries to deliver, but does not insist on promises that can't be kept. It understands the fundamental imperative of development for developing countries. It recognizes the need to deliver large-scale assistance to many countries around the world. It acknowledges that a regime premised on an absolute separation of responsibilities based on a snapshot of the world in 1992 makes no sense. And it is committed to meeting the single most important objective of the Framework Convention: to avoid dangerous climate change." ▤

The Secretary-General's Point Man on Climate Policy

Karen Freeman

Following are excerpts from an interview with Robert C. Orr, the UN assistant secre-tary-general for policy coordination and strategic planning and Secretary-General Ban Ki-moon's chief strategist on climate change negotiations. The telephone interview, conducted for "A Global Agenda" by Karen Freeman, took place on April 17, 2010.

Q: Since the Copenhagen Accord was adopted outside the procedure set up for the UN Framework Convention on Climate Change (UNFCCC) conference last December, is the accord inside or outside the UN?

A: Why is Copenhagen a bit confusing? At this point there are 117 countries [now 138] that have formally supported it in writing to the UNFCCC secretariat—the Web site has the latest. That constitutes over 80 percent of global emissions and the global economy.

The Copenhagen accord is where we are right now: the deals stand. No one has walked away. That doesn't mean everything is clear. Some commitments are condi-tional, so that's one source of uncertainty. The second source is how to turn this political agreement into a legally binding agreement. That's the holy grail. One big debate that came out of Copenhagen is what to do with the Kyoto Protocol. The first commitment period for Kyoto ends in 2012. Do we get a new treaty that supersedes it, or do we get a second Kyoto commitment period? Or allow another treaty that wouldn't supersede Kyoto?

Another sore point is the process used in Copenhagen. The Danish presidency, when things did not move as hoped, turned to the ministerial level, then to heads of state. We had an unprecedented 30 leaders in a room for almost 48 hours of negotiations. The representativity of that group has been questioned by some, but officially represented were 140 countries, at a minimum.

But governments got the accord only hours before they were supposed to agree, so it left a bad taste. The debate is now over how to incorporate the accord into a formal legal negotiating track. Does it get incorporated in as a whole? In pieces? Who gets to decide?

Q: This year's big UN Framework Convention on Climate Change conference will be in Cancún, Mexico, from Nov. 29 to Dec. 10. What's the outlook?

A: The betting for Cancún is not that we're going to be able to get a formal legal-ly binding agreement that is a top-to-bottom agreement—while that is the goal—but agreement on significant chunks of substance, some from the Copenhagen Accord and some from a formal negotiating track.

The secretary-general says the ultimate goal is a comprehensive legally binding agreement. One reason for expecting something less than total success in one gulp is that this is the most comprehensive, complex negotiation in history. The secretary-general has launched the advisory group on financing to find ways to raise $100 billion per year by 2020; that would be a huge achievement. But is it realistic to have agreement on all those pieces in the next few months? Can we get deeper agreements if not the final word?

There's one more issue. In the accord, a broad body of countries agrees to keep the increase in global temperature to below 2 degrees Celsius. Yet I don't think anyone would say that the current commitments on the table are going to get us there. We have to line up goals with commitments.

UN Photo/Devra Berkowitz

Robert C. Orr, Secretary-General Ban Ki-moon's chief strategist on climate policy, addresses a news conference in June 2010. Orr acknowledges that the climate change deal reached in Copenhagen in 2009 "left a bad taste," but he notes that countries accounting for more than 85 percent of global emissions have since embraced it in some way.

Q: Can we get an agreement matching up goals with commitments in Cancún?

A: No, I think it's going to be an ongoing process. For Cancún and beyond, a much broader set of countries with a much broader set of interests will have obligations to achieve the goals, compared with Kyoto, so countries are going to have to have more degrees of freedom to decide on strategies.

Q: What about the big UN Framework Convention on Climate Change meeting in South Africa at the end of 2011? Will a comprehensive treaty be possible by then?

A: I would hesitate to say it's all going to happen in Cancún or in South Africa. But if a large set of the chunks happened in Cancún and/or in South Africa, you might get over a threshold where you'd say, "Yes, there is now a comprehensive, or relatively comprehensive, treaty." It takes a little bit of the high drama away to not have an agreement on one treaty at one time with a big press conference at the end. But it's more likely to be an iterative set of agreements.

Q: Groups outside the UN seem to be getting into the climate change arena in a major way: regional groups, the Major Economies Forum, the Group of 8, the Group of 20 and the like. Could that leave the UN on the sidelines?

A: Well they're not getting into it; they've been in it. Just to be clear on that: It is universally recognized by all governments—and at this point by 99-point-something percent of the pundits—that there is no place outside the UNFCCC where you can get an agreement. Right after Copenhagen, everyone heard about the idea that this could somehow be done outside the UN or the UNFCCC, but you just don't hear that these days. So if the G-20, for example, had some kind of an understanding on financing, that would be very helpful, given that they account for over 80 percent of the world's economy. But the reality is you can't have a treaty that affects everybody and needs everyone in it outside a treaty format.

Q: Is the UN increasing its public relations efforts to counter global warming skeptics?

A: The global understanding of the climate challenge is still not up to the severity of the issue. Is the UN making efforts? Absolutely. And I do think that progress on the science has been helpful in the last two or three years to take certain issues off the table. Is climate change happening? No one serious is asking that anymore. That is an advance, and that is due to a lot of communications work in addition to the science. ■

Help, My Island Is Sinking!

Mirva Lempiainen

Fragile is the word for the Maldives Republic, an island nation in the Indian Ocean where water constitutes 99 percent of the surface area and land 1 percent. The 200 inhabited islands are scattered over 115 square miles, an area nearly twice the size of the District of Columbia.

As global warming continues, the water level is creeping up on the Maldives. The rising sea may eventually submerge much of the Maldives, whose highest peak is only seven feet above sea level. The United Nations has estimated that the country may be uninhabitable by the year 2100, making its citizens some of the first environmental refugees in the world—if nothing is done to turn off the tap.

The country's uncertain future has prompted the Maldives' citizens and government to launch a broad assault on climate change on every possible level, ranging from local awareness projects to a national drive to achieve carbon neutrality, and to an international lobbying campaign for strong global curbs on greenhouse gas emissions.

"We don't want to just sit around and say, 'O.K., we are too small, nobody will notice us,'" said Ibrahim Asneem Adam, a photographer and father of two boys, aged 7 and 11. He recently helped organize "350 Postcards from the Frontline," a project that raised awareness of the Maldives' plight by displaying a collage of postcards depicting everyday life in the islands at an open-air exhibition in Malé, the capital. The number represents the concentration of greenhouse gases in the atmosphere that many scientists consider a reasonably safe upper limit for the world. That would mean limiting the rise in average global temperatures to 1.5 degrees Celsius.

Joe Romm, a physicist and climate-change activist, said, "Small island nations are going to be destroyed by global warming." As for the Maldivians, he said, "I think they're going to have to move." Romm, a top US Energy Department official in the Clinton Administration, added: "It's a great tragedy. They are the innocent victims."

A Big Bump in the Average

Over the past century, the sea level has risen globally at an average of 0.08 inches a year, according to a 2007 Report of the International Panel on Climate Change, established in 1988 by the World Meteorological Organization and the United Nations Environment Program. Data from 1993 to 2009 suggest that sea levels are rising faster than predicted, but there is a lot of geographical fluctuation. The Western Pacific sea level, for example, may be rising up to three times as fast as the global average.

The seas today may be nearly eight inches higher, on average, than they were a century ago, and nearly two inches higher than just 15 years ago, and climate experts say global warming is a major factor behind any such rise. As increasing levels of greenhouse gases warm the atmosphere, the oceans heat up. Warm water takes up more space than cold; at the same time, warmer air melts mountain glaciers and ice sheets, adding to the oceans' volume.

This is dire news for the Maldives, where the average elevation is five feet above sea level. Abdul Ghafoor Mohamed, the nation's representative at the United Nations, said: "We do have the very real risk of losing our land and . . . becoming what you might call environmental refugees."

Warming poses a clear economic threat to the Maldives, whose white sand beaches and coral reefs attract more than 600,000 international visitors a year, making tourism the largest economic activity. Yet the republic still ranks among the poorest third of the world's countries, with a per capita gross domestic product of $4,200 in 2009. Zoona Naseem, who works at the Banyan Tree Resort on Vabbinfaru island, said: "Our repeater guests who come to the Maldives to visit our island, very often they will say, 'Where's the beach? Where's the beach that was there last year?'"

If current emissions trends continue, global sea levels will rise four to five feet this century, Romm estimates. That's enough to wipe out such Pacific Ocean island nations as Fiji, Samoa and Tonga as well as the Maldives.

And although islands face the greatest threat from global warming, rising sea levels also pose difficulties for low-lying coastal areas of Bangladesh, Vietnam, San Francisco Bay and Florida, among many other places. The International Organization for Migration estimates climate change may create as many as a billion refugees around the world by 2050.

Some Are Evacuating Now

Some people have already had to pack their bags. The Carteret Islands in Papua New Guinea are expected to be uninhabitable by 2015 as they are slowly swallowed up by the ocean, a phenomenon local officials blame on global warming. The government helped the first five Carteret Island families move to the much larger nearby island of Bougainville in 2009, and the 2,000 remaining inhabitants are expected to follow within five years.

For the 396,000 people estimated to live in the Maldives, moving to another part of the country is not an option. "There is no higher ground we can move to, there is no safe island within the archipelago," Ambassador Ghafoor said.

Rising seas are not a new threat in the Maldives, whose inhabitants lived in fear of severe storms, tidal surges and tsunamis long before global warming became a worldwide preoccupation. After heavy flooding in 1987, an 11.5-foot-high sea wall was built around the capital island, Malé, to guard against a recurrence.

It was the country's former president, Maumoon Abdul Gayoom, who brought the Maldives into the climate change spotlight two decades ago. At the 1992 UN Earth Summit, Gayoom called himself "a representative of endangered people." In 1998, he was the first president to sign the Kyoto Protocol on climate.

The current president, Mohamed Nasheed, whose victory in 2008 in the country's first democratic elections ended Gayoom's 30-year rule, has kept up the tradition. In November 2008, Nasheed announced that he wanted to buy space for a new home country and was eyeing land in India, Sri Lanka and Australia. He has also pushed for the establishment of a relocation fund, financed by the tourism industry.

Ambassador Ghafoor said Maldivians would prefer a global agreement on climate change to moving to another land. He wants the world to commit to "no more than a 1.5 degree increase in temperature and 350 parts per million of carbon," he said. "That's what we can live with—that's the highest."

A Carbon-Neutral Goal

The government has decided that one good way to garner support for its cause is to lead by example. President Nasheed declared in March 2009 that the Maldives over the next decade would become the world's first carbon-neutral country.

The country took a big first step eight months later, when the Maldives' State Electric Company Limited launched a project to build a 75-megawatt wind farm in Gaafaru Island, North Malé atoll. The $200 million foreign direct investment project, estimated to reduce the country's carbon dioxide emissions by up to 25 percent, will power up Malé, the airport island of Hulhule and a number of resorts.

A few weeks before the wind farm announcement, the government held a widely publicized cabinet meeting underwater. The president and 11 ministers donned diving gear and sat on tables at the bottom of a 12-foot lagoon for 30 minutes, signing an SOS note.

The meeting was dismissed as a baseless public relations stunt by Nils-Axel Mörner, a retired Swedish oceanographer and a specialist in sea level changes. Until 2003 he was president of the Commission on Sea Level Change for the International Union for Quaternary Research. The members of the union study environmental changes over 2.6 million years.

Mörner, in a letter to the national newspaper of the Maldives in October, argued that the country's plight was greatly exaggerated. Sea levels are now barely rising and as recently as 1970 have been higher than they are today, he said.

But Lubna Moosa, a local environmental consultant, said action against climate change was past due. "This is not the time for debating the issue," she said. "We really want to focus on taking adaptive measures now." ■

SUDAN

Omar Hassan al-Bashir, the president of Sudan, at a meeting of the New Partnership for Africa's Development, in Addis Ababa, Ethiopia, in January 2009. The International Criminal Court issued an arrest warrant for al-Bashir in 2009 on charges he organized atrocities in Sudan's Darfur region. The warrant was the court's first issued for a head of state, but al-Bashir remains at large.

Perfecting the Pursuit of Global Atrocities

112 International Criminal Court: Growing Up
Matthew Heaphy

116 'Ignorance Is the Worst Enemy' – A Profile of ICC's President
Suh-Yong Chung

International Criminal Court: Growing Up

Matthew Heaphy

Barely a dozen years after its creation as the first permanent global criminal court, the International Criminal Court is entering a new era. Three trials are under way. It has issued 12 arrest warrants for suspects in cases of genocide, war crimes and crimes against humanity connected to four crises, and has begun a formal investigation of charges of atrocities in Kenya after 2007 elections. The 111 nations that have ratified its governing treaty, the Rome Statute, reviewed the treaty in May and June 2010. It now has initially strong support from the United States, which has said that it would end its hostility toward the court and begin a new and cooperative relationship with it.

Relationship with the UN

The United Nations General Assembly established the court by adopting its governing treaty in 1998 at a conference in Rome. While the court is independent of the UN, the two institutions cooperate. The court's work is in many ways considered a part of the UN's agenda, and the UN through its expertise and field operations contributes to the work of the court. The two have a formal agreement defining their relationship, and the court's Assembly of States Parties, its governing body, composed of its member countries, often meets at UN headquarters in New York.

Late in 2010, the court's president, Judge Sang-Hyun Song, will present the court's annual report to the General Assembly under the assembly's agenda item, "The promotion of justice and international law."

The two institutions have also agreed to cooperate, coordinate their activities where appropriate, exchange information and collaborate on judicial matters. In addition, UN officials may testify in court proceedings. In January 2010, Radhika Coomaraswamy, the UN secretary-general's special representative for children and armed conflict, testified as an expert in the court's first trial, of Thomas Lubanga Dyilo, a former rebel leader charged with recruiting child soldiers in Congo. Other UN officials are likely to testify in the future trials, in addition to providing field support and information about evidence.

The court also has a special relationship with the Security Council, based on the council's request in March 2005 that the court investigate atrocities in Sudan's western region of Darfur. That investigation has resulted in arrest warrants for a militia leader, a senior government minister and Omar Hassan al-Bashir, president of Sudan, none of whom has been apprehended. The Bashir warrant is the court's first for a head of state. A council resolution invites the court's prosecutor to report to it every six months on actions taken in response to the referral resolution. The court's prosecutor, Luis Moreno-Ocampo, is expected to brief the

Security Council on this in December 2010, and he is expected to seek political support for making arrests under the warrants.

Post-Election Issues in Kenya

In November 2009, Moreno-Ocampo requested that an investigation be opened into charges of crimes against humanity in Kenya in the post-election period in 2007-08. In March 2010, a pre-trial judges' conference authorized the prosecutor to open the investigation. This marks the first time the court has opened an investigation at the request of its prosecutor, all other cases so far having been opened after a referral from the Security Council or a country that is a member of the court.

The role of the pre-trial judges is part of a mechanism in the governing treaty designed to prevent politicized prosecutions by the court. The court's prosecutor is also accountable to the Assembly of States Parties.

The investigation, which began in May 2010 with a visit by the prosecutor to Kenya, follows continued inaction by Kenyan officials in response to violence after the 2007 elections, which involved accusations of fraud and vote-rigging. According to the authorities, more than 1,200 people were killed, 3,500 injured and 350,000 left homeless. Some of the post-election violence was reported to have been organized and carried out by government and business leaders. Kofi Annan, the former UN secretary-general, played a significant role in pushing for creation of a coalition government and in lining up political support for action by the court. Despite early signs of cooperation with the court, the government appeared unable to deal with atrocities that might involve senior officials. As a result, an African Union Panel of Eminent African Personalities, which Annan chaired, provided the prosecutor with a sealed envelope listing potential suspects.

The prosecutor has said his office plans to complete most of the investigations in 2010, and potential cases could be presented to judges by early 2011. While the government has vowed to share information with the court, the prosecutor may face challenges in obtaining the evidence needed to try government officials. Since the court relies on its member countries' cooperation and has no police force of its own, it may have trouble securing the arrest of figures who are well-connected or are part of the government. The court will also need to demonstrate its value to Kenyans who are divided over whether, and what kind of justice should be done.

First Review Conference

In May and June 2010, the court's governing treaty came up for review at a conference in Kampala, Uganda, convened by Secretary-General Ban Ki-moon. The conference, open both to countries that are members of the court and observer countries, considered amendments to the treaty and assessed the court's contribution to the system of international justice.

The conference was required by the Rome Statute. It was originally intended only to consider amendments and to review whether to keep a provision enabling countries, when they join the court, to reject its jurisdiction over war crimes for seven years. The provision was intended to make it easier for countries to join the court while they made necessary changes to their domestic war-crimes laws.

The most important amendment before the conference was a provision on the court's jurisdiction over the crime of aggression, which could be activated some time after Jan. 1, 2017. The crime of aggression is now defined for the purposes of the court as the "planning, preparation, initiation or execution" of "the use of armed force by a state against the sovereignty, territorial integrity or political independence of another state."

While aggression has always been listed among the crimes in the court's jurisdiction, that jurisdiction was suspended until the treaty could be amended to define the crime and determine how the court would pursue it. After years of negotiations in a working group open to all UN members, the conference endorsed the draft amendment, subject to a further decision of the court's governing body. The crime of aggression will therefore eventually be one of the crimes the court investigates and prosecutes. The review conference's decision on this amendment will dramatically reshape the court's future work and realizes a longtime dream of court advocates.

The conference also adopted a proposed amendment to expand the list of war crimes to include the use of certain poisons and other weapons, such as flattening bullets, in domestic conflicts. Amendments not considered at the review conference will be taken up at a meeting at UN Headquarters in December 2010.

Senior government representatives attending the review conference also adopted a declaration reaffirming their collective commitment to the Rome Statute and opposition to impunity for the most serious crimes. The conference also held a special session enabling member nations' most senior officials, such as heads of state and government, to address the conference and to make commitments pledging support to the court. Another session took stock of the state of international criminal justice, focusing on the topics of national cooperation with the court; the court's relationship with domestic courts; victims and communities affected by atrocities in the court's jurisdiction; and the question of reconciling peace and justice.

Challenges Ahead

Besides the day-to-day challenges of operating an international court and investigating and prosecuting the most serious of international crimes, the court as an institution will face other tests. Proposals that the court be empowered to deal with such matters as terrorism and nuclear weapons, for example, could deeply divide the nations that have joined the court. As some countries press the court to adopt their priorities as its own, there is a risk of asking it to do too much.

More broadly, the conference's decision to activate the court's jurisdiction over the crime of aggression means that some major powers, including the US, may be more wary of a close relationship with the court. Now that the amendment has been approved, its proponents will have to work for its acceptance. However, the amendment applies only to nations that ratify it, and even they can decide not to be bound by it.

The court also will be expected to do more and work faster. The first cases have understandably moved at a slow pace since they present new and complex legal questions. However, public patience for long delays is limited. Court officials, judges and prosecutors will face increasing pressure to complete trials more quickly and with fewer resources. This will require streamlined procedures and smart work by experienced jurists, while ensuring the rights of the accused and their victims.

Further on the horizon, six new court judges and a new chief prosecutor will take office for nine-year terms in the first half of 2012. Much of the groundwork for the elections, expected to be held late in 2011, will take place over the next year and could have an extraordinary impact on the court's future, in particular on its proceedings. The elections are likely to be held at UN headquarters in New York and, if so, may be extensively influenced by UN politics. There will be a major effort by outside groups that monitor the court to ensure that governments nominate and elect only the most qualified candidates.

Last, the court and the US will continue their period of reacquaintance. Following an Obama administration decision late in 2009 to attend court meetings after eight years of staying away, Washington participated in the review conference in Kampala and has repeatedly pledged to cooperate with the court. While it is too early to say how the Kampala conference will affect its long-term relations with the court, it appears that the US will try to continue a constructive relationship, which could lead in time to discussion of joining it. ▓

'Ignorance Is the Worst Enemy' — A Profile of ICC's President

Suh-Yong Chung

Judge Sang-Hyun Song stood before a tough crowd in the Democratic Republic of Congo, trying to persuade the group that a fellow Congolese, the warlord Thomas Lubanga, who was being held in an international detention center, belonged there. Song, who recounted this story in a recent interview in Korea, said he risked his life in December 2009 as he spoke in Lubanga's own village as a judicial representative from the International Criminal Court in The Hague.

In a speech translated into numerous languages, he said, he tried to persuade the villagers that Lubanga had gone so bad that justice had to be served. But the Congolese just grew more clamorous, furious that a foreigner had come to talk to them about taking down a leader of their own. They wanted the International Criminal Court's president out.

Not a man easily intimidated or used to giving up, Song kept going for three hours, relying on his persuasive skills to present his arguments and dispel misunderstandings. At last the crowd saw it his way, even standing to applaud, overcoming apprehensions about the International Criminal Court and its being used as a tool to control Africans. In this visit, Song, president of the court, managed to convey to the crowd, so accustomed to being manipulated by outsiders as well as their own rulers, that he was there to tell them that justice was being done. The arrest warrant for Lubanga, who had been held in The Hague detention center since 2006, did not preclude a fair trial, he said.

As Song said of his mission, "Ignorance is the worst enemy."

Lubanga, the first suspect to be tried by the court, has been on trial since January 2009, with some interruptions. He is accused of recruiting and sending children under 15 years old into battle. The trial is still in session, with the defense currently presenting its case.

Dedicated to Law

Judge Song, a 68-year-old South Korean, started his career at the International Criminal Court on March 11, 2003, with a three-year term. He was re-elected in 2006 for a term of nine years. In March 2009, he was elected president, with a three-year term in the Appeals Division. As president, Judge Song is responsible for administering (except for the prosecutor's office) and carrying out the functions listed in the Rome Statute, the court's governing treaty. As president, he also works closely with the chief prosecutor, Luis Moreno-Ocampo, though he has no authority over Moreno-Ocampo's office.

Song's life work as a lawyer expert in court management, civil and criminal procedures and the law of evidence began in the army of the Republic of Korea, where he worked both in the judge-advocate office as a prosecutor and as a military

Suh-Yong Chung

Judge Sang-Hyun Song, president of the International Criminal Court. Song taught for more than 30 years at Seoul National University Law School before being elected to the court in 2003. He was chosen its president in March 2009.

judge, trying criminal cases. He serves on the advisory committee to the Korean Supreme Court and the Ministry of Justice in South Korea. As such, he took an initiative in the reform of the national litigation system and the criminal justice system, notably in affecting the penal code, the code and the court rules of criminal procedure and the prison system.

He is a distinguished legal scholar and taught for more than 30 years at Seoul National University Law School as a professor of procedural law and evidence. He has also taught as a visiting professor at many law schools, including Harvard University, New York University, Columbia University and the University of Melbourne.

He graduated from Seoul National University Law School in 1963 and continued his study in the United States, receiving a S.J.D (doctorate) from Cornell Law School in 1970. He is the vice president of the UN Children's Fund, Unicef, in Korea and a member of the Lawyers Committee of Amnesty International in Korea as well.

Judge Song's experience in international law, primarily in international humanitarian law and human rights law, catapulted him into the International Criminal Court.

How the Court Functions

The judge savors talking about the court, particularly its complementary principle, which provides that even where the court has jurisdiction, it will not necessarily act. For example, if a crime occurs in the territory of a country or is committed by a country, it is the primary responsibility of the country's judicial system to investigate first. But if a country or its judicial apparatus is incapable or unwilling to take action for political or other reasons, the International Criminal Court can carry out an investigation on its own or take up a prosecution.

All of which means that the court works within a strict framework, adhering to guidelines that are meant to keep countries' sovereignty paramount. As Judge Song says, "The ICC is the court of last resort."

He emphasizes that the court's jurisdiction is not universal. This means that the court may exercise jurisdiction only if the accused is a citizen of a country that is a court member; if the crime took place in a member country; or if the Security Council has referred the situation to the prosecutor, as in the case of the arrest warrant issued for Omar Hassan al-Bashir, Sudan's president, in 2009.

Although the court is an independent organ and not part of the UN, the two work together in establishing and maintaining an international criminal justice system. The court's mission, Judge Song reiterates, is purely judicial. While the International Court of Justice deals primarily with disputes among countries and is a UN institution, the International Criminal Court deals only with individuals who have committed certain heinous and serious acts—genocide, crimes against humanity and war crimes.

As president, Judge Song foresees an international criminal justice system emerging in 15 years or so as a three-tier arrangement: the International Criminal Court, national courts, and truth and reconciliation commissions, all working in complementary ways, with The Hague court as centerpiece.

But the court alone cannot manage all of the world's international criminal justice issues, Judge Song is quick to point out. Countries, local and regional communities, private organizations and others must work with the court to ensure that it functions effectively as an international body.

In the Lubanga case, the trial is being watched closely as the world studies how this new court conducts itself.

Since the birth of the court in July 2002, Judge Song has been motivated by the growing interest among the academics, lawyers and judges around the globe. Currently there are only two courtrooms in The Hague, and almost every day both are busy with trials or hearings.

"Even when I deliver a judgment to a chamber," Judge Song said, "many groups of graduate students and young lawyers come and watch. As soon as hard copies of judgments become available, they all just sit around in the ICC conference rooms and have discussions or seminars about that particular judgment until as late as 9 p.m."

He considers this an encouraging sign that there is concerted interest in the court, and even more important, in international criminal justice. ▩

Evo Morales, Bolivia's president, addresses a meeting of the Group of 77 at UN headquarters in New York in May 2010. The Group of 77, a bloc of developing nations that includes China, has opposed many key UN reform initiatives.

Changing with the Times

122 Healing the UN: A Prescription
Thomas G. Weiss

125 The Reform Agenda
David E. Birenbaum

129 G20: In Need of a UN Embrace
Park Soo Gil

**131 New UN Women's Agency Sets Sail
on Uncharted Course**
Barbara Crossette

Healing the UN: A Prescription

Thomas G. Weiss

The diagnosis seems clear: The United Nations is paralyzed.

But before setting a course of treatment, one must first understand the underlying causes.

Four disorders afflict the United Nations. The first is the enduring concept of the international community as a system of sovereign states, an idea dating from the 1648 Treaties of Westphalia. This is of course the basis for the UN Charter and membership in the world body. As a result of sovereignty's continuing grip, the gap is steadily growing between virtually all of the life-threatening challenges facing the planet and the ability of the international decision-making process to deal with them. Narrowly defined vital interests are the norm. The UN remains a formidable bastion of sacrosanct state sovereignty, even as technological advances, globalization and trans-boundary problems proliferate and national frontiers make less and less sense.

The second problem stems from the performance that passes for diplomacy in UN circles. It centers on the artificial divide between the aging acting troupes from the industrialized North and those from the developing countries in the global South. The once creative voices of the nonaligned movement and the Group of 77 developing countries, alliances formed in the 1950's and 1960's as a way to create diplomatic space for negotiations on international security and the economy, have now become prisoners of their own rhetoric. Such rigid and counterproductive groups—and the artificial divisions they create—end up constituting almost insurmountable barriers to diplomatic initiatives. Serious conversation is displaced by posturing.

Incoherent, Uncoordinated

The third condition is structural, arising from the overlapping jurisdiction of UN bodies, the lack of coordination of activities and the absence of centralized financing. The UN's moving parts work at cross purposes instead of in an integrated, mutually reinforcing and collaborative fashion. All agencies relentlessly pursue cut-throat fundraising to finance expanding mandates and missions. While the UN's organizational chart refers to a "system," implying coherence and cohesion, the organization in reality has more in common with feudalism than with a modern organization.

The final disorder is the overwhelming weight of the UN bureaucracy, its low productivity and an underperforming leadership in the international secretariats. The stereotype of a bloated administration is in some ways inaccurate—it overlooks many talented and dedicated individuals. But recruitment and promotion methods are certainly part of what ails the UN. When success occurs, it usually reflects personalities and serendipity rather than recruitment of the best people for the right reasons and institutional structures designed to foster collaboration.

Staff costs account for the lion's share of the UN's budget, and the international civil service is a potential resource whose composition, productivity and culture could change and change quickly. The current lackluster leadership, however, will continue for at least two years more, perhaps even until the middle of the next decade.

In fact, there could not be a better design for futile complexity than the current array of agencies, each focusing on a substantive area, often situated in a different city from relevant UN partners, and with separate budgets, governing boards, organizational cultures and independent executive heads. Dealing with crucial global challenges such as climate change, pandemics, terrorism and weapons of mass destruction requires multidisciplinary perspectives, efforts across sectors with firm central direction, plus inspired leadership. The UN rarely supplies any of this.

Lines of Therapy

Can we fix the UN? Are there palliatives if not cures?

The first remedy requires further building upon the spotty yet significant progress in recasting national interests in terms of good global citizenship and enhanced international responsibilities. The prescription for the Westphalian system's ailments consists of yet more energetic recalculations of the shared benefits of fostering global good works and respecting international commitments. Democratic member states, whether large or small, should theoretically find this pill relatively easy to swallow because they have a long-term, rational and vital interest as well as a moral responsibility to promote cooperation.

As corny as it sounds, there is also a therapeutic benefit from "good international citizenship," an expression coined by Gareth Evans, the former Australian foreign minister and one-time president of the International Crisis Group. This vision underpins the conviction that there is a relationship between the provision of basic rights and wider international security. Nothing illustrates this better than "the responsibility to protect," known colloquially as R2P. This redefines sovereignty as contingent upon respect for human rights, rather than as absolute. While R2P imposes initial and primary responsibility for human rights on the state, it argues that if a state does not honor its responsibilities, or itself is the perpetrator of atrocities, then the responsibility to protect shifts upward to the international community of states. The doctrine illustrates how to move in the direction of reframing state sovereignty, a values breakthrough after centuries of mindless acceptance of the proposition that state sovereignty is a license to kill.

Building New Bridges

Moving beyond the North-South quagmire is the second prescription. On occasion, states have forged creative partnerships across the fictitious borders that supposedly divide the industrialized and developing countries. Less posturing and role-playing is a prerequisite for the future health of the world organization, and examples of wide-ranging coalitions across continents and ideologies include those that negotiated the treaty to ban landmines and agreed to establish the International Criminal Court. Similar bridges should be built across the divides on climate change, development finance, nonproliferation, reproductive rights and terrorism, to name a few.

The third line of treatment would be to pursue the approach of making the UN work more coherently, as advocated in "Delivering as One," one of the last reports initiated by Kofi Annan before his departure as UN secretary-general. Eyes usually glaze over at mention of "reform" to improve coordination among UN agencies, because nothing to date has even modestly alleviated the turf battles and unproductive competition for funds that characterize the UN. Basically donors would have to stop talking out of two sides of their mouths and insist on the centralization and consolidation that they often preach. This is not an impossible task, nor is adopting modest alternative means of financing the UN, such as infinitesimal percentage taxes on financial transfers or airline tickets.

The final therapy consists of taking steps to reinvigorate the UN staff. There is an urgent need to revive the notion of an autonomous international civil service as championed by the UN's second secretary-general, Dag Hammarskjold. Competence and integrity should outweigh nationality and gender considerations as well as cronyism, which have become the principal criteria for recruitment and promotion. In fact, the ideal goes back to what a Carnegie Endowment working group during World War II called the "great experiment" of the League of Nations.

Moving back to the future would involve recruiting people of integrity and talent. There are numerous ways to attract more mobile and younger staff with greater turnover and fewer permanent contracts while providing better career development for the world organization of the 21st Century. The UN staff accounts for 90 percent of the organization's expenditures, and strengthening performance and productivity by improving output and efficiency should be at the top of its to-do list. ■

The Reform Agenda

David E. Birenbaum

Progress in carrying out the United Nations reform agenda was modest at best in 2009. At this point, the outlook for 2010 is for more of the same. The agenda this year will be headed by reviews of progress made toward goals already set, as well as a look at human-resource management.

The lack of major progress reflects the reality that much of what was proposed as reform steps at the 2005 World Summit had already been done by previous General Assemblies or by the secretary-general. One important reform—a review of the more than 7,000 General Assembly mandates five or more years old—has pretty much been abandoned because of the Secretariat's inability to determine what it would cost to fulfill the mandates and the recalcitrance of the Group of 77, the bloc of developing nations (which includes China). The purpose of the review was to eliminate outdated and duplicated programs.

Despite the generally improved atmosphere of the assembly's budget commit-tee, formally the Fifth Committee, no movement has been made on the difficult issue of micromanaging of the Secretariat by the General Assembly. The thorn is politics: the Group of 77 is reluctant to relinquish power over the secretary-general, whom they believe is in the thrall of the developed world.

On Security Council reform, the long-stalled plan to expand the council and improve its working methods has gone through the same rigamarole as earlier efforts. Committees meet, debates proceed and facilitators ease the way, but the crucial political decisions remain unmade.

The latest phase involves a paper that was circulated that reflects the positions of the participating countries, which means that the debate is centered on a text rather than being conducted in face-to-face negotiations. There is also no con-sensus so far on any of the approaches under consideration, with each facing substantial opposition. The outlook is more likely to turn on an interim solution involving the creation, on a transitional basis, of semipermanent seats without the right of veto, with a review in 5 to 10 years on possible new permanent seats. The council has 15 members, 5 of whom—Britain, China, France, Russia and the United States—have permanent seats with veto power, while the 10 others serve two-year nonrenewable terms.

Management and Financial Reform

The Fifth Committee is the main group involved in management and financial reform. The panel's 64th annual session, beginning Sept. 15, 2009, focused on two main measures: the biennial budget and the scale of assessments used to deter-mine UN members' annual dues. The budget debate was not contentious and included no noteworthy reforms. In keeping the current scale of assessments, the committee, led by the Group of 77, rejected a bid by Europeans to reduce their aggregate assessments. (The European Union contributes 40 percent of the regular budget but has 30 percent of global income.) It also rejected a bid by the Russians to use a price-adjusted rate of exchange, a method that would have lowered the dues paid by Moscow, among others. The committee provided for a review of the methodology before the 66th session ends, in September 2012. The scale of assessments for peacekeeping, which is set separately, was left as is.

The key reform measure approved by the committee was a proposal from the secretary-general for an accountability system for the Secretariat. This has been in the works for 17 years, during which essential elements went into place: namely the ethics office, whistleblower protection, financial disclosure rules, protection against sexual harassment and senior-manager performance compacts. The new system incorporates these steps into a framework based on three pillars: performance, compliance and integrity.

Each pillar is supported by institutional and individual standards, including a focus on accountability, transparency and results. In approving this system, the committee broadened the definition of accountability to emphasize the professional responsibility of the Secretariat and its staff in making decisions and stressed the importance of results.

In accepting the secretary-general's proposal, the developed nations overcame the initial skepticism of countries in the developing world. If the new system is able to hold the Secretariat accountable to the General Assembly in terms of attaining results, the politics of reform will be tested anew, since developed countries will push for the assembly to back off from micromanaging.

A revamped information technology system, meanwhile, will increase institutional and individual accountability. A new Enterprise Resource Planning project, when fully operating, will enable the Secretariat to integrate and track core administrative services across the organization, including peacekeeping operations.

One potentially significant shortcoming will be the lack of metrics in the secretary-general's results-focused framework; it will be difficult to assess performance. And what cannot be measured cannot be evaluated. To be sure, determining results in the public sector is a challenge, to say the least, yet a serious effort to find a proper evaluation method is essential.

Security Council: Debate Continues

The debate on Security Council reform focused on five issues: categories of membership, the veto question, regional representation, a larger council and its working methods, and the relationship of the council to the General Assembly. Under Ambassador Zahir Tanin of Afghanistan, who is chairing the intergovernmental negotiations, all five matters were debated.

On May 10, Tanin issued his draft. Not surprisingly, it revealed a wide divergence of positions on all the issues. For the most part, countries have reiterated familiar stances. The one area of potential progress is the willingness of several nations to consider a transitional plan whereby a group of semipermanent seats would be created, provided a review in 10 to 15 years is mandated. These seats would not hold vetoes but would extend for longer terms than the current non-permanent seats' two-year terms.

The United States has taken a minimalist approach to Security Council reform. In doing so, it is endorsing modest expansion of both permanent and nonpermanent members but only on a country-by-country basis, rather than on a selection by regional groups, the current arrangement. As for the veto structure and the relationship of the Security Council to the General Assembly, these matters remain untouched.

There may be progress on the council's working methods, however. The Tanin draft reveals wide agreement on the need to enhance the council's transparency through more open meetings, strengthened reporting on its activities and enhanced participation. The five permanent members have made clear their determination to preserve their privileges and status, but an effort to continue the council's transparency could be worked out.

UN Photo/Martine Perret

UN peacekeepers on a cease-fire monitoring patrol try to push their car out of the sand in Oum Dreyga, Western Sahara, in June 2010. UN reform initiatives can run into stiff resistance as they wend their way through a global bureaucracy, leaving the world body spinning its wheels.

The fall session of the General Assembly will focus on carrying out reforms related to human-resources management rather than on new reform proposals.

The secretary-general is to report on the progress of the performance-appraisal system. Based on the report, the Fifth Committee will address the secretary-general's proposals on converting from fixed-term contracts to continuing staff contracts, determining who should be awarded permanent positions and measuring staff performance, succession planning (for the retirement of senior personnel) and recruitment. One important issue that may not be taken up is staff rotations, which would be unfortunate, given the emphasis on culture change and job performance in the new accountability system. Rotating personnel so that they have maximum exposure in the field, where engagement with the UN's mission is direct and fruitful, could contribute substantially to positive change. The secretary-general has made major proposals in this regard but has met with resistance from the Group of 77. He should persist.

A Fight Over Files

The General Assembly is also slated to review the internal justice system, which resolves employment-related disputes with UN staff. This could focus attention on recent reports of a dispute between the secretary-general and the judges about handing over files concerning staff members who are brought before administrative tribunals. The secretary-general has refused to yield the files, citing executive privilege of sorts, thus creating an impasse.

The Peacebuilding Commission is also up for review this year by both the Security Council and the General Assembly. Debate in the council has already begun, and the assembly has established a review procedure. It is not clear how the two bodies will work together, as there is no established practice and much potential for friction.

The review offers the first chance to examine the Peacebuilding Commission's performance since it started operating in 2005. So far, the commission has worked in four countries: Sierra Leone, Burundi, Guinea-Bissau and Central African Republic. While the review is still in its early stages, the sense is that the commission has succeeded in these countries, particularly in Burundi, but that it has not met all expectations.

The review is expected to focus on the commission's working methods and its interaction with other UN bodies, in particular, those concerned with peacekeeping and financial support. Among other issues to be addressed will be how to ensure a country's involvement and support in the peace-building planning and process. The review is supposed to be finished by the end of the fall session. ■

G20: In Need of a UN Embrace

Park Soo Gil

The Group of 20, usually known as the G20, has since its formation in 1999 demonstrated its potential as the major international economic forum. This organization of the developed and developing nations is now expected to become more involved in global economics and development, after winning praise for helping the world economy pull out of the 2008 financial crisis.

For this reason, it is often said that the G20 has taken the place of the Group of Eight, whose members are enfolded by the G20. This older association of industrialized nations consisted of Britain, Canada, France, Germany, Italy, Japan, Russia and the United States. In economic cooperation, the displacement is true and is welcome in view of the growing weight of the emerging economies in the international economic system.

The G20 unites the European Union and 19 major developed and developing countries: Argentina, Australia, Brazil, Britain, Canada, China, France, Germany, India, Indonesia, Italy, Japan, Mexico, Russia, Saudi Arabia, South Africa, South Korea, Turkey and the US. Together these economies account for 90 percent of the global gross national product and two-thirds of the world's population.

The G20, a high achiever with barely 10 years of history, is also a work in progress that could benefit from a formal relationship with the United Nations, just as the UN would be helped by closer ties with the G20.

Key Challenges

The G20 faces two key challenges in 2010: to evolve with the changes in the global economic system, and to reach out to nonmembers. The UN, as an institution of 192 nations, can help the G20 on both challenges: it can help to broaden G20's agenda and harness the assets of nonmembers in addressing major problems. The UN can also help the group carry out its decisions more effectively.

The group has no permanent staff. The chair rotates among its members yearly. South Korea is the chair in 2010 and France takes over in 2011.

When set up in 1999, the group worked at the level of finance ministers and central bankers to help emerging and advanced economies cope with global economic woes. Its members have since met annually to seek ways toward economic cooperation, growth, development and stability.

In September 2008, the group was elevated to the level of leaders in view of the size of the challenges posed by the financial and economic crisis, which was later dubbed the Great Repression. So far, G20 leaders have met in Washington in 2008, in London and Pittsburgh in 2009 and in Toronto in 2010. A second 2010 summit is scheduled for Seoul in November.

With respect to the scope of G20 issues, the top priority at its first three summits was to stave off a crash of the world economy. Having helped manage the crisis, its agenda should evolve to post-crisis management and the promotion of sustainable growth. In this connection, President Lee Myung-bak of South Korea, who will chair the Seoul summit, hopes to focus on closing the gap between developed and developing nations and on establishing a global financial safety net.

A Wider View

By working more closely with the UN, the group can benefit from the UN's broader agenda. Full participation of the UN secretary-general in G20 summits would enable the group to take better account of the full range of UN concerns, from peace and security to climate change and health, from combating poverty to food and fuel security, human development and the Millennium Development Goals.

Toward that end, G20 leaders have already asked the UN to develop an advanced technological system linking all the UN family's early-warning databases. With real-time data, this system would help world leaders respond effectively in a crisis. It would also help policymakers reach the populations they have had the hardest time reaching. At the G20 summit in November, the secretary-general will be able to update world leaders on his progress on this initiative.

With the growing importance of reaching out as the G20 broadens its agenda, it must pay more attention to countries that are not members or risk alienating them or undermining its own legitimacy. The Norwegian Foreign Minister, Jonas Gahr Støre, for example, has already questioned the group's legitimacy and called for changes in its membership structure. A central challenge is to find the right balance between being representative and being effective. One way to achieve this is to forge close cooperation with the UN, which has both universal membership and global legitimacy.

Just One Step Further

UN Secretary-General Ban Ki-moon has been invited to all four G20 summits to date. Thus far, however, the invitation has been extended on an ad hoc basis. The UN's engagement with the G20 should be formalized to ensure that the voices of non-G20 members can be heard.

The UN should be involved in summit preparations, the meeting itself and in carrying out recommendations after the meeting. While Ali Abdussalam Treki of Libya, the General Assembly president for the session ending in September 2010, publicly praised the G20's work in 2008, he has also criticized the group for failing to act in the best interests of the UN's 192 nations.

The UN can help in wider and more meaningful implementation of G20 decisions, because they can be communicated to all UN members and addressed in the larger UN context in their implementation. ■

New UN Women's Agency Sets Sail on Uncharted Course

Barbara Crossette

After 65 years of relegating the crucial issues of women's rights and status in society to powerless and underfunded offices in the United Nations, in July 2010 the General Assembly created a new women's agency with the promise of vastly increased financial strength and a high-level under secretary-general to lead it. It will be known as UN Women, and should be fully functional by January 2011.

That, however, is just the beginning of what will be critical months ahead for insuring that the new agency gets a strong staff and sufficient independence to move ahead decisively and not be burdened by a potentially unwieldy governing board and a heavy dependence on voluntary contributions from donor governments.

The importance of women in global development is now recognized. It is not coincidental that the laggards in progress toward the Millennium Development Goals are those areas where women are central. The dismal failure to cut maternal mortality in many countries is only one example of how the goals are undercut by women's powerlessness over their own lives.

Passing on the Bad and the Good

In meeting almost every goal, whether or not women are specifically factored into the targets and indicators, their lives have an important impact. Women without the right to demand safe sex figure in the spread of AIDS and the virus that causes it. As farmers and suppliers of water and basic energy for their homes—often fuel gathered in dwindling woodlands—they understand environmental degradation. When educated, they have smaller, healthier families, and send their children to school.

Since the late 1990s, women have also been identified by the Security Council as the missing factor in peace negotiations to end the civil wars that have marked the post-cold war era, and in the nation-building that follows. Women are not only sidelined but also widely abused. In 2000, ironically the same year in which the Millennium Development Goals were adopted by the General Assembly, the Security Council adopted a resolution abhorring the violence against women that had become prevalent during conflict. This was seen as necessary although sexual assault as a tactic had already been declared an international war crime after horrific accounts of atrocities against women and girls in the Balkans, Rwanda and the Democratic Republic of Congo.

For millions of women, violence is the central problem in their lives, and it is not just in time of conflict. Abuse of women remains a pandemic, whether in time of war or peace. For UN Women, there is no shortage of agenda items to tackle. France has already suggested that a survey of laws that harm women should be undertaken, with governments put on notice that their adherence to a lengthening list of conventions had to be real.

Until this year, it is estimated that less than $10 million annually has been spent on women's programs at the UN, not counting special events like international conferences. The hope for UN Women is that it will have a starting budget close to $500 million, with an estimated $125 million from the UN's assessed funds. Work in the field around the world will have to rely on $375 million from voluntary donations. Advocates for the new agency had campaigned for a start-up budget of $1 billion.

Staff from the Old Agencies?

In terms of structure, UN Women—formally titled in the General Assembly resolution as the tongue-twisting "United Nations Entity for Gender Equality and the Empowerment of Women"—will consolidate four existing offices and bodies: the Office of the Special Adviser on Gender Issues and Advancement of Women; the Division for the Advancement of Women; the UN Development Fund for Women; and the UN International Research and Training Institute for the Advancement of Women. A question has already arisen about the extent to which staff members in those offices will simply transfer to the new agency, or whether the under secretary-general appointed to run it will have what advocates consider the essential latitude to form her own team.

The governing board of UN Women will be independent; there had been suggestions that the board be folded into a combined UN Development Program-UN Population Fund board. But the UN Women's board will be very large, with 41 members appointed by governments.

There will also be a predictable voting majority drawn from developing nations in Africa, Asia and Latin America. That is not a problem in itself, given that those areas most need to enhance the status of women. But there is a record of regional blocs ganging up to back unqualified candidates: the Human Rights Council is the best example of this, as regional groups perennially send countries with records of abuse to sit on that council on the theory that everybody gets a turn.

The board will earmark 10 seats for Africa; 10 for Asia, which includes the Middle East; 4 from Eastern Europe; 6 from Latin America and the Caribbean; 5 from the group called Western Europe and Others, which includes the United States, Canada, Australia and New Zealand, and 6 seats for large donor countries, two of which must be from outside Europe and North America. Technically, the 54-nation Economic and Social Council will elect board members to three-year terms. It, however, has been a center of horse-trading for decades, and there is scant hope of open competition.

Patronage a Barrier to Service

To ensure that UN Women will not get bogged down in standoffs between the staff and the board, governments must be pressed to appoint strong qualified women and men to the governing body. There are plenty of qualified women in developing countries worldwide, but politicking and patronage too often deny them the chance to serve in the UN system.

The compromise resolution finally adopted by the General Assembly on July 2 made clear that governments want to have considerable control or influence over the agency's activities. The resolution says that the agency can provide a country with guidance and technical support only if invited to do so. It will also be expected to work primarily with official women's organizations or other focal points designated by governments.

Advocates for a strong agency had wanted it to have the freedom to work with private groups of all kinds. The founding resolution recognizes the positive input of women's organizations and other groups, but specifies that any new mandates "will be subject to approval by intergovernmental process."

The resolution, an omnibus document dealing more broadly with coherence in the UN system, has in its section on the reform of gender architecture a lot of worn-out language about "gender mainstreaming" in the UN, a concept that has been around for years to little effect. Advocates of the new agency have consistently made a point of that problem. For example, it is difficult to find coherent—the new buzzword—links to women on the UN's main Web site, or even in the online pages of agencies and programs.

Changes in Peacekeeping Corps

The Department of Peacekeeping Operations, custodians of pledges to increase the participation of women in peacekeeping troops and UN police through a series of Security Council resolutions, has not in the past demonstrated such progress clearly in comprehensible statistics. The peacekeeping department's new head of police, Ann-Marie Orler, a lawyer and officer in the Swedish national police, has begun to change that. [See "Women Peacekeepers: Not Tokens but Essential Workers," P. 35]

Advocates of a new women's agency, while pleased that it has finally become a reality, are now focused on the work ahead globally: promoting the agency, lobbying governments to nominate credible members to its board and supporting the new head of UN Women, who will inevitably be challenged as she begins to make the agency's presence known and felt. "We know this is only the beginning," Rachel Harris of the Women's Environment and Development Organization said in a statement on the day the agency was created. "We must continue to ensure that we are building a United Nations that really works for all women." ▦

A UN peacekeeper from
Brazil helps a street mer-
chant in Port-au-Prince,
the Haitian capital, after
a fire that ravaged 50
shops in June 2004.

Appendices

136 **Appendix A: Important Dates in United Nations History**
Compiled by Max McGowen

140 **Appendix B: The UN System**

141 **Appendix C: Composition of the Secretariat**
Compiled by Simon Minching

142 **Appendix D: Operations and Budgets**
Compiled by Simon Minching

154 **Appendix E: Acronyms and Abbreviations**

163 **Appendix F: Glossary**
Compiled by Christopher J. Tangney

178 **Appendix G: Nobel Prizes**

Appendix A: Important Dates in United Nations History

Compiled by Max McGowen

June 12, 1941 Inter-Allied Declaration signed in London, encouraging free people to work together in war and peace.

Jan. 1, 1942 Representatives of 26 Allied nations meet in Washington to sign Declaration of United Nations, in which US President Roosevelt coins the term "United Nations."

Sept. 21-Oct. 7 1944 US, Soviet Union, Britain and China agree on basic blueprint for a world organization at Dumbarton Oaks mansion near Washington.

Feb. 11, 1945 Roosevelt, Churchill and Stalin meet in Ukraine, resolving to establish "a general international organization to maintain peace and security."

June 25, 1945 United Nations Charter unanimously adopted by delegations of 50 nations in San Francisco.

Oct. 24, 1945 The five permanent members of the Security Council and a majority of other signers ratify Charter, creating the UN we know today.

Feb. 1, 1946 Trygve Lie of Norway becomes first secretary-general of United Nations.

Jan. 17, 1946 Security Council, in London, holds first meeting, establishing its procedural rules.

Jan. 24, 1946 General Assembly adopts first resolution, focused on peaceful uses of atomic energy and abolition of weapons of mass destruction.

Dec. 1946 United Nations International Children's Emergency Fund created to provide food, clothing and health care to children suffering famine and disease. Name is later changed to UN Children's Fund but acronym remains Unicef.

Dec. 10, 1948 General Assembly adopts Universal Declaration of Human Rights.

Aug. 21, 1950 Secretariat workers move into offices in the new headquarters complex in New York. Campus eventually comprises Secretariat, General Assembly, Conference Area and Library.

1954 Office of UN High Commissioner for Refugees wins first of two Nobel Peace Prizes, for European work.

Aug. 30, 1955 First United Nations Congress on the Prevention of Crime and the Treatment of Offenders adopts standard minimum rules for treatment of prisoners.

Nov. 7, 1956 General Assembly holds first emergency special session in Suez Canal crisis. Two days before, it established first UN peacekeeping force, called the UN Emergency Force.

Nov. 20, 1959 General Assembly adopts Declaration of the Rights of the Child.

Sept. 1960 Seventeen newly independent states, all but one in Africa, join UN. It marks biggest increase in membership in a single year.

Sept. 18, 1961 Secretary-General Dag Hammarskjold dies in plane crash on mission to the Congo. U Thant, Burmese diplomat, named to succeed him.

Dec. 21, 1965 General Assembly adopts International Covenant on Social, Economic and Cultural Rights along with counterpart, International Covenant on Civil and Political Rights.

Nov. 22, 1967 After Six-Day War in the Middle East, Security Council adopts Resolution 242, stipulating requirements for end of hostilities.

June 12, 1968 General Assembly approves Treaty on Nonproliferation of Nuclear Weapons.

Jan. 4, 1969 International Convention on the Elimination of All Forms of Racial Discrimination goes into effect.

Oct. 21, 1971 General Assembly admits representative from People's Republic of China, displacing Republic of China on Taiwan.

June 1972 First UN Environment Conference held in Stockholm, bringing establishment of the UN Environment Program.

Nov. 13, 1974 General Assembly recognizes Palestine Liberation Organization as "the sole legitimate representative of the Palestinian people."

Nov. 5-16, 1974 UN conducts conference in Rome on food and agriculture, declaring freedom from hunger as a universal human right.

June-July 1975 UN holds first conference on women, in Mexico City, coinciding with International Women's Year.

May-June 1978 General Assembly holds first special session on disarmament.

May 8, 1980 World Health Organization declares smallpox eliminated.

1981 UN High Commissioner for Refugees receives second Nobel Peace Prize, this for work with Asians.

Nov. 25, 1981 General Assembly adopts Declaration on the Elimination of All Forms of Intolerance and Discrimination Based on Religion or Belief.

Dec. 10, 1982 A hundred and seventeen states and two entities sign UN Convention on the Law of the Sea, largest number of signatures affixed to a treaty in one day.

Dec. 10, 1984 Convention Against Torture and Other Cruel, Inhuman or Degrading Treatment or Punishment adopted by General Assembly.

Sept. 1987 Treaty on Protection of the Ozone Layer, also known as Montreal Protocol, signed.

1988 UN Peacekeeping receives Nobel Peace Prize.

Sept. 2, 1990 Convention on Rights of the Child enters into effect.

April 1991 UN Iraq-Kuwait Observation Mission established to carry out elimination of weapons of mass destruction in Iraq after the Gulf War.

Jan. 31, 1992 Leaders from all 15 members of the Security Council attend first Security Council Summit in New York. The meeting leads to Secretary-General Boutros Boutros-Ghali's report, "An Agenda for Peace."

June 1992 Rio de Janeiro is host to more than 100 countries at the UN Conference on Environment and Development, popularly known as the Earth Summit. Recognition of the importance of sustainable development is major outcome.

Feb. 22, 1993 Security Council establishes first international tribunal to examine human rights violations in the former Yugoslavia.

April 5, 1994 José Ayala-Lasso of Ecuador becomes first UN High Commissioner for Human Rights.

May 6, 1994 Secretary-General Boutros Boutros-Ghali issues Agenda for Development plan to improve human condition.

Nov. 8, 1994 Security Council establishes second international tribunal to investigate Rwandan genocide.

March 1995 World Summit for Social Development held in Copenhagen seeking new commitment to combat poverty, unemployment and social exclusion.

June 1996 Second UN Conference on Human Settlements convenes in Turkey.

Sept. 10, 1996 General Assembly adopts Comprehensive Test-Ban Treaty. It remains to be entered into force.

July 18, 1998 International Criminal Court is established by Rome Statute.

March 1, 1999 Ottawa Convention on antipersonnel mines enters into force.

Sept. 2000 General Assembly adopts Millennium Declaration starting the clock for eight Millennium Development Goals to reduce worldwide poverty by 2015.

Nov. 12, 2001 Security Council adopts Resolution 1377, calling on all nations to intensify their efforts to eliminate "the scourge of international terrorism" in the aftermath of the Sept. 11 terrorist attacks in the US.

July 1, 2002 Rome Statue enters into force, and the International Criminal Court begins work.

Aug. 19, 2003 Twenty-two staff members and officials, including Ambassador Sergio Vieira de Mello, killed in a terrorist attack on UN headquarters in Iraq.

Sept. 2005 Secretary-General Kofi Annan presents his report, "In Larger Freedom:

Toward Security, Development and Human Rights for All," to a special session of the General Assembly, where member nations discuss significant reform of UN.

Jan. 27, 2006 Nearly 2,000 people gather in the General Assembly Hall for International Holocaust Remembrance Day.

Feb. 27, 2006 The 50th session of the Commission on the Status of Women convenes to review the progress and chart new goals.

March 15, 2006 A 47-nation Human Rights Council is created by a vote of the General Assembly to replace the Human Rights Commission, abolished due to its declining credibility.

Jan. 1, 2007 Ban Ki-moon of South Korea succeeds Kofi Annan as the eighth Secretary-General.

Sept. 24, 2007 The Future in Our Hands, called to discuss leadership issues relating to climate change, brings together representatives of more than 150 member states.

Jan.1, 2008 UN establishes Joint United Nations/African Union Mission in Darfur to assume responsibility for the war-torn region from the African Union. The peacekeeping operation was UN's largest.

May 30, 2008 A hundred and seven states adopt Convention on Cluster Munitions, first agreement to seek a ban on a particular class of weapons worldwide.

Dec. 10, 2008 A year of celebrations across the UN system culminates on the 60th anniversary of signing of the Universal Declaration of Human Rights, a key step in the founding of the United Nations and important in international law.

Sept. 14, 2009 The United Nations announces it will merge four existing agencies and offices into a single new entity to promote the rights and well-being of women worldwide and advance gender equality.

Dec. 23, 2009 The General Assembly establishes a new assistant secretary general position to raise the profile of human rights and strengthen the link between UN headquarters in New York and the UN High Commissioner for Human Rights in Geneva.

Jan. 12, 2010 An earthquake of 7.0 magnitude hits Haiti, resulting in hundreds of thousands of deaths, including the largest one-day toll in the UN's history. Among the 101 UN dead were Hedi Annabi, the UN peacekeeping chief in Haiti, and his deputy, Luiz Carlos da Costa. Brazil lost 18 security workers in its peacekeeping mission.

Sources: www.unhchr.ch/chrono.htm
www.un.org/issues/gallery/history/index.html www.un.org/Overview/milesto4.htm
UNA-USA e-news updates

Appendix B: The United Nations System Today

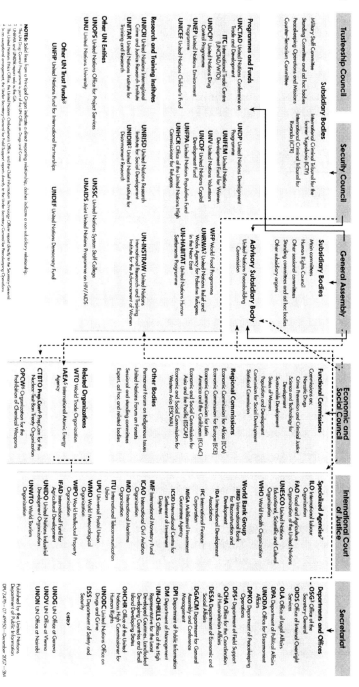

Trusteeship Council

Security Council

Military Staff Committee

Standing Committee and ad hoc bodies

Peacekeeping Operations and Missions

Counter-Terrorism Committee

Subsidiary Bodies

International Criminal Tribunal for the former Yugoslavia (ICTY)

International Criminal Tribunal for Rwanda (ICTR)

General Assembly

Subsidiary Bodies

Main committees

Human Rights Council

Other sessional committees

Standing committees and ad hoc bodies

Other subsidiary organs

Advisory Subsidiary Body

United Nations Peacebuilding Commission

Programmes and Funds

UNCTAD United Nations Conference on Trade and Development

  ITC International Trade Centre (UNCTAD/WTO)

UNDCP¹ United Nations Drug Control Programme

UNEP United Nations Environment Programme

UNICEF United Nations Children's Fund

UNDP United Nations Development Programme

  UNIFEM United Nations Development Fund for Women

  UNV United Nations Volunteers

  UNCDF United Nations Capital Development Fund

UNFPA United Nations Population Fund

UNHCR Office of the United Nations High Commissioner for Refugees

WFP World Food Programme

UNRWA² United Nations Relief and Works Agency for Palestine Refugees in the Near East

UN-HABITAT United Nations Human Settlements Programme

Research and Training Institutes

UNICRI United Nations Interregional Crime and Justice Research Institute

UNITAR United Nations Institute for Training and Research

UNRISD United Nations Research Institute for Social Development

UNIDIR³ United Nations Institute for Disarmament Research

UN-INSTRAW United Nations International Research and Training Institute for the Advancement of Women

Other UN Entities

UNOPS United Nations Office for Project Services

UNU United Nations University

UNSSC United Nations System Staff College

UNAIDS Joint United Nations Programme on HIV/AIDS

Other UN Trust Funds⁸

UNFIP United Nations Fund for International Partnerships

UNDEF United Nations Democracy Fund

Economic and Social Council

Functional Commissions

Commissions on:

Narcotic Drugs

Crime Prevention and Criminal Justice

Science and Technology for Development

Sustainable Development

Status of Women

Population and Development

Commission for Social Development

Statistical Commission

Regional Commissions

Economic Commission for Africa (ECA)

Economic Commission for Europe (ECE)

Economic Commission for Latin America and the Caribbean (ECLAC)

Economic and Social Commission for Asia and the Pacific (ESCAP)

Economic and Social Commission for Western Asia (ESCWA)

Other Bodies

Permanent Forum on Indigenous Issues

United Nations Forum on Forests

Sessional and standing committees

Expert, ad hoc and related bodies

Related Organizations

WTO World Trade Organization

IAEA⁶ International Atomic Energy Agency

CTBTO Prep.Com⁶ PrepCom for the Nuclear-Test-Ban Treaty Organization

OPCW⁶ Organization for the Prohibition of Chemical Weapons

International Court of Justice

Specialized Agencies⁷

ILO International Labour Organization

FAO Food and Agriculture Organization of the United Nations

UNESCO United Nations Educational, Scientific and Cultural Organization

WHO World Health Organization

World Bank Group

IBRD International Bank for Reconstruction and Development

IDA International Development Association

IFC International Finance Corporation

MIGA Multilateral Investment Guarantee Agency

ICSID International Centre for Settlement of Investment Disputes

IMF International Monetary Fund

ICAO International Civil Aviation Organization

IMO International Maritime Organization

ITU International Telecommunication Union

UPU Universal Postal Union

WMO World Meteorological Organization

WIPO World Intellectual Property Organization

IFAD International Fund for Agricultural Development

UNIDO United Nations Industrial Development Organization

UNWTO World Tourism Organization

Secretariat

Departments and Offices

OSG⁹ Office of the Secretary-General

OIOS Office of Internal Oversight Services

OLA Office of Legal Affairs

DPA Department of Political Affairs

UNODA Office for Disarmament Affairs

DPKO Department of Peacekeeping Operations

DFS⁹ Department of Field Support

OCHA Office for the Coordination of Humanitarian Affairs

DESA Department of Economic and Social Affairs

DGACM Department for General Assembly and Conference Management

DPI Department of Public Information

DM Department of Management

UN-OHRLLS Office of the High Representative for the Least Developed Countries, Landlocked Developing Countries and Small Island Developing States

OHCHR Office of the United Nations High Commissioner for Human Rights

UNODC United Nations Office on Drugs and Crime

DSS Department of Safety and Security

⟨SRS⟩

UNOG UN Office at Geneva

UNOV UN Office at Vienna

UNON UN Office at Nairobi

Published by the United Nations Department of Public Information

DPI/2470—07-49950—December 2007—3M

NOTES: Solid lines from a Principal Organ indicate a direct reporting relationship; dashes indicate a non-subsidiary relationship.

1. The UN Drug Control Programme is part of the UN Office on Drugs and Crime.
2. UNRWA and UNIDIR report only to the GA.
3. The United Nations Ethics Office, the United Nations Ombudsman's Office, and the Chief Information Technology Officer report directly to the Secretary-General.
4. IAEA reports to the Security Council and the General Assembly (GA).
5. The CTBTO Prep.Com and OPCW report to the GA.
6. Specialized agencies are autonomous organizations working with the UN and each other through the coordinating machinery of the ECOSOC at the intergovernmental level, and through the Chief Executives Board for coordination (CEB) at the inter-secretariat level.
7. UNFIP is an autonomous trust fund operating under the leadership of the United Nations Deputy Secretary-General. UNDEF's advisory board recommends funding proposals for approval by the Secretary-General.

Appendix C: Composition of the Secretariat

Compiled by Simon Minching

These figures cover the period from July 1, 2008 to June 30, 2009, unless otherwise noted.

The 39,978 worldwide total of staff members in the Secretariat is based as follows:

12,236 at headquarters
2,593 at regional commissions
21,746 in peacekeeping missions
1470 in other field locations
1933 in tribunals

As of June 30, 2009, they held posts at these levels:

Total, under secretaries-general and assistant secretaries-general	126 (0.3%)
Total, director category	589 (1.5%)
Total, professional category	10,839 (27.1%)
Total, general category	28,424 (71.1%)

As of June 30, 2009, the distribution of staff in professional or higher posts:

Post Level	Quantity in Post
Professional 1/2	1,324
P-3	3,240
P-4	2,894
P-5	1,358
Director-1	440
D-2	149
assistant secretaries-general	62
under secretaries-general	64

Professional and higher-level gender breakdown:

Post Level	Male Quantity / (%)	Female Quantity / (%)
P- 1/2	620 / 46.8%	704 / 53.2%
P-3	1,844 / 56.9%	1,396 / 43.1%
P-4	1,832 / 63.3%	1,062 / 36.7%
P-5	940 / 69.2%	418 / 30.8%
D-1	315 / 71.6%	125 / 28.4%
D-2	111 / 74.5%	38 / 25.5%
USG & ASG	101 / 80.2%	25 / 19.8%

Note: Nationals of all 192 countries are represented among the Secretariat staff. A total of 177 countries are represented by staff in posts subject to geographical distribution. There are more than 1,000 nationals in the Secretariat from each of these countries: Afghanistan, the Democratic Republic of Congo, France, Haiti, Kenya, Lebanon, Liberia, Sudan and the United States.

Source: General Assembly document, A/64/352, Sept. 15, 2009.

Appendix D: Operations & Budgets

Compiled by Simon Minching

TABLE 1: REGULAR BUDGET APPROPRIATIONS FOR 2010-2011

(estimated*, in US$ millions; all figures rounded to the nearest $10,000; extrabudgetary appropriations not included in total; these are forecasted costs not included in the regular budget.)

Regular Budget Expenditures:

Part I: Overall Policy Making, Direction and Coordination

1. Overall policy making, direction and coordination
Appropriation for 2008-09: **75.78**
2010-11 proposal: **100.85**
Net change / (percent): **+25.07** / (**+33.08%**)

2. General Assembly affairs and conference services
Appropriation for 2008-09: **662.26**
2010-11 proposal: **676.59**
Net change / (percent): **+14.33** / (**+2.16%**)

Total: $777.4 million

Part II: Political Affairs

3. Political affairs
Appropriation for 2008-09: **962.58**
2010-11 proposal: **1,109.99**
Net change / (percent): **+147.41** / (**+15.31%**)

4. Disarmament
Appropriation for 2008-09: **22.46**
2010-11 proposal: **22.30**
Net change / (percent): **-0.16** / (**-0.007%**)

5. Peacekeeping operations
Appropriation for 2008-09: **105.79**
2010-11 proposal: **107.71**
Net change / (percent): **+1.92** / (**+0.018%**)

6. Peaceful uses of outer space:
Appropriation for 2008-09: **7.64**
2010-11 proposal: **8.44**
Net change / (percent): **+0.80** / (**+10.47%**)

Total: $1,248.44 million

Part III: International Justice and Law

7. International Court of Justice
Appropriation for 2008-09: **45.13**
2010-11 proposal: **51.01**
Net change / (percent): **+5.88** / (**+13.03%**)

8. Legal affairs
>Appropriation for 2008-09: **47.71**
>2010-11 proposal: **45.85**
>Amount change / (percent): **-1.86** / (**+3.9%**)

Total: $96.86 million

Part IV: International Cooperation for Development

9. Economic and social affairs
>Appropriation for 2008-09: **165.53**
>2010-11 proposal: **166.22**
>Net change / (percent): **+.69** / (**+0.004%**)

10. Least-developed countries, landlocked developing countries and small island developing states
>Appropriation for 2008-09: **5.86**
>2010-11 proposal: **7.42**
>Net change / (percent): **+1.56** / (**+26.62%**)

11. UN support to the New Partnership for Africa's Development
>Appropriation for 2008-09: **12.21**
>2010-11 proposal: **12.79**
>Net change / (percent): **+.58** / (**+4.75%**)

12. Trade and development
>Appropriation for 2008-09: 133.09
>2010-11 proposal: 140.43
>Net change / (percent): +7.34 / (+5.52%)

13. International Trade Center, UNCTAD/WTO
>Appropriation for 2008-09: **30.87**
>2010-11 proposal: **30.54**
>Net change / (percent): **-0.33** / (**-1.07%**)

14. Environment
>Appropriation for 2008-09: **14.06**
>2010-11 proposal: **14.4**
>Net change / (percent): **+0.34** / (**+2.42%**)

15. Human Settlements
>Appropriation for 2008-09: **20.8**
>2010-11 proposal: **21.51**
>Amount change / (percent): **+0.71**/(**+3.41%**)

16. International drug control, crime and terrorism prevention and criminal justice
>Appropriation for 2008-09: **37.58**
>2010-11 proposal: **41.0**
>Net change / (percent): **+3.42** / (**+9.1%**)

Total: $434.31 million

17. Economic and social development in Africa
Appropriation for 2008-09: **128.64**
2010-11 proposal: **132.7**
Net change / (percent): **+4.06** / (**+3.16%**)

18. Economic and social development in Asia and the Pacific
Appropriation for 2008-09: **92.42**
2010-11 proposal: **93.92**
Net change / (percent): **+1.5** / (**+1.62%**)

19. Economic and social development in Europe
Appropriation for 2008-09: **64.73**
2010-11 proposal: **67.88**
Net change / (percent): **+3.15** / (**+4.87%**)

20. Economic and social development in Latin America and the Caribbean
Appropriation for 2008-09: **103.16**
2010-11 proposal: **111.65**
Net change / (percent): **+8.49** / (**+8.23%**)

21. Economic and social development in Western Asia
Appropriation for 2008-09: **64.72**
2010-11 proposal: **66.6**
Net change / (percent): **+1.88** / (**+2.9%**)

22. Regular program of technical cooperation
Appropriation for 2008-09: **54.83**
2010-11 proposal: **53.71**
Net change / (percent): **-1.12** / (**+2.04%**)

Total: $526.46 million

23. Human rights
Appropriation for 2008-09: **127.35**
2010-11 proposal: **142.74**
Net change / (percent): **+15.39** / (**+12.08%**)

24. Protection of and assistance to refugees
Appropriation for 2008-09: 80.0
2010-11 proposal: 80.54
Net change / (percent): **+0.54** / (**+0.007%**)

25. Palestine refugees
Appropriation for 2008-09: **45.07**
2010-11 proposal: **48.74**
Net change / (percent): **+3.67** / (**+8.14%**)

26. Humanitarian assistance
  Appropriation for 2008-09: **29.86**
  2010-11 proposal: **29.9**
  Net change / (percent): **+0.04** / (**+0.001%**)

Total: $301.92 million

Part VII: Public Information

27. Public information:
  Appropriation for 2008-09: **189.37**
  2010-11 proposal: **186.71**
  Net change / (percent): **+2.66** / (**+1.4%**)

Total: $186.71 million

Part VIII: Common support services

28. Management and central support services
  Appropriation for 2008-09: **492.43**
  2010-11 proposal: **505.81**
  Net change / (percent): **+13.38** / (**+2.72%**)

29. Office of Information and Communications Technology
  Appropriation for 2008-09: **73.33**
  2010-11 proposal: **72.16**
  Net change / (percent): **-1.17** / (**-1.6%**)

Part IX: Internal oversight

30. Internal oversight
  Appropriation for 2008-09: **37.48**
  2010-11 proposal: **39.44**
  Net change / (percent): **+1.96** / (**+5.23%**)

Total: $39.44 million

Part X: Jointly financed administrative activities and special expenses

31. Jointly financed administrative activities
  Appropriation for 2008-09: **12.46**
  2010-11 proposal: **12.11**
  Net change / (percent): -0.35 / (**-2.81%**)

32. Special expenses
  Appropriation for 2008-09: **100.37**
  2010-11 proposal: **113.14**
  Net change / (percent): **+12.77** / (**+12.72%**)

Total: $125.25 million

33. Construction, alteration, improvement and major maintenance
Appropriation for 2008-09: **62.2**
2010-11 proposal: **61.27**
Net change / (percent): **-0.93** / (**-1.5%**)

Total: $61.27 million

34. Safety and security
Appropriation for 2008-09: **207.93**
2010-11 proposal: **239.29**
Net change / (percent): **+31.36** / (**+15.08%**)

Total: $239.29 million

35. Development account
Appropriation for 2008-09: 18.65
2010-11 proposal: **23.65**
Net change / (percent): **+5.0** / (**+26.81%**)

Total: $23.65 million

36. Staff assessment
Appropriation for 2008-09: **510.94**
2010-11 proposal: **517.02**
Net change / (percent): **+6.08** / (**+1.19%**)

Total: $517.02 million

Total 2008-09 Regular Budget Appropriation: $4,865,080,200*
Total 2010-11 Regular Budget Projection: $5,156,029,100*
Net Change / (Percent): +$290,948,900 / (+5.98%)

1. Support Activities
Appropriation for 2008-09: **831.74**
2010-11 proposal: **1,047.59**
Net change / (percent): **+215.85** / (**+25.95%**)

2. Substantive Activities
Appropriation for 2008-09: **1,560.21**
2010-11 proposal: **1,610.44**
Net change / (percent): **+50.23** / (**+3.22%**)

3. Operational Activities
Appropriation for 2008-09: **6,268.54**
2010-11 proposal: **6,783.92**
Net change / (percent): +**515.38** / (+**8.22%**)

Total 2008-09 Extrabudgetary Appropriation: $8,660,492.3**
Total 2010-11 Extrabudgetary Projection: $9,441,446.2**
Net Change / (Percent): +$781,453,900 / (+9.02%)

Estimates of income

1. Income from staff assessment
2008-09: **515.55**
2010-11 estimate: **521.18**
Net change / (percent): +**5.63** / (+**1.09%**)

2. General income
2008-09: **39.73**
2010-11 estimate: **31.18**
Net change / (percent): -**8.55** / (-**21.52%**)

3. Services to the public
2008-09: **1.1**
2010-11 estimate: **1.81**
Net change / (percent): +**0.71** / (+**64.55%**)

Total 2008-09 Income: $556,380,000
Total 2010-11 Estimate of Income: $554,170,000
Net Change / (Percent): -$2,210,000 / (-0.004%)

*These regular budget figures represent estimates provided by UN documents. Any actual difference in UN sums from those compiled here are a result of rounding to the nearest $10,000. 2008-2009 appropriations reflect a UNA-USA analysis of UN data from document A/64/6, "Proposed program budget for the biennium 2010-2011." 2010-2011 figures represent the latest proposal made by the Fifth Committee in document A/C.5/64/L.19, Dec. 28, 2009.

** These extrabudgetary figures represent exact estimates as provided by UN documents. Any actual difference in UN sums from those compiled here are a result of rounding to the nearest $10,000. 2008-2009 appropriations and 2010-2011 proposals can be found in document A/64/6, "Proposed program budget for the biennium 2010-2011."

Sources:
General Assembly document A/64/6, "Proposed program budget for the biennium 2010-2011," June 5, 2009.
Fifth Committee document A/C.5/64/L.19, "Program budget for the biennium 2010-2011," Dec. 28, 2009.

TABLE 2: PEACEKEEPING OPERATIONS BUDGET (07/09-06/10)

Figures in US$ millions

United Nations Truce Supervision Organization (UNTSO)
Since May 1948*
2008-2009 Appropriation: **66.22**
2010-2011 Appropriation: **60.7** (gross)

United Nations Military Observer Group in India and Pakistan (UMOGIP)
Since January 1949*
2008-2009 Appropriation: **16.96**
2010-2011 Appropriation: **16.14** (gross)

United Nations Peacekeeping Force in Cyprus (UNFICYP)
Since March 1964
Approved budget 07/09–06/10: **$54,412,700** (gross)
— including voluntary contributions of one-third from Cyprus
and **$6.5** million from Greece

United Nations Disengagement Observer Force (UNDOF)
Since June 1974
Approved budget 07/09–06/10: **$45,029,700** (gross)

United Nations Interim Force in Lebanon (UNIFIL)
Since March 1978
Approved budget 07/09–06/10: **$589,799,200** (gross)

United Nations Mission for the Referendum in Western Sahara (MINURSO)
Since April 1991
Approved budget 07/09–06/10: **$53,527,600** (gross)

United Nations Interim Administration Mission in Kosovo (UNMIK)
Since June 1999
Approved budget 07/09–06/10: **$46,809,000** (gross)

United Nations Organization Stabilization Mission in the Democratic Republic of Congo (MONUSCO)- Since November 1999
Approved budget 07/09–06/10: **$1,346,584,000** (gross)

United Nations Mission in Liberia (UNMIL)
Since September 2003
Approved budget 07/09–06/10: **$560,978,700** (gross)

United Nations Operation in Côte d'Ivoire (UNOCI)
Since April 2004
Approved budget 07/09–06/10: **$491,774,100** (gross)

United Nations Stabilization Mission in Haiti (MINUSTAH)
Since June 2004
Approved budget 07/09–06/10: **$611,751,200** (gross)

United Nations Mission in the Sudan (UNMIS)
Since March 2005
Approved budget 07/09–06/10: **$958,350,200** (gross)

United Nations Integrated Mission in Timor-Leste (UNMIT)
Since August 2006
>Approved budget 07/09–06/10: **$205,939,400**

African Union/United Nations Hybrid operation in Darfur (UNAMID)
Since July 2007
>Approved budget 07/09–06/10: **$1,598,942,200**

United Nations Mission in the Central African Republic and Chad
(MINURCAT)- Since September 2007
>Approved budget 07/09–06/10: **$690,753,100**

Subtotal of missions: (09-10): $7,254,651,100

>Support account: 09-10: **$322,547,400**

>UN Logistics Base at Brindisi (UNLB) 2009-10: **$57,954,100**

>UN Support for African Union Mission in Somalia (AMISOM)
>2009-10: **$213,580,000**

TOTAL: 2009-2010 PEACEKEEPING BUDGET: $7,848,732,600**
2010-11: ABOUT $8.4 BILLION (PROPOSED)

*UNTSO and UNMOGIP are funded from the United Nations regular biennial budget. Costs to the United Nations for the other operations are financed from separate accounts on the basis of legally binding assessments on all member states. For these missions, budget figures are made on a one-year basis (07/09-06/10).

**Removed from this total is the 2009-2010 funding allocated for the United Nations Observer Mission in Georgia (UNOMIG). According to its Web site, "UNOMIG came to an end on June 2009 due to a lack of consensus among Security Council members on mandate extension."

Sources:

Fifth Committee document A/C.5/64/15, "Approved resources for peacekeeping operations for the period from 1 July 2009 to 30 June 2010," Jan. 22, 2010.

http://www.un.org/en/peacekeeping/missions/past/unomig/

TABLE 3: INTERNATIONAL WAR CRIMES TRIBUNALS APPROPRIATIONS
(in US$ millions)

International Criminal Tribunal for Rwanda
Appropriation for 2008-09: **$282.6 (net)**
Initial Appropriation for 2010-11: $227.25 (net)
Change / (percent): **-55.35 / (-19.59%)**

Source: http://www.un.org/News/Press/docs//2008/ga10804.doc.htm
http://www.ictr.org/default.htm (general information)

International Tribunal for former Yugoslavia
Appropriation for 2008-09: **$342.3 (net)**
Initial Appropriation for 2010-11: $301.9 (net)
Change / (percent): **-40.4 / (-11.8%)**

Source: http://www.un.org/News/Press/docs//2008/ga10804.doc.htm
http://www.icty.org/sid/325

The Special Court for Sierra Leone
(Financed by voluntary contributions)
Requested 2009 budget: $27.97
Requested 2010 budget: $12.71
Change / (percent): -15.26 / (-54.56%)

Source: Sixth Annual Report of the President of the Special Court, 2008-2009

Extraordinary Chambers in the Courts of Cambodia:
2009 UN funding estimate: $29.39
2009 Cambodian funding estimate: $6.98
Total 2009 funding estimate: $36.37
(2010 Figures not available)

Source: http://www.unakrt-online.org/Docs/Other/2005-2009%20ECCC%20Approved%20Budget.pdf,
Revised Budget Estimates 2005-09, UNAKRT Online (UN Assistance to the Khmer Rouge Trials)

TABLE 4: SCALE OF TOP 10 BUDGET CONTRIBUTIONS BY COUNTRIES (assessed by UN)

Country	Regular Budget (2010-2012)
US*	22.000 percent
Japan	12.530
Germany	8.018
Britain*	6.604
France*	6.123
Italy	4.999
Canada	3.207
China*	3.189
Spain	3.177
Mexico	2.356

*Security Council permanent members. Russia, the fifth permanent member, contributes 1.602%.
Note: Maximum assessment rate is 22%; minimum assessment rate is 0.001%.

Source: General Assembly resolution, A/RES/64/248

UN Photo/Evan Schneider

The 15-nation UN Security Council meets in April 2010 to discuss the situation in Somalia.

TABLE 5: TOP 10 COUNTRIES WITH THE HIGHEST UN REGULAR BUDGET ARREARS (US $ MILLIONS) AS OF JUNE 30, 2009

	Regular Budget	Tribunals	DPKO	Total
United States	846.01	65.1	324.05	1,235.20
Japan	210.68	-	69.37	280.05
Germany	78.44	-	-	78.44
China	24.78	-	-	24.78
Argentina	19.87	.66	1.30	21.83
Greece	10.90	-	12.94	23.84
Iran	10.52	1.16	5.11	16.79
Chile	5.37	.80	5.53	11.70
Venezuela	3.66	.41	2.66	6.73
Slovenia	1.76	.15	.32	2.23

Source: ST/ADM/SER.B/768
http://www.un.org/ga/search/view_doc.asp?symbol=ST/ADM/SER.B/768

*DPKO figures were calculated from the debts owed toward peacekeeping operations and UN support to the African Union's Mission in Somalia. Omitted are debts from political/peacekeeping missions and the peacekeeping support account. Other member states have larger peacekeeping arrears, but this list is sorted first by the largest regular budget arrears.

Note: An assessment of contributions is done monthly, but June 2009 is the latest report available on the UN Web site. More recent data has been compiled but is not electronically available. Furthermore, as of Jan. 1, 2010, all printing of UN official documents was discontinued in efforts to become environmentally friendly.

Top 10 Contributors to the UN Regular Budget for Year 2010
(Millions of US$)—Rounded to Nearest $10,000

United States	517.13
Japan	294.53
Germany	188.47
Britain	155.23
France	143.93
Italy	117.51
Canada	75.38
China	74.96
Spain	74.68
Mexico	55.38

ST/ADM/SER.B/789
Source: http://www.un.org/zh/members/contribution_2010.pdf

Libyan leader Muammar
el-Qaddafi addresses the
64th session of the UN
General Assembly in
September 2009. Behind
him are Secretary-
General Ban Ki-moon
(left) and Ali Abdussalam
Treki of Libya, the
General Assembly's presi-
dent for the session.

Appendix E: **Acronyms and Abbreviations**

ACABQ Advisory Committee on Administrative and Budgetary Questions

ACC Administrative Committee on Coordination

ACPR Advisory Committee of Permanent Representatives

ADB Asian Development Bank

ADN European Agreement Concerning the International Carriage of Dangerous Goods by Inland Waterways

ADR European Agreement Concerning the International Carriage of Dangerous Goods by Road

AFDB African Development Bank

ALADI Asociación Latino Americana de Integración

AMAP Arctic Monitoring and Assessment Programme

AMIS African Union-led Mission in the Sudan

APCAEM Asian and Pacific Center for Agricultural Engineering and Machinery

APCC Asian and Pacific Coconut Community

APCICT Asian and Pacific Training Center for Information and Communications Technology for Development

APCTT Asian and Pacific Center for Transfer of Technology

APEC Asia-Pacific Economic Cooperation

APO Asian Productivity Organization

ASEAN Association of South East Asian Nations

AU African Union

BCEAO Central Bank of West African States

BCIE Central American Bank for Economic Integration

BINUBUN Integrated Office in Burundi

BIPM International Bureau of Weights and Measures

BIS Bank for International Settlements

BONUCA UN Peacebuilding Office in the Central African Republic

CAAC Working Group on Children and Armed Conflict

CABI CAB International

CAPSA Centre for Alleviation of Poverty through Secondary Crops Development in Asia and the Pacific

CARICOM Caribbean Community and Common Market

CAT Committee Against Torture

CBD Convention on Biological Diversity

CBF Committee on Budget and Finance

CBSS Council of the Baltic States

CCAMLR Commission for the Conservation of Antarctic Living Marine Resources

CCE Committee on Central American Economic Cooperation

CCPCJ Commission on Crime Prevention and Criminal Justice

CD Conference on Disarmament

CDB Caribbean Development Bank

CDCC Caribbean Development and Cooperation Committee

CEBUN System's Chief Executives Board for Coordination

CEC Commission for Environmental Cooperation (North America)

CEDAW Convention on the Elimination of All Forms of Discrimination Against Women

CEGAN Committee of High-Level Government Experts

CERD Committee on the Elimination of Racial Discrimination

CERN European Organization for Nuclear Research

CESCR Committee on Economic, Social and Cultural Rights

CFA Committee on Food Aid Policies and Programmes

CFF Compensatory Financing Facility

CGAP Consultative Group to Assist the Poorest

CGIAR Consultative Group on International Agricultural Research

CHR Commission on Human Rights

CIRDAP Center on Integrated Rural Development for Asia and the Pacific

CIS Commonwealth of Independent States

CITES Convention on International Trade in Endangered Species of Wild Fauna and Flora

CMS Convention on the Conservation of Migratory Species of Wild Animals

CMW Committee on the Protection of the Rights of All Migrant Workers and Members of their Families

CND Commission on Narcotic Drugs

CNGO Committee on Nongovernmental Organizations

COE Council of Europe

COMESA Common Market for Eastern and Southern Africa

COPUOS Committee on the Peaceful Uses of Outer Space

CPA Comprehensive Peace Agreement

CPC Committee for Program and Coordination

CPF Collaborative Partnership on Forests

CPLP Community of Portuguese Speaking Nations

CPR Committee of Permanent Representatives

CRC Committee on the Rights of the Child

CRIC Committee for the Review of the Implementation of the Convention (to Combat Desertification in Countries Experiencing Serious Drought and/or Desertification. especially in Africa)

CSD Commission on Sustainable Development

CSocD Commission for Social Development

CST Committee on Science and Technology

CSTD Commission on Science and Technology for Development

CSW Commission on the Status of Women

CTBTO Comprehensive Nuclear Test Ban Treaty Organization

CTC Counter-Terrorism Committee

CTED Counter-Terrorism Committee Executive Directorate

CWC Convention on the Prohibition of the Development, Production, Stockpiling and Use of Chemical Weapons

DESA Department of Economic and Social Affairs

DFS Department of Field Support

DGACM Department for General Assembly and Conference Management

DM Department of Management

DPA Department of Political Affairs

DPI Department of Public Information

DPKO Department of Peacekeeping Operations

DRC Democratic Republic of Congo

DSS Department of Safety and Security

EBRD European Bank for Reconstruction and Development

ECA Economic Commission for Africa

ECB European Central Bank

ECE Economic Commission for Europe

ECHR European Court of Human Rights

ECLAC Economic Commission for Latin America and the Caribbean

ECOWAS Economic Community of West African States

EFTA European Free Trade Association

EPO European Patent Office

EPTA Expanded Program of Technical Assistance (UN)

ESCAP Economic and Social Commission for Asia and the Pacific

ESCWA Economic and Social Commission for Western Asia

EU European Union

EUTELSAT European Telecommunications Satellite Organization

FAO Food and Agriculture Organization of the United Nations

GATT General Agreement on Tariffs and Trade

GEF Global Environment Facility

GHS Globally Harmonized System of Classification and Labeling of Chemicals

HELCOM Helsinki Commission- Baltic Marine Environment Protection Commission

HIPCs Heavily Indebted Poor Countries

HLCM High Level Committee on Management

HLCP High Level Committee on Programs

HONLEA Heads of National Drug Law Enforcement Agencies

HRC Human Rights Campaign

IADB Inter-American Development Bank

IAEA International Atomic Energy Agency

IATTC Inter-American Tropical Tuna Commission

IBE International Bureau of Education

IBRD International Bank for Reconstruction and Development

IBSFC International Baltic Sea Fishery Commission

ICAO International Civil Aviation Organization

ICCAT International Commission for the Conservation of Atlantic Tunas

ICCROM International Center for the Study of the Preservation and Restoration of Cultural Property

ICES International Council for the Exploration of the Sea

ICO International Coffee Organization

ICOM International Council of Museums

ICOMOS International Council on Monuments and Sites

ICSG International Copper Study Group

ICSID International Center for Settlement of Investment Disputes

ICC International Criminal Court

ICTR International Criminal Tribunal for Rwanda

ICTY International Criminal Tribunal for the former Yugoslavia

IDA International Development Association

IDC International Data Center

IEFR International Emergency Food Reserve

IFAD International Fund for Agricultural Development

IFC International Finance Corporation

IGCP International Geoscience Program

IHO International Hydrographic Organization

IIC InterAmerican Investment Corporation

ILO International Labor Organization

ILPES Latin American and Caribbean Institute for Economic and Social Planning

IMF International Monetary Fund

IMFC International Monetary and Financial Committee

IMO International Maritime Organization

INCB International Narcotics Control Board

INDES Inter-American Institute for Social Development

INSTRAW International Research and Training Institute for the Advancement of Women

INTAL Institute for the Integration of Latin America and the Caribbean

INTERPOL International Criminal Police Organization

IOM International Organization for Migration

IOTC Indian Ocean Tuna Commission

IPCC Intergovernmental Panel on Climate Change

IPHC International Pacific Halibut Commission

ISA International Seabed Authority

ISDB Islamic Development Bank

ITC International Trade Center

ITU International Telecommunication Union

IWC International Whaling Commission

JAG Joint Advisory Group (of the ITC)

JIU Joint Inspection Unit

LDCs Least Developed Countries

MAB International Coordinating Council of the Program on Man and the Biosphere

MAC Military Armistice Commission

MDGs Millennium Development Goals

MIF Multilateral Investment Fund

MIF Multinational Interim Force (Haiti)

MIGA Multilateral Investment Guarantee Agency

MINURCAT United Nations Mission in the Central African Republic and Chad

MINURSO United Nations Mission for the Referendum in Western Sahara

MINUSTAH United Nations Stabilization Mission in Haiti

MONUSCO United Nations Organization Stabilization Mission in the Democratic Republic of Congo

NAALC Commission for Labor Cooperation (North America)

NEPAD New Partnership for Africa's Development

NPT Nuclear Non-Proliferation Treaty

OAU Organization of African Unity

OCHA Office for the Coordination of Humanitarian Affairs

ODA Office for Disarmament Affairs

OECD Organization for Economic Cooperation and Development

OHCHR Office of the UN High Commissioner for Human Rights

OIOS Office of Internal Oversight Services

OLA Office of Legal Affairs

ONUB United Nations Operation in Burundi

OPCW Organization for the Prohibition of Chemical Weapons

OPEC Organization of Petroleum Exporting Countries

OSG Office of the Secretary-General

PBC Peacebuilding Commission

POC Postal Operations Council

SBC Secretariat of the Basel Convention on the Control of Transboundary Movements of Hazardous Wastes and their Disposal

SBSTTA Subsidiary Body on Scientific, Technical and Technological Advice

SDRs Special Drawing Rights (IMF and Asian Development Bank)

SIAP Statistical Institute for Asia and the Pacific

STAP Scientific and Technical Advisory Panel

STRP Scientific and Technical Review Panel

TDB Trade and Development Board (of UNCTAD)

TSAG Telecommunication Standardization Bureau

UNAIDS Joint UN Program on HIV/AIDS

UNAMI UN Assistance Mission for Iraq

UNAMID UN/African Union Hybrid Operation in Darfur

UNAMIS UN Advance Mission in Sudan

UNAMSIL UN Assistance Mission in Sierra Leone

UNAT UN Administrative Tribunal

UNC UN Command-Korea

UNCC UN Compensation Commission

UNCCD UN Convention to Combat Desertification

UNCDF UN Capital Development Fund

UNCIP UN Commission for India and Pakistan

UNCITRAL UN Commission on International Trade Law

UNCLOS UN Convention on the Law of the Sea

UNCTAD UN Conference on Trade and Development

UNDC UN Disarmament Commission

UNDCP UN International Drug Control Program

UNDEF UN Democracy Fund

UNDG UN Development Group

UNDOF UN Disengagement Observer Force

UNDP UN Development Program

UNECE UN Economic Commission for Europe

UNEP UN Environment Program

UNESCO UN Educational, Scientific and Cultural Organization

UNFCCC UN Framework Convention on Climate Change

UNFF UN Forum on Forests

UNFICYP UN Peacekeeping Force in Cyprus

UNFIP UN Fund for International Partnerships

UNFPA UN Population Fund

UNGEGN UN Group of Experts on Geographical Names

UN-HABITAT UN Human Settlements Program

UNHCR UN High Commissioner for Refugees

UNICEF UN Children's Fund

UNICRI UN Interregional Crime and Justice Research Institute

UNIDIR UN Institute for Disarmament Research

UNIDO UN Industrial Development Organization

UNIDROIT International Institute for the Unification of Private Law

UNIFEM UN Development Fund for Women

UNIFIL UN Interim Force in Lebanon

UNIOSIL UN Integrated Office in Sierra Leone

UNIPOM UN India-Pakistan Observation Mission

UNITAR UN Institute for Training and Research

UNMEE UN Mission in Ethiopia and Eritrea

UNMIK UN Interim Administration Mission in Kosovo

UNMIL UN Mission in Liberia

UNMIN UN Mission in Nepal

UNMIS UN Mission in Sudan

UNMIT UN Integrated Mission in Timor-Leste

UNMOGIP UN Military Observer Group in India and Pakistan

UNMOT UN Mission of Observers in Tajikistan

UNMOVIC UN Monitoring, Verification and Inspection Commission

UNOCI UN Operation in Côte d'Ivoire

UNODA UN Office for Disarmament Affairs

UNODC UN Office on Drugs and Crime

UNOG UN Office at Geneva

UNOGBIS UN Peacebuilding Support Office in Guinea-Bissau

UNOHRLLS Office of the High Representative for the Least Developed Countries, Landlocked Developing Countries, and Small Island Developing States

UNOL UN Peacebuilding Support Office in Liberia

UNOMIG UN Observer Mission in Georgia

UNON UN Office at Nairobi

UNOPS UN Office for Project Services

UNOSAT UN Institute for Training and Research (UNITAR) Operational Satellite Applications Program

UNOTIL UN Office in Timor-Leste

UNOV UN Office at Vienna

UNPOS UN Political Office for Somalia

UNRISD UN Research Institute for Social Development

UNRWA UN Relief and Works Agency for Palestine Refugees in the Near East

UNSCEAR UN Scientific Committee on the Effects of Atomic Radiation

UNSCO Office of the United Nations Special Coordinator for the Middle East Peace Process

UNSCOM UN Special Commission (Iraq)

UNSDRI UN Social Defense Research Institute

UNSMA UN Special Mission to Afghanistan

UNSSC UN Systems Staff College

UNTOP UN Tajikistan Office of Peacebuilding

UNTSO UN Truce Supervision Organization

UNU UN University

UNV UN Volunteers

UNWTO World Tourism Organization

UPOV International Union for the Protection of New Varieties of Plants

UPU Universal Postal Union

WEOG Western European and Others Group

WHC World Heritage Committee

WHO World Health Organization

WFP World Food Programme

WIPO World Intellectual Property Organization

WMDs Weapons of Mass Destruction

WMO World Meterological Organization

WSIS World Summit on the Information Society

WSSD World Summit on Sustainable Development

WTO World Trade Organization

Appendix F: Glossary

Compiled by Christopher J. Tangney

absolutism A theory of government vesting unrestrained power in a person, a dynasty, a party or an administration.

acclamation An overwhelmingly affirmative vote. If no opposition is indicated, an item of business is declared adopted "by acclamation."

accord A diplomatic agreement that stipulates action on the part of the signers. It does not have the force of a treaty but is often treated similarly (e.g., the Camp David Accords signed by Israel and Egypt in 1978).

act of state The actions of a government for which no individual can be held accountable.

ad hoc Latin phrase meaning "to this." For a specific or temporary purpose. An ad hoc committee is not a standing committee.

ad litem Latin phrase meaning "for the litigation."

aegis Greek for a "shield," thus a power or influence that organizes, protects or shields. Nations join in peacekeeping under the aegis of the United Nations.

African Development Bank Established in 1964, it provides loans for and invests in its African member states, offers technical assistance for development, promotes investment for development and helps coordinate regional policies and plans. Its members, or shareholders, consist of 53 African countries and 14 non-African countries.

African Union Created in July 2002 to replace the Organization of African Unity. Promotes democracy, human rights and development across the continent and works to increase foreign investment through the New Partnership for Africa's Development.

aggression An act of force; a belligerent action by one state against another.

allegiance Loyalty to a principle, leader or country.

alliance A union of powers or countries created to undertake joint action.

ambassador The highest ranking diplomat who can be sent by one government to another or to an international organization.

amicus or amici curiae In Latin, "friend or friends of the court." Someone who is not party to a legal proceeding. Often identified as "third parties."

amnesty A pardon given by a government to a group or class of people, usually for political reasons.

anarchy Absence of government; a state of lawlessness or political disorder.

annexation An act in which a country proclaims sovereignty over territory beyond its domain. Unlike secession, whereby territory is given or sold by a treaty, annexation is a unilateral act made effective by actual possession and legitimized by general recognition.

appeasement The policy of giving in to the demands of another.

Arab League Established on March 22, 1945. Formed to consider cultural cooperation among the Arab states. Its headquarters are in Cairo.

arbitration A way to settle disputes outside ordinary court procedures by giving an agreed-upon third party authority to make a legally binding decision.

area of operation The portion of an arena of conflict necessary for the conduct of a peacekeeping operation.

area of separation The area between the forces of parties in a conflict where they have agreed not to deploy troops. Sometimes called a demilitarized zone.

aristocracy Government by a small privileged class; power is vested in a minority considered to be those best qualified.

arrears The unpaid portion of an assessment for a given financial period.

appropriations Funds set aside for a specific use.

assessment The amount a member state must pay toward the expenses of the UN in a financial period, as specified in the relevant budget adopted by the General Assembly.

asylum Protection granted by a country to the citizen of another (usually a political refugee).

atrocities Acts of unusual cruelty or brutality, usually inflicted on large groups of defenseless people.

authoritarianism A system of government with a concentration of power in a leader or small elite not constitutionally responsible to the people.

autonomy The right of self-government.

back-channel diplomacy Secret lines of communication, often through an informal intermediary.

barter system The exchange of goods or services without use of money or other medium of exchange, either based on established rates of exchange or bargaining.

Beijing Declaration An international agreement signed at the Fourth World Conference on Women in Beijing in 1995 affirming the equal rights of men and women and calling upon nations to promote gender equality and the empowerment of women.

bilateral A two-way agreement or exchange.

biological warfare Use of disease-producing agents, like bacteria and viruses, on humans, animals or plants.

bloc An informal grouping of countries.

blockade A maneuver to prevent ships or other carriers from getting goods into a port or region.

Bonn Agreement An agreement on Dec. 5, 2001, creating an interim administration to lead Afghanistan for two years until a representative government could be elected. Elections were held in October 2004.

breach A failure to observe agreed-upon terms; a break or interruption in friendly relations.

Bretton Woods institutions Financial bodies, including the World Bank and International Monetary Fund, which were set up at a meeting of 43 countries in Bretton Woods, N.H., in July 1944 to help rebuild postwar economies and promote economic cooperation.

buffer zone Also known as an area of separation, a neutral space between hostile parties; as a demilitarized zone, an area in which the parties have agreed not to deploy military forces.

bureaucracy An administrative structure usually composed of officials in a hierarchy.

Bush Doctrine Also known as the new National Security Strategy of the US, adopted in September 2002, providing for the pre-emptive use of force.

cease-fire An end or pause in hostilities.

censorship The suppression or prohibition of material considered harmful by those in control.

Central American Free Trade Agreement This US-proposed agreement, modeled after the North American Free Trade Agreement, promotes trade liberalization between the US and Costa Rica, the Dominican Republic, El Salvador, Guatemala, Honduras and Nicaragua.

chemical warfare Hostile use of chemical compounds, usually toxic agents.

civil disobedience The refusal to obey the demands or commands of a government or occupying power; violence or active measures of opposition are not used.

civil society The institutions, organizations and behaviors among the government, business world and family. Civil society includes voluntary and nonprofit organizations, philanthropic institutions and social and political movements.

coalition A temporary alliance between two or more political units for the purpose of joint action. In the 2003 Iraq war, the "coalition of the willing" involved primarily the US, Britain, Australia and Poland.

Coalition Provisional Authority A temporary administration set up in Iraq by the US and its allies in May 2003 to maintain stability, security and institutional structures until an interim government was established in June 2004.

coercion Forced compliance through fear and intimidation.

Cold War The rivalry after World War II between the US and the Soviet Union and their respective allies.

collective security A concept that seeks to ensure peace through enforcement by the community of nations.

commission A body created to perform a function, administrative, legislative or judicial.

Commonwealth of Independent States A union of 12 of the 15 former Soviet republics, created in December 1991 to promote common policies.

communiqué An official document, usually an announcement to the public or press.

Comprehensive Nuclear Test-Ban Treaty Opened for signatures on Sept. 10, 1996, it established a global verification mechanism for nuclear weapons. The treaty says that signers agree not to carry out explosions of nuclear weapons and to prohibit and prevent such explosions anyplace under its jurisdiction or control.

conciliation The process of bringing two sides in a dispute to agree to a compromise.

conservatism An ideology generally characterized by a belief in individualism, with minimal government intervention in the economy and society.

consolidated appeals process A mechanism used by aid organizations to plan, carry out and monitor their activities; they use this data to produce a Common Humanitarian Action Plan and appeal to be presented to the international community yearly.

constituency A body of citizens that elects a representative to a public body.

constitution The fundamental rules and principles under which a state is organized.

constitutionalism The belief that governments will defer to the rules and principles of their constitutions and uphold the rule of law.

convention A practice or custom followed by nations. Some international laws are called conventions, like the Convention on the Rights of the Child.

Convention on the Elimination of All Forms of Discrimination Against Women Adopted by the General Assembly in 1979 as an international bill of rights for women, defining what constitutes discrimination and setting up an agenda for national action to end such differentiation.

coup d'état French for "blow to the state": a sudden overthrow of a government.

cross-borrowing Borrowing from one account to meet the needs of another.

Dayton Peace Accords An agreement among Bosnia, Herzegovina, Croatia and the Federal Republic of Yugoslavia in 1995 to respect one another's sovereignty and to settle future disputes peacefully.

delegate A representative.

delegation A group of representatives.

demilitarized zone The area between parties in a conflict where they have agreed not to deploy military forces. It may be placed under control of peacekeepers.

democracy A form of government in which political decisions are made by all citizens. In direct democracy, citizens exercise their control directly through the process of majority rule. In representative democracy, citizens exercise the same right through representatives chosen by election.

Department of Peacekeeping Operations The main UN office dealing with peacekeeping and peace-building.

developed countries Those with more fully industrialized economies, more productive agriculture and a relatively high standard of living.

developing countries Those not fully industrialized, with limited specialization and financial savings. These countries are identified by a population that is out-growing its resources and who have a low standard of living.

diplomacy The conduct of relations between nations, often through representatives empowered to seek agreements.

diplomatic immunity Special rights for official representatives of foreign governments, including immunity from laws in the country to which they are assigned.

directive A communication in which policy is established or a specific action is ordered concerning conduct or procedure.

disarmament The reduction or removal of armed forces and armaments.

displaced person Someone left homeless as a result of war or disaster. A person fleeing war or disaster who crosses a national border is considered a refugee. People who take flight but never leave their country are considered internally displaced persons.

draft resolution A document prepared for formal debate; it is written in the form of a resolution but has not been adopted by the committee.

dumping In relation to trade, the selling of goods in a foreign market below the cost of production, or for less than they are sold in the home market.

Economic and Social Council A 54-member body elected by the General Assembly to three-year terms. It is responsible for coordinating and overseeing UN economic and social work.

economic growth An increase in a nation's production of goods and services, often measured by gross national product.

embargo A government order prohibiting entry or departure of foreign commercial carriers, especially as a war measure. Also refers to a restriction imposed on commerce by law.

embassy A body of diplomatic representatives, specifically one headed by an ambassador.

eminent domain Also called condemnation or expropriation, this describes the power of government to take private property for public use without the owner's consent.

envoy A diplomatic agent of any rank.

epidemic An infectious disease widespread among the population of a community or region.

ethnic cleansing The expulsion, imprisonment or killing of members of one ethnic group by another seeking ethnic homogeneity.

ethnocentrism Belief in the inherent superiority of one's own cultural or ethnic group.

European Union With its headquarters in Brussels, this organization of 27 countries seeks economic and social progress for a strong European presence in the world and a free and secure citizenship.

exile A prolonged stay away from one's country or community, usually forced. The term can also refer to banishment but is sometimes self-imposed.

extort To get money or other items of value through violence, threats or misuse of authority.

extremist One who supports ideas, doctrines or policies beyond the norm, usually in politics or religion.

facilitator In diplomacy, a neutral person or country bringing warring parties to a meeting with the goal of exchanging views and, possibly, finding preliminary agreement. The facilitator's role is less formal than that of a mediator or a broker in a treaty negotiation.

faction An association of people hoping to influence a government toward actions favorable to their interests; known also as an interest group.

famine An acute general shortage of food.

federalism A system of government in which sovereignty is distributed among a central government and provincial or state governments.

Food and Agriculture Organization Headquartered in Rome, FAO was founded in 1945 with a mandate to raise levels of nutrition and standards of living, to improve agricultural productivity and to better the condition of rural populations.

free trade Trade carried on without governmental regulations, especially international trade conducted without protective tariffs and customs duties.

Group of Seven (G7) First made up of the seven most industrialized nations—Britain, Canada, France, Germany, Italy, Japan and the US—the group now includes Russia and is more often referred to as the Group of Eight (G8).

Group of Eight (G8) See G7.

Group of 20 (G20) A group of nations created in 1999 that includes the world's leading industrialized countries (G8), the European Union, the International Monetary Fund and the World Bank. The G20 is a forum to promote dialogue between developed and developing countries on key issues of economic growth and the financial system.

Group of 77 (G77) A group established in 1964 by 77 developing countries that now has 130 members. As the largest coalition in the UN, it provides a way for the developing world to promote its collective economic interests and enhance its negotiating strength.

General Agreement on Tariffs and Trade, or GATT. This 1948 agreement was incorporated into and superseded by the World Trade Organization in January 1995. The 100-plus members of GATT established rules for international trade, with the aim of reducing trade barriers. The World Trade Organization offers a dispute-settlement system to enforce those rules.

General Assembly The central deliberative organ of the UN. Each of the 192 member states is represented equally and has a vote.

genocide Systematic killing to eliminate a whole people or nation.

Global Fund The Global Fund for HIV/AIDS, Tuberculosis and Malaria is a non-UN body initiated by Secretary-General Kofi Annan to raise money to fight deadly diseases in developing nations.

grassroots Originating among ordinary citizens.

gross domestic product An economic measure embracing the total value of all products manufactured and goods provided within a territory (often, per year). Like the gross national product (see below) it is used to assess a nation's economy.

gross national product The value of all goods and services produced by a country's nationals.

guerrilla A member of an irregular force of soldiers, usually volunteers.

habeas corpus Latin for "you have the body." A legal action demanding that a prisoner be brought before the court.

The Hague Home to many international courts and tribunals, particularly the International Criminal Court.

head of government The person in effective charge of the executive branch of a government. In a parliamentary system, the prime minister.

head of state The person who represents the state but may not exercise political power. In a parliamentary system, it may be a president or a monarch.

human rights law Obligations regulating government behavior toward groups and individuals in political, civil, economic, social and cultural spheres.

ideology A system of beliefs and values.

immunity Exemption from the application of a rule or jurisdiction.

indictment A formal written statement by a court or other authority calling upon a prosecutor to start a trial on specified charges.

indigenous Born, growing or produced naturally in a region or country; native.

inter alia Latin term for "among other things."

interdependence Dependence on each other or one another; mutual dependence.

intergovernmental organization Any body with two or more member states.

International Atomic Energy Agency Established in 1957. With headquarters in Vienna, this agency serves as the world center for nuclear information and cooperation. It is also the chief inspector of the world's nuclear facilities.

International Court of Justice Also known as the World Court, this is the main judicial organ of the UN for settling disputes between member countries and giving advisory opinions to the UN and its agencies. It does not hear cases brought by or against individual people or private organizations nor does it hear criminal cases.

International Criminal Court A permanent court established in 1998 with jurisdiction over individual people accused of war crimes, crimes against humanity or genocide.

international criminal law This involves violations of international law that point to individual criminal accountability. It provides a legal basis for trying heads of state and the like on charges of genocide, war crimes and crimes against humanity.

International Criminal Police Organization or Interpol Established in 1956, it promotes international cooperation among police authorities. Interpol has 181 members.

International Criminal Tribunal for the former Yugoslavia Established by the Security Council in 1993, this organization was created to prosecute those responsible for serious violations of international humanitarian law since 1991 in the territory that was formerly Yugoslavia.

International Criminal Tribunal for Rwanda Established by the Security Council in 1994, this organization was created to prosecute those responsible for genocide and other serious violations of international humanitarian law committed in the year 1994 in Rwanda, or by Rwandans in neighbor states.

International Development Association Created in 1960, it provides interest-free loans to the world's poorest countries. It is part of the World Bank group.

International Finance Corporation A member of the World Bank Group, this corporation was founded in 1956. It is currently the largest multilateral source of financing for private-sector projects in the developing world.

international humanitarian law Also called the law of war or armed conflict law, this aims to protect those who are not taking part in hostilities and restricts the methods of fighting between countries or other combatants.

International Labor Organization Set up in 1919, it became a specialized agency of the UN in 1946. It seeks to improve working and living conditions by establishing standards that reduce social injustice in areas like employment, pay, health, job safety and freedom of association among workers.

international law Traditionally defined as the agreements and principles governing relations between countries; increasingly it regulates state behavior toward nonstate actors.

International Law Commission Established in 1947 with a membership of 15 people competent in international law, it encourages progressive development of international law and its codification.

internally displaced person See displaced person.

International Monetary Fund Established at the Bretton Woods Conference in 1944, it provides financial advice and financing to countries having trouble with their balance of payments.

interstate Actions between two or more states or countries.

Intifada The word has come to symbolize the Palestinian uprising against Israeli occupation.

intrastate Actions within a state or country.

Joint United Nations Program on HIV/AIDS This body began work in 1995 as the main advocate for global action on HIV/AIDS under the sponsorship of the UN Children's Fund, the UN Development Program, the UN Population Fund, the UN Educational, Scientific and Cultural Organization, the World Health Organization and the World Bank. Today, the UN Office on Drugs and Crime, the International Labor Organization and the World Food Program also sponsor it.

junta A Spanish word for a group or council holding governmental power. After a revolution or coup d'état, frequently a group of military officers.

Kyoto Protocol 1997 A treaty resulting from the UN Framework Convention on Climate Change, this agreement outlines goals to limit greenhouse gas emissions and honor commitments to reduce greenhouse gas by the signing nations.

League of Arab States See Arab League.

League of Nations Organization created after World War I to achieve international peace and security.

least-developed country A country characterized by a low standard of living, limited industrial capacity and long-term barriers to economic growth.

loya jirga A Pashtun phrase meaning "grand council." For centuries, leaders in Afghanistan have convened loya jirgas to choose new kings, adopt constitutions and decide important political matters. The most recent such process was set in motion by the Bonn Agreement of Dec. 5, 2001.

mandate As it applies to the UN, it is an authoritative command given by the Security Council or General Assembly to a UN mission or representative.

maquiladora Assembly production of products in Mexico using US resources.

member state One of the 192 countries now belonging to the UN.

microcredit The lending of small amounts of money to people unable to provide traditional collateral or security. Microcredit has emerged in places like Bangladesh as a way for people to set up a business and escape poverty.

Millennium Development Goals Eight benchmarks and accompanying targets agreed upon at the Millennium Summit of 2000. It set goals to be reached by 2015 for poverty eradication and developmental progress worldwide.

Millennium Summit Conference A meeting on Sept. 6-8, 2000, at UN headquarters. It gathered 150 heads of state and government to tackle global challenges. The Millennium Declaration outlines the eight Millennium Development Goals.

Montreal Protocol Signed in 1987 and amended in 1990 and 1992, this pact aims to protect the stratospheric ozone layer.

most-favored nation The clause in a treaty by which one party or both agree to grant to the other all privileges granted to any third party.

multilateral Involving or participated in by more than two nations or parties.

nation Individuals in a specific geographical area who share a strong historical continuity, common culture and language and are under the rule of one government.

nation-state A sovereign state whose citizens or subjects are relatively homogeneous in factors like language or common descent.

nationalism Loyalty and devotion to a nation, especially a sense of national consciousness exalting one nation above all others and placing primary emphasis on promotion of its culture and interests.

national interest Interests specific to a nation-state, especially including survival and maintenance of power.

nationalize To take over ownership, performed by a national government.

Nonaligned Countries An alliance of third-world nations seeking to promote the political and economic interests of developing countries. At the UN, this alliance is referred to as the nonaligned movement.

nongovernmental organization A nonprofit organization that contributes to development through cooperative projects, financial and material aid, education and the dispatch of personnel. Some NGOs are accredited by the UN system and can represent their interests before the Economic and Social Council.

North American Free Trade Agreement An agreement that became effective in January 1994 among Canada, the US and Mexico.

North Atlantic Treaty Organization or NATO A military alliance formed in 1949 when 12 democratic nations signed the treaty. NATO now has 28 members.

Nuclear Nonproliferation Treaty Taking effect in 1970, this treaty was intended to limit the number of countries with nuclear weapons to five: the US, Soviet Union, Britain, France and China. Since then, more than 140 countries have pledged not to acquire nuclear weapons and to accept the safeguards of the International Atomic Energy Agency.

observer mission Unarmed officers sent to observation posts to monitor cease-fires and armistices.

Official Development Assistance Loans, grants, technical assistance and other forms of cooperation extended by governments to developing nations to promote progress.

Organization of American States A regional organization created in 1948 to promote Latin American development. It has 35 members. Cuba remains a member but has been excluded from participation since 1962.

Organization of the Islamic Conference An association of 57 countries and three observer Islamic countries seeking Muslim cohesion in social, economic and political matters.

pandemic An infectious disease affecting a large part of the population in a wide geographical area, often on a global scale.

peace enforcement Also known as third-generation peacekeeping. This does not require consent from the conflicting parties and is undertaken to protect the populace from an aggressor or a civil war.

peacekeeper A person assigned to help maintain peace where conflict has just ended. Peacekeepers can include civilian staff; "peacekeeping soldiers" do not.

peacekeeping operation This involves military personnel operating under the precepts of impartiality and neutrality, undertaken by the UN to help maintain or restore international peace and security. Second-generation peacekeeping, which includes preventive diplomacy and post-conflict peacebuilding, is based on the consent of the parties involved and incorporates a multi-faceted UN role.

peacebuilding mission A project aimed at development activities in post-conflict regions to ensure that conflicts do not resume and that reconstruction efforts are fair.

peacemaking A diplomatic process of brokering an end to conflict, principally through mediation and negotiation. Military activities contributing to peace-making include military-to-military contacts, security assistance, shows of force and preventive deployments.

permanent five The five permanent members of the UN Security Council, now the US, Britain, Russia, China and France.

political asylum Protection granted to a person by a foreign government when the applicant demonstrates that he or she would be persecuted or harmed if returned to the country of origin.

political office UN political offices work to support the peace missions through reconciliation and negotiation.

preventive deployment The interposition of a military force to deter violence in a zone of potential conflict.

preventive diplomacy Also known as conflict prevention, this form of diplomacy is geared to prevent disputes from arising.

protectionism The practice of protecting domestic products from foreign competition by placing tariffs and quotas on imports.

protocol A document that records basic agreements reached in negotiations before the formal document is ready for signing.

quorum The number of members of an organization required to be present for conduct of business.

recosting A UN budgetary practice providing for adjustment of foreign exchange rates and inflation assumptions in a budgetary cycle.

referendum The practice of submitting to popular vote a measure proposed by a legislative body or sought by part of the public; a referendum is a direct vote in which an entire electorate is asked to accept or reject a proposal.

refugee See displaced person.

regular budget At the UN, includes costs of the Secretariat in New York, the UN offices in Geneva, Vienna and Nairobi, the regional commissions, the International Court of Justice and the Center for Human Rights. More than 70 percent of the UN regular budget is earmarked for staff costs. The scale of assessment (how much each country owes) is based on the principle of capacity to pay.

repatriate To restore or return to the country of origin, allegiance or citizenship.

resolution A document adopted by a committee or body that expresses the opinions and decisions of the UN.

rule of law The principle that authority is legitimately exercised only in accordance with written, publicly disclosed laws adopted and enforced in accordance with established procedural steps.

sanction An economic or military measure, usually by several nations in concert, to force a nation violating international law to desist.

Security Council The UN organ responsible for maintaining peace and security. It is composed of five permanent members—Britain, China, France, Russia and the US—and 10 rotating members elected to two-year terms by the General Assembly to represent equitable geographic distribution.

Secretariat The UN organ that runs the daily affairs of the organization. It consists of international civil servants and is led by the secretary-general.

Secretary-General Defined in the UN Charter as the chief administrative officer of the UN and head of the Secretariat. The secretary-general acts as the primary spokesperson and de facto leader of the UN.

self-determination The choice of a people in a given area to select their own political status or independence.

sovereign Supreme power, especially over a body politic; political authority free from external control.

sovereignty Autonomy; the right to control a government, a country, a people or oneself.

state-building (nation-building) The concept of rebuilding a post-conflict country, most often so that its sovereignty is recognized by the international community.

state party Countries that are party to—or have joined as a member—a particular group or have signed a particular protocol or other document.

sustainable development A term for economic progress that meets the needs of the present without compromising the potential of future generations.

terrorism The systematic use of unpredictable violence against governments or people to attain a political objective.

treaty A formal, binding international agreement. In the US, treaties proposed by the executive branch that have been negotiated with a foreign country or international organization must be approved by a two-thirds majority in the Senate and then signed by the president.

tribunal A committee or board appointed to judge a particular matter.

truce A suspension of fighting by agreement.

Trusteeship Council A principal organ of the UN, it was established to help ensure that nonself-governing territories were administered in the best interests of the inhabitants, peace and security. The council suspended operation in 1994 after the independence of Palau, the last remaining UN trust territory.

United Nations Charter It established the UN and its method of operating and was drawn up and signed by representatives of 50 countries in 1945.

United Nations Children's Fund or Unicef Founded in 1946 as the UN International Children's Emergency Fund. With headquarters in Paris, it is the only UN organization devoted solely to children and their rights.

United Nations Development Fund for Women Created in 1976, the fund fosters the empowerment of women and gender equity.

United Nations Development Program The main body for UN development work and the largest provider of developmental grant assistance in the UN system.

Universal Declaration of Human Rights A proclamation of the basic rights and freedoms of all people, adopted by the General Assembly on Dec.10, 1948, and commemorated every year on Human Rights Day.

United Nations Educational, Scientific and Cultural Organization (Unesco) A specialized agency working for world peace and security by promoting collaboration in education, science, culture and communication.

United Nations Environment Program Headquartered in Nairobi, Kenya, this project provides leadership and encourages partnerships to protect the environment.

United Nations Framework Convention on Climate Change To counter global warming, this agency seeks to stabilize greenhouse-gas concentrations in the atmosphere and to disseminate technology and information to help developing countries adapt to climate change.

United Nations High Commissioner for Human Rights A UN office established in 1993 to protect human rights.

United Nations High Commissioner for Refugees A UN office created by the General Assembly in 1951 to help refugees.

United Nations Population Fund The largest internationally financed source of population assistance for developing countries. It began its work in 1967.

United Nations University An international educational institution engaged in scholarly work on pressing global problems. Its two main goals are to strengthen research and educational abilities of institutions in developing countries and make policy-relevant contributions to the UN's work. It was established in 1972 and has its headquarters in Tokyo.

war crime A crime that breaches the laws of international armed conflict as defined by the Geneva Conventions, Hague Conventions and, most recently, the Rome Statute. War crimes include, but are not limited to, willful killing, torture or inhumane treatment, unlawful deportation, various abuses against prisoners of war, taking of hostages and extensive destruction and appropriation of property not justified by military necessity and carried out unlawfully and wantonly.

weapons of mass destruction Weapons, biological, chemical and nuclear, designed to kill large numbers of people at once.

World Bank Established at the Bretton Woods Conference in 1944. As a multilateral lending agency, it seeks to reduce poverty by promoting sustainable growth.

World Food Program The frontline UN organization fighting to eradicate hunger. Its headquarters are in Rome and it began work in 1963.

World Health Organization Founded in 1948 with headquarters in Geneva, this organization promotes technical health cooperation among nations, carries out programs to control and eradicate disease and works to improve the quality of life.

World Trade Organization An international organization meant to liberalize trade. It is a forum for governments to negotiate trade agreements and settle disputes.

Zionism Zionist ideology holds that Jews are a people or nation and should gather in a single homeland. Zionism evolved into an international movement for the establishment of a Jewish community in Palestine and later for the support of modern Israel.

Appendix G: And the Prize Goes to . . .

The selection of Martti Ahtisaari, a former UN under secretary-general, for the 2008 Nobel Peace prizes, brings the total to three prizes in the last five years that have been awarded to people directly related or affiliated with the UN. These accomplishments underscore the organization's role as the world's foremost peacekeeper.

2008: Ahtisaari joined the UN in 1976 in the UN Institute for Namibia, when it was established as the first university in southwest Africa. (It is now called the University of Namibia.) Ahtissari then rose through UN ranks, ultimately becoming under secretary-general for administration and management in 1987 Under Secretary-General Javier Pérez de Cuéllar. Ahtisaari won the Peace Prize in recognition of his mediation efforts in Asia, Africa and Europe.

2007: The UN's Intergovernmental Panel on Climate Change and former US vice president Al Gore were jointly awarded the prize for their work on global warming. The panel was honored for bringing thousands of scientists and officials together to establish certainty on climate change.

2005: The International Atomic Energy Agency (IAEA) and its director general, Mohamed ElBaradei, were honored for their work on nuclear nonproliferation. ElBaradei was a diplomat at Egypt's permanent mission to the UN in New York and worked as senior fellow in charge of the international law program at the UN Institute for Training and Research before heading the IAEA.

2001: The UN and Kofi Annan, the secretary-general at the time, were both awarded the prize "for their work for a better organized and more peaceful world," the Nobel Committee said. Annan was cited for rejuvenating the UN, particularly in working on peace, security and human rights as well as the challenges of HIV/AIDS and terrorism. The committee citation proclaimed that "the only negotiable route to global peace and cooperation goes by way of the United Nations."

1988: UN peacekeeping forces were recipients for operating "under extremely difficult conditions" while contributing to "reducing tensions where an armistice has been negotiated but a peace treaty has yet to be established" and therefore making a decisive effort towards "the initiation of actual peace negotiations."

1981: The Office of the UN High Commissioner for Refugees "carried out work of major importance to assist refugees, despite the many political difficulties with which it has had to contend," namely coping with increasing numbers of refugees flowing from Vietnam and the exodus from Afghanistan and Ethiopia.

1969: On its 50th anniversary, the International Labor Organization, a specialized agency, was honored for succeeding in "translating into action the fundamental moral idea on which it was based"—that is, "if you desire peace, cultivate justice."

1965: Unicef, for acting as a "peace factor of great importance" and for forging a link of solidarity between rich and poor countries and the caring for children.

1961: Dag Hammarskjold, the second secretary-general of the UN, from 1953 until his death in 1961, was the only person to receive the Nobel Peace Prize posthumously (though he had been nominated before he died). He was instrumental in establishing the first UN peacekeeping force and became deeply involved in the Congo war in the early 1960s and died in a plane crash while on a UN mission in the region.

1954: To the UN High Commissioner for Refugees for its work helping refugees and displaced people in Europe in the aftermath of World War II.

1950: Ralph Bunche, UN mediator in Palestine, received the prize for his mediation of the 1949 armistice between Israel and seven Arab countries. By carrying out these difficult talks, the committee stated, and "by exercising infinite patience," Bunche "finally succeeded in persuading all parties to accept an armistice."

Members of a Jordanian
Special Weapons and
Tactics (SWAT) team take
position during a drug
seizure exercise staged in
Les Cayes, Haiti, in
December 2008 by the
UN Stabilization Mission
in Haiti.

Charts and Tables

182   **Peacekeeping Missions**
Compiled by Simon Minching

184   **Top Contributors of Peacekeeping Funding**
Compiled by Simon Minching

185   **Top Contributors of Uniformed Personnel**
Compiled by Simon Minching

186   **Global Summary of the AIDS Pandemic**
Compiled by Simon Minching

187   **Consolidated Appeals**
Compiled by Simon Minching

188   **Millennium Development Goals and Targets**
Compiled by Max McGowen

Ongoing UN Peacekeeping Operations, as of September 2009

The United Nations deployed approximately 122,000 personnel to 15 peacekeeping operations as of September 2009. This table shows the location, distribution of personnel, type of mandate and size of each operation. (Dollars in millions)

Name of Operation/ Location/ Start Date	2009-2010 Budget	Troops and Military Observers	Police	Civilians (International, Local, and UN Volunteers)	Total	Mandate Type and Number of Tasks
UN Truce Supervision Organization in Palestine (UNTSO) 1948-	60.70ᵃ	153	0	211	364	Traditional 2
UN Military Observer Group in India and Pakistan (UNMOGIP) Jammu, Kashmir and Pakistan 1949-	16.15ᵇ	44	0	70	114	Traditional 1
UN Peacekeeping Force in Cyprus (UNFICYP) 1964-	54.41	850	69	152	1071	Traditional 3
UN Disengagement Observer Force (UNDOF) Israel-Syria: Golan Heights 1974-	45.03	1044	0	143	1187	Traditional 2
UN Force for Southern Lebanon (UNIFIL) 1978-	589.80	11,504	0	981	12,485	Multidimensional 6
UN Mission for the Referendum in Western Sahara (MINURSO) 1991-	53.53	219	5	276	500	Multidimensional 2
UN Interim Administration Mission in Kosovo (UNMIK) 1999-	46.81	9	7	455	471	Limited² 3
United Nations Organization Mission in the Democratic Republic of the Congo 1999-	1,346.58	19,357	1216	4320	24,893	Multidimensional 12

Source: UNA-USA analysis of UN data, and: http://www.un.org/en/peacekeeping/bnote.htm

a Figures are rounded to nearest $10,000.

1 UNTSO and UNMOGIP are funded from the United Nations regular biennial budget. Costs to the United Nations of the other current operations are financed from their own separate accounts on the basis of legally binding assessments on all Member States. For these missions, budget figures represent the 2010-2011 appropriation. All others are for one year (07/09-06/10) unless otherwise specified.

2 Since the deployment of EULEX in December 2008, UNMIK's mandate has been limited to "an increasingly diplomatic and political role targeted on facilitating dialogue and external relations, and fostering minority rights." For more, see: http://www.unmikonline.org/news.htm#1706

continued

Name of Operation/Location/ Start Date	2009-2010 Budget	Troops and Military Observers	Police	Civilians (International, Local, and UN Volunteers)	Total	Mandate Type and Number of Tasks
UN Mission in Liberia (UNMIL) 2003-	560.98	9109	1318	1651	12,078	Multidimensional 10
United Nations Operation in Côte d'Ivoire (UNOCI) 2004-	491.78	7390	1154	1384	9928	Multidimensional 9
United Nations Stabilization Mission in Haiti (MINUSTAH) 2004-	611.75	7032	2055	1941	11,028	Multidimensional 11
United Nations Mission in the Sudan (UNMIS) 2005-	958.35	9867	674	3832	14,373	Multidimensional 14
United Nations Integrated Mission in Timor L'este (UNMIT) 2006-	205.94	33	1488	1430	2951	Multidimensional 10
African Union/United Nations Hybrid Operation in Darfur (UNAMID) 2007-	1,598.42	17,125	4675	4065	25,865	Multidimensional 13
United Nations Mission in the Central African Republic and Chad (MINURCAT) 2007-	690.75	3554	259	1075	4888	Multidimensional 7
TOTAL		**87,290**	**12,920**	**21,986**	**122,196**	

Top 10 Contributors of Peacekeeping Funding

Compiled by Simon Minching

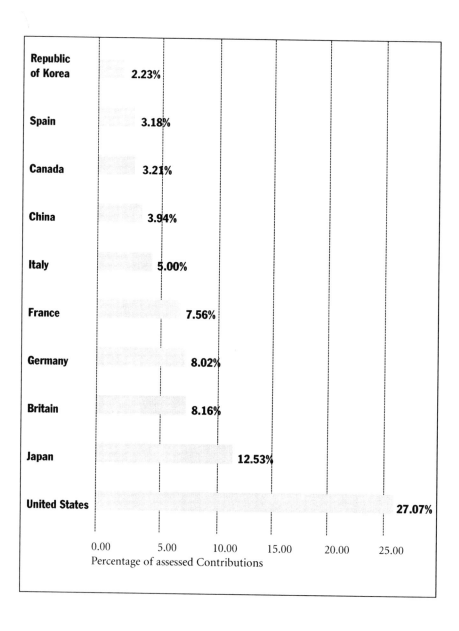

Republic of Korea	2.23%
Spain	3.18%
Canada	3.21%
China	3.94%
Italy	5.00%
France	7.56%
Germany	8.02%
Britain	8.16%
Japan	12.53%
United States	27.07%

0.00   5.00   10.00   15.00   20.00   25.00

Percentage of assessed Contributions

Top Contributors of Uniformed Personnel to
UN Peacekeeping Operations (as of December 31, 2009)

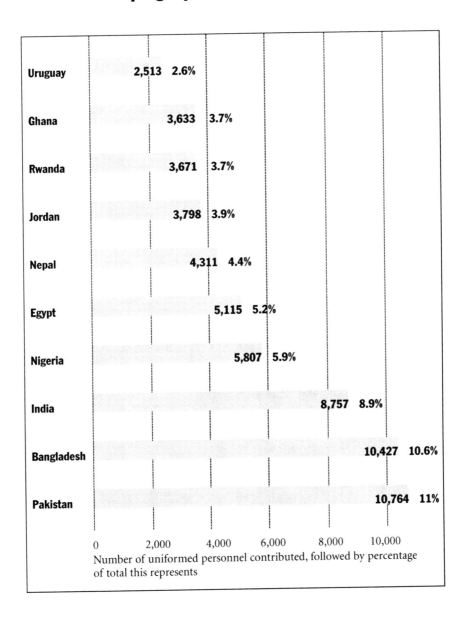

Uruguay	2,513 2.6%
Ghana	3,633 3.7%
Rwanda	3,671 3.7%
Jordan	3,798 3.9%
Nepal	4,311 4.4%
Egypt	5,115 5.2%
Nigeria	5,807 5.9%
India	8,757 8.9%
Bangladesh	10,427 10.6%
Pakistan	10,764 11%

0   2,000   4,000   6,000   8,000   10,000

Number of uniformed personnel contributed, followed by percentage
of total this represents

Global Summary of the AIDS Pandemic
Compiled by Simon Minching

Number of people living with HIV in 2008	**Total**	**~33.4 million**
	Adults	~31.3 million
	Women	~15.7 million
	Under 15	~2.1 million
People newly infected with HIV in 2008	**Total**	**~2.7 million**
	Adults	~2.3 million
	Under 15	~430,000
AIDS deaths in 2007	**Total**	**~2.0 million**
	Adults	~1.7 million
	Under 15	~280,000

Source: 2009 AIDS Epidemic Update, http://data.unaids.org/pub/Report/2009/JC1700_Epi_Update_2009_en.pdf
Note: The ~ symbol represents an approximation, and the figure that follows is the median in the range of UNAIDS/WHO estimates, based on the best available information.

In Nepal, a UN fact-finding team visits the remote mountain community of Rasuwa in February 2008 as part of preparations for April elections.

UN Photo/Tilak Pokharel

Consolidated Appeals

Compiled by Simon Minching

Since its creation by the General Assembly in 1991, the consolidated appeals process has improved cooperation among donors, UN agencies, aid groups and governments struck by grave humanitarian crises. The UN Office for the Coordination of Humanitarian Affairs manages the appeals, which help aid organizations, donors and recipients work together to better plan, carry out and monitor their activities as well as raise money. Here is a snapshot of recent years' financial requests.

(#'s in millions of US$)

2010
Original requirements: $7,749
Revised requirements: $8,863
Commitments, contributions and carryover: $3,080
Amount covered: 35%
Unmet requirements: $5,782
Uncommitted pledges: $117.65

2009
Original requirements: $7,015
Revised requirements: $7,100
Commitments, contributions and carryover: $50.4
Amount covered: 1%
Unmet requirement: $7,050
Uncommitted pledges: $3.8

2008
Original requirements: $5,674
Revised requirements: $7,163
Commitments, contributions and carryover: $5,009
Amount covered: 70%
Unmet requirement: $2,154
Uncommitted pledges: $181.1

2007
Original requirements: $4,455
Revised requirements: $5,142
Commitments, contributions and carryover: $3,724
Amount covered: 72%
Unmet requirement: $1,148
Uncommitted pledges: $21.7

Source: ReliefWeb Financial Tracking Service
Charts compiled by the UN Office for the Coordination of Humanitarian Affairs (OCHA)

Millennium Development Goals and Targets

Compiled by Max McGowen

GOAL 1: ERADICATE EXTREME HUNGER AND POVERTY

Target 1. By 2015, halve the proportion of people whose income is less than $1 a day.

Target 2. By 2015, halve the proportion of people who suffer from hunger.

GOAL 2: ACHIEVE UNIVERSAL PRIMARY EDUCATION

Target 3. Ensure that by 2015, boys and girls everywhere will be able to complete a full course of primary schooling.

GOAL 3: PROMOTE GENDER EQUALITY AND EMPOWER WOMEN

Target 4. Eliminate gender disparity in primary and secondary education, preferably by 2005, and in all levels of education no later than 2015.

GOAL 4: REDUCE CHILD MORTALITY

Target 5. By 2015, reduce the under-five mortality rate by two-thirds.

GOAL 5: IMPROVE MATERNAL HEALTH

Target 6. By 2015, reduce the maternal mortality ratio by three-quarters.

GOAL 6: COMBAT HIV/AIDS, MALARIA AND OTHER DISEASES

Target 7. By 2015, have stopped and begun to reverse the spread of HIV/AIDS.

Target 8. By 2015, have stopped and begun to reverse the incidence of malaria and other major diseases.

GOAL 7: ENSURE ENVIRONMENTAL SUSTAINABILITY

Target 9. Integrate the principles of sustainable development into country policies and programs and reverse the loss of environmental resources.

Target 10. By 2015, halve the proportion of people without sustainable access to safe drinking water and basic sanitation.

Target 11. By 2020, achieve a major improvement in the lives of at least 100 million slum dwellers.

GOAL 8: DEVELOP A GLOBAL PARTNERSHIP FOR DEVELOPMENT

Target 12. Develop further an open, rule-based, predictable, nondiscriminatory trading and financial system (includes a commitment to good governance, development and poverty reduction, both nationally and internationally).

Target 13. Address the special needs of least-developed countries (includes tariff- and quota-free access for least-developed countries' exports, enhanced program of debt relief for heavily indebted poor countries and cancellation of official bilateral debt and more generous official development assistance for countries committed to poverty reduction).

Target 14. Address the special needs of landlocked developing countries and small island developing states (through the Program of Action for the Sustainable Development of Small Island Developing States and 22nd General Assembly provisions).

Target 15. Deal comprehensively with the debt problems of developing countries through national and international measures to make debt sustainable in the long term.

Target 16. In cooperation with developing countries, develop and carry out strategies for decent and productive work for youth.

Target 17. In cooperation with pharmaceutical companies, provide access to affordable essential drugs in developing countries.

Target 18. In cooperation with the private sector, make available the benefits of new technologies, especially information and communications technology.

Source: UN Millennium Project, 2006

"A Global Agenda" Index

A

Afghanistan
aid issues, 58, 61, 62-63
CIA and, 63
drone attacks, 65
economy, 64-65
elections, 62
Fahim, Marshal, 63
future prospects, 62-66
Ghani, Ashraf, 64
international troop support, 63
Karzai, Ahmad Wali, 63
London conference, 61
loya jirga, 62
opium trade, 61, 64-65
Pakistan and, 65
poverty indicators, 65
Provincial Reconstruction
    Teams, 64
Pushtuns, 65
refugees, 92
UN role, 6, 43, 62, 66
US role, 62-66
Africa
Central African stability, 21
education, 72-73
illicit transactions, 7
peacekeeping, 6-7, 16, 18
poverty, 56, 57
West Africa, 21-22
African Union
African Union Panel of Eminent
    African Personalities, 113
Darfur, role in, 22
regional partnerships, 24-25
Somalia, mission in, 23-24
AIDS, 57, 186
Al Qaeda, *See* Terrorism
Angola
Chemical Weapons Convention
    and, 12
Annan, Kofi
Commission on Human Rights,
    78, 86
Iraq invasion, 42
Kenya and, 113
Middle East, 31
MDGs, 67
Responsibility to Protect and,
    xxiv
Robinson, Mary, appointment
    of, 79
UN reform and, 124
Arbour, Louise, 78-79
Assad, Hafez, 30

B

Baghdad
terrorist attacks, 6
Bakiyev, Kurmanbek S.,
    66
Bali Action Plan, 96

Ban Ki-moon
climate change, 94, 99, 101, 105
G20 and, 130
ICC review conference and, 113
Iraq report, 70
Nuclear security summit, 53
Palestinians and, 30
peacekeeping partnerships, 24
primary education and, 72
Responsibility to Protect and, 32
Sachs, Jeffrey D. and, 56
World Food Program,
    investigation of, 61
Barosso, José Manuel, 98
Bashir, Omar Hassan al-, 22, 110,
    112, 118
BASIC group, 98, 101
Biological and Toxin Weapons
    Convention, 11-12
ratification of, 11
US and compliance with, 11
Biological weapons. *See* weapons of
    mass destruction
Blair, Tony, 31
Bokova, Irina, 73
Bolton, John, 43, 48
Bono, 58
Bosnia
genocide, 39
Brahimi, Lakhdar, iv, 16, 39
Brazil
economic growth, 2
BRIC coalition, 101
Britain
nuclear state, 8
permanent Security Council
    member, 8
peacekeeping and, 17
Brown, Gordon, 53
Bunche, Ralph, 29
Bush, George W.
abortion issues, 49
"axis of evil," 66
Commission on Human Rights,
    abolition of, 86
exceptionalism and, 85
HIV/AIDS funding, 42
Human Rights Council and, 48
Middle East progress, 31
UN relationship, 42-44, 47

C

Carter, Jimmy, 46
Center for Sustainable
    Development in the Americas,
    102
Central African Republic
    peacekeeping, 7
Chad
UN mission, 23
Chambers, Raymond, 67

Chemical weapons. *See* weapons of
    mass destruction
Chemical Weapons Convention,
    11-12
failure to join, 12
progress, 12
Chemical Weapons Convention
    Coalition, 12
China
economic growth, 2, 56
climate change, 97-98, 100-01,
    103
Group of 77 (G77), 101, 120, 125
nuclear state, 8
permanent Security Council
    member, 8
sovereignty principle and, 18, 33
state censorship, 84
Climate change
2007 Report of the International
    Panel on Climate Change, 107
adaptation strategies, 100
Boer, Yvo de, 102
Cancún conference, 99, 104-06
Copenhagen Accord, 96-100,
    103-04
Copenhagen conference, xxiv,
    96-103
Developed-developing country
    divide, 96-98
Figueres, Christiana, 102
Fourth Assessment Report,
    101-02
global consumption and, 3
Intergovernmental Panel on
    Climate Change, 2-3, 96-97,
    101
Kyoto Protocol, 96-100, 102-03,
    104, 106, 108
mitigation strategies, 100
Pew Center on Global Climate
    Change, 100
Stern, Todd, 97-98, 103
Clinton, Bill, 31, 49
Clinton, Hillary, 31, 48, 52, 86
Collier, Paul, 59
Commission on Human Rights,
    78-79, 82
Commission on Sea Level Change
    for the International Union for
    Quarternary Research, 109
Consolidated appeals, 187
Conventional Armed Forces in
    Europe Treaty, 10
Conventional arms, 8-10
trade, 10, 13
Convention for the Elimination of
    All Forms of Discrimination
    Against Women, 46-47, 87
Convention for the Protection and
    Assistance of Internally

Displaced Persons in Africa, 89
Convention on Cluster Munitions,
  10-13
Convention on the Rights of the
  Child, 87
Coomaraswamy, Radhika, 112
Copenhagen Accord, 96-100,
  103-04
Copenhagen Green Climate Fund,
  100
Côte d'Ivoire, 21-22
  elections, 22
  Independent Electoral
    Commission, 22
  political struggle, 21-22
  regional organizations in, 24
  UNOCI, 22
Counterterrorism
  2006 Global Counter-Terrorism
    Strategy, 4-5
  Executive Directorate, 5
  generally, 4-7
  information-sharing, 5-6
  UN Counter-Terrorism
    Implementation Task Force,
    5-6
Cuba
  Human Rights Council and, 79
  Nuclear Nonproliferation Treaty
    Review Conference (2010), 8

D
Darfur. *See also* Sudan
  armed conflict, 22
  atrocities, 22, 112
  Bashir, Omar Hassan al-, 22,
    110, 112, 118
  comprehensive peace
    agreement, 23, 52
  female peacekeepers, 36
  peacekeeping, 16
"Delivering as One," 6, 124
Democratic Forces for the
  Liberation of Rwanda, 20
Democratic Republic of Congo
  "Africa's first world war," 20
  armed groups, 20-21
  elections, 21
  independence, 20
  Lubanga, Thomas 112, 116, 119
  peacekeeping, 7, 16, 20-21, 38
  UN mission in, 20
    budget, 20
    personnel, 20
    women and, 131
Development
  AidData Web site, 60
  aid debate, 56-60
  AIDS figures, 57
  Ethiopia, 58
  Ghana, 58
  Haiti, vi, 27, 60
  Iraq, 70-71
  literacy, 72-73
  maternal death, 57-58
  Nigeria, 74-75
  poverty level, 57

primary education, 72-73
Sanchez, Pedro, 67
sea level, elevation of, 107-109
sustainable development, 67-69
Dhanapala, Jayantha, iv, 45
Disarmament, 8-10, 11-13
Division for the Advancement of
  Women, 132
Duflo, Esther, 59-60
Dyilo, Thomas Lubanga, *See*
  Lubanga, Thomas

E
Earth Institute, 68
Earth International, 98
Easterly, William, 56-57, 61
Economic Community of West
  African States, 21, 24
Education for All, 72-73
Egypt
  Chemical Weapons Convention
    and, 12
  Human Rights Council and, 79
Eshkol, Levi, 30
European Union
  Nuclear Nonproliferation Treaty
    Review Conference (2010), 8
  peacekeeping partnership, 24
  quartet on the Middle East, 31
  Sudan human rights monitor, 83
  UN contributions and, 125-126
Evans, Gareth, 123

F
Food and Agriculture
  Organization, 28
France
  permanent Security Council
    member, 8
  peacekeeping and, 17

G
Galbraith, Peter, 63
Gasana, Eugene-Richard, 33
Gayoom, Maumoon Abdul, 108
Gbagbo, Laurent, 22
General Assembly
  counterterrorism role, 4-5
  elimination of weapons of mass
    destruction, 8, 44
  Fifth Committee, vi, 125-26, 128
  Human Rights Council and, 78,
    85, 87
  International Criminal Court,
    creation of, 112
  institutional arrangement, 17
  internal justice system review,
    128
  mandate review, 125
  Middle East, role in, 29, 82
  Millennium Development Goals
    and, 67
  Office of the High Commissioner
    for Human Rights, 79-80
  Peacebuilding Commission
    review, 128
  UN Women and, 131-33

"Global War on Terror," 4
Goldstone Report, 31, 46, 81-82
Gore, Al, 101
Governance and Economic
  Management Assistance
  Program, 18
Gration, Gen. Scott, 49, 52
"Great Games," 2
Group of 20 (G20), 101, 106,
  129-30
Group of 77, (G77), 101, 120, 122,
  125, 128
Guatemala,
  corruption and, 6
Guterres, António, 92

H
Hague Code of Conduct Against
  Ballistic Missile Proliferation
  (2002), 10
Haiti
  Action Plan for National
    Recovery and Development, 27
  aid issues, 58, 60
  earthquake, vi, 26-28, 54
  peacekeeping, 16
  UN mission, 26
Hammarskjold, Dag, 29-30, 124
Hancock, Graham
  on "Lords of Poverty," 28
Haq, Ameerah, 35
Hezbollah
  2006 War, 13, 30, 43
Holbrooke, Richard, 48
Holmes, John, 21
Houphouët-Boigny, Félix, 21
Human Rights Council
  composition, 78-80
  criticisms, 78-85, 132
  five-year review, v-vi, 85-86
  freedom of expression, 80
  Gaza war and, 81-82
  global economic crisis and, 81
  Goldstone Report, 31
  internally displaced persons, 88
  Israel and, 46, 79, 81-82, 86-87
  special sessions, 80-81
  "traditional values" workshop, 80
  Universal Periodic Review,
    83-87
  US participation, 48-49
Human Rights Watch
  Democratic Republic of Congo
    and, 20-21
Hutchinson, Clare, 35

I
India
  climate change, 97-98, 101-03
  economic growth, 2, 56
  education gap, 73
  nuclear state, 8
InterAcademy Council, 101
Inter-Agency Standing Committee,
  91
Intergovernmental Panel on
  Climate Change, 2-3, 96-97, 101

Internally displaced persons, 88-91
International Atomic Energy
  Agency congressional funding
  of, 44
International Commission Against
  Impunity, 6
International Court of Justice, 118
International Criminal Court
  Assembly of States Parties, 112
  Bashir, Omar Hassan al-, 22,
    110, 112, 118
  court functions, 118-19
  first review conference, 113-14
  future challenges, 114-15
  Gaza war crimes, 46, 82
  Kenya and, 113
  Moreno-Ocampo, Luis, 112-13,
    116
  Rome Statute, 43, 87, 112-14,
    116
  Song, Sang-Hyun, 112, 116-19
  US policy and, 43
International Crisis Group, 123
International Maritime
  Organization, 6
International Monetary Fund
  Haiti and, 26
  poverty alleviation, 27, 58
Iran
  "axis of evil," 66
  Nuclear Nonproliferation Treaty
    Review Conference (2010), 8
  UN sanctions, 45, 48
Iraq
  Canal Hotel bombing, 71
  elections, 70
  Iraqi National Development
    Plan, 71
  McNab, Christine, 71
  oil production, 71
  refugees, 92-93
  UN Assistance Mission, 70
  UN Development Assistance
    Framework, 71
  US-led invasion, 70
Israel
  2006 War, 13
  2008-2009 Gaza War, 31, 81-82
  Chemical Weapons Convention
    and, 12
  cluster bombs, use of, 13
  Gaza blockade, 46
  Human Rights Council and, 46,
    81-82, 86-87
  nuclear state, 8
  US relationship, 45-46

J
Jarring, Gunnar, 29-30
Jonathan, Goodluck Ebele, 9
Jordan
  mine clearing, 13

K
Kabila, Joseph, 20
Kagame, Paul, 56-57
Kälin, Walter, 88-89

interview, 89-91
Karimov, Islam, 66
Karzai, Ahmad Wali, 63
Karzai, Hamid
  approval rating, 63
  drug trade, 65
  election fraud allegations, 62
  Iran and, 66
  rule of law and, 61, 63
Killen, Brenda, 58-59
Kissinger, Henry A., 8, 30
Kyoto Protocol, 96-100, 102-04,
    106, 108

L
Lamamra, Ramtane, 24
Lavrov, Sergey, 31
League of Nations, 34, 124
Lebanon
  1982 Israeli invasion, 30
  peacekeeper contributions, 17
  terrorist attacks, 6
Liberia
  civil wars, 21, 38
  Truth and Reconciliation
    Commission, 21
  UN mission, 21
Libya
  Nuclear Nonproliferation Treaty
    Review Conference (2010), 8
  sanctions and, 4
Lie, Trygve, 29-30
Loj, Ellen Margrethe, 35
Lord's Resistance Army, 20-21
Lubanga, Thomas, 112, 116, 119

M
Madagascar
  counterterrorism and, 6
Major Economies Forum, 101
Maldives
  sea level, elevation of, 107-09
McArthur, John, 49
McChrystal, Stanley A., 64
McLay, Jim, 33-34
Meir, Golda, 30
Melkert, Ad, 70-71
Merkel, Angela, 63
Middle East
  1956 Suez Crisis, 29
  1967 Six Day War, 29-30, 45
  2006 war, 13
  2008-09 Gaza war, 31, 81-82
  Arab-Israeli conflict, 31
  nuclear free, 8
  quartet on the Middle East, 31
  UN Emergency Force, 30
  UN role in, 29-31, 46
  US invasion of Iraq, 42
Millennium Cities Initiative, 68-69
Millennium Development Goals,
    51, 57 59-60, 130
  "bottom billion" and, 2, 59, 67
  creation of, 67
  Group of Eight pledge, 59
  list of, 188-89
  progress, 68, 69

universal primary education,
    72-73
  women and, 131
Millennium Promise, 67
Millennium Villages Project, 67-69
mine ban treaty, 10, 12-13
Mohamed, Abdul Ghafoor, 108-09
Morales, Evo, 120
Moreno-Ocampo, Luis, 112-13,
    116
Moyo, Dambisa
  "Dead Aid," v, 56, 58
Mugabe, Robert, 57
Multilateralism
  counterterrorism and, 4-7
  global security and, 2-3
Muñoz, Heraldo, 49
Myanmar
  Chemical Weapons Convention
    and, 12
  Responsibility to Protect and,
    xxiv, 33
Myung-bak, Lee, 130

N
Nasheed, Mohamed, 108-109
Nasser, Gamal Abdel, 30
Nationalism
  statehood and, 2
Nigeria
  Alidu, Wirba, 75
  civil unrest, 74
  counterterrorism and, 6
  oil production, 74
  poverty ranking, 74
  Sowore, Omoyele, 75
  UN Development Program
    business program, 74-75
NATO
  Nuclear Nonproliferation Treaty
    Review Conference (2010), 8
Netanyahu, Benjamin, 46
North Korea
  Chemical Weapons Convention
    and, 12
  mines and, 13
  nuclear state, 8
Norwegian Refugee Council, 89
Nuclear Nonproliferation Treaty, 8,
    11, 44
Nuclear Nonproliferation Treaty
  Review Conference (2010), 8, 45
Nunn, Sam, 8

O
Obama Administration
  Afghanistan withdrawal, 66
  Gaza blockade incident and, 46
  Human Rights Council and, 46,
    79, 86-87
  ICC and, 115
  multilateralism, 4, 31, 43
  oil spill, 103
Obama, Barack
  climate change and, iv, 98-99,
    102-03
  General Assembly address, 40

mine ban and, 12-13
Nobel Peace Prize, 42, 44, 47
nuclear-free world, iv, 8, 44-45
Security Council meeting, 44, 53
UN relationship, 42-45, 47
Office of the High Commissioner
for Human Rights, 79, 83
Office of the Special Adviser on
Gender Issues and the
Advancement of Women, 132
Organization for Economic
Cooperation and Development,
58-59
Organization for Security and
Cooperation in Europe, 24
Organization for the Prohibition of
Chemical Weapons, 12
Organization of Islamic States, 81
Orr, Robert C.
climate change and, 97-99, 101,
104-106
interview, 104-106
Ould-Abdallah, Ahmedou, 24

P
Pachauri, Rajendra, 101-02
Pakistan
Afghanistan relationship, 65-66
nuclear state, 8
Pushtuns, 65
terrorist attacks, 6
Paris Declaration on Aid
Effectiveness, 60
Peacebuilding Commission, 128
Peacekeeping operations, 7, 16-39
budget and costs, 16, 18, 148-49,
182-84
conflict data, 37
institutional challenges, 17-18
female peacekeepers, 35-36,
133
in Côte d'Ivoire, 22
in Democratic Republic of
Congo, 20-21
in Haiti, 26, 180
in Lebanon, 30
in Liberia, 21
missions table, 182-183
operational challenges, 16-17
personnel, xxiv, 16, 35-36, 185
political challenges, 18-19
sovereignty and, xxiv-xxv,
18-19
Perry, William J., 8
Petraeus, David H., 64
Pfutze, Tobias, 61
Phillips, Captain Richard, 24
Pillay, Navanethem
appointment of, 78-79
criticisms, 79
Office of the High Commissioner
for Human Rights, defense
of, 80
Posner, Michael, 86
Prost, Kimberly, 5
Protocol on Blinding Laser
Weapons, 11

Q
Qaddafi, Muammar el-, 153

R
Rasmussen, Lars Løkke, 102
Reagan, Ronald, 44
Red Cross\Red Crescent, 91
Responsibility to Protect
creation, xxiv, 32
doctrine, 32-34,123
Rice, Susan, 32, 43, 48-50
interview, 51-53
Robinson, Mary, 79, 81
Rome Statute, 43, 46-47, 87,
112-14, 116
Rule of Law Coordination and
Resource Group, 7
Russia
Chemical Weapons Convention
and, 12
Human Rights Council and, 79
permanent Security Council
member, 8
quartet on the Middle East, 31
sovereignty principle and, 33
Strategic Arms Reduction
Treaty, 8, 44
Rwanda
genocide, xxiv, 33, 39, 49
women and, 131

S
Sachs, Jeffrey D.
aid debate, 56-58
Millennium Development Goals
and, 67
"The End of Poverty," 56
Secretary-General. *See also* Ban
Ki-moon
Advisory Board on
Disarmament Matters, 10
Advisory Group on Climate
Change Financing, 100
UN Charter, 29
UN reform, vi, 125-26, 128
Security Council
Counter-Terrorism Committee, 4
counterterrorism strategy, 4-5
institutional arrangement, 17
Middle East, role in, 29, 31,
45-46
peacekeeping mission in the
Democratic Republic of
Congo and, 21
permanent members
credibility, xxiii, 39
military spending, 8
reform, 125, 127
Responsibility to Protect and,
32
Peacebuilding Commission
review, 128
Peacekeeping and, 16-18, 37, 39
peacekeeping mission in Liberia
and, 21
reform, 125-27
Resolution 242, 29

resolution, female peacekeepers,
35
Responsibility to Protect and,
32-33
sanctions, 4
Somalia, 23
women and, 131
September 11 attacks, 4
Shell Petroleum Development Co.
in Nigeria, 74
Shultz, George P., 8
Sierra Leone, 21, 24
Silva, Luiz Inácio Lula da, 99
Sirleaf, Ellen Johnson, 21, 56
Solheim, Erik, 94
Somalia
aid issues, 61
Black Hawk Down affair, 23, 38
Chemical Weapons Convention
and, 12
Eritrea-Ethiopia war, 23
humanitarian aid, 38, 90
piracy, 6, 23-24
refugees, 92
regional organizations in, 24-25
Security Council and, 23
UN weapons ban, 23
Song, Sang-Hyun, 112, 116-19
Soros, George, 100
South Africa
economic growth, 2
South Korea
G20 summit, 129-30
mines, and, 13
Stockholm International Peace
Research Institute, 8
Støre, Jonas Gahr, 130
Sudan. *See also* Darfur
2005 North-South peace
agreement, 22-23
Bashir, Omar Hassan al-, 22,
110, 112, 118
elections, 22-23
Janjaweed militias, 22
North-South conflict, 22-23
peacekeeping, 7, 22-23
regional organizations in, 24
sanctions and, 4
secession referendum, 22
Syria
Chemical Weapons Convention
and, 12

T
Tajikistan
civil war, 66
Islamic fundamentalism, 65
Taliban. *See* Terrorism
Tamil Tigers. *See* Terrorism
Tanin, Zahir, 126-27
Tarp, Finn, 59
Taylor, Charles, 21
Terrorism
Al-Shabaab, 23
Al Qaeda, 4-6, 65
international cooperation, 2
nuclear weapons, 3

Taliban, 4-5, 61, 63, 65-66
Tamil Tigers, 33, 81, 89
Thant, U, 29-30
The One Campaign, 58
Transparency International
  Corruption Perceptions Index, 61
  "Preventing Corruption in
    Humanitarian Operations," 60
Treaties of Westphalia (1648),
  122-23
Treki, Ali Abdussalam, 130
Two-time refugees, 92-93

U

UN Assistance Mission for Iraq, 70
UN Charter
  conventional weapons, 8
  human rights, 78
  peace and security, xxiv, 2, 37,
    39, 42
  secretary-general mandate, 29
  sovereignty and, xxiv-xxv, 122
UN Children's Fund Unicef
  congressional allocation for, 44
UN Counter-Terrorism
  Implementation Task Force, 5-6
UN Department of Peacekeeping
  Operations, 18
  Office of Rule of Law and
    Security Institutions, 18
  women and, 133
UN Development Assistance
  Framework, 71
UN Development Fund for
  Women, 132
UN Development Program
  Bush, George W. and, 44
  Haiti, 54
  Nigeria, 74
  poverty alleviation, 27-28, 58
  sustainable development, 69
  UN Women and, 132
UN Disengagement Observer
  Force, 30
UN Economic and Social Council,
  78
UN Educational, Scientific, and
  Cultural Organization
  Bush, George W. and, 42
  Education for All program,
    72-73
  Global Monitoring Report,
    72
UN Emergency Force, 29-30
UN Environmental Program, 107
UN Framework Convention on
  Climate Change, 97, 99, 101-06
UN High Commissioner for
  Human Rights, 79
UN High Commissioner for
  Refugees, 92-93
  Mahecic, Andrej, 92
UN Industrial Development
  Organization, 68
UN Interim Force in Lebanon, See
  Peacekeeping Operations
UN International Research and

Training Institute for the
  Advancement of Women, 132
UN Millennium Project, 67-68
UN Mission in Liberia, See
  Peacekeeping Operations
UN Mission in Côte d'Ivoire, See
  Peacekeeping Operations
UN Office for Project Services, 75
UN Office on Drugs and Crime, 4,
  6, 11
UN Peacebuilding Commission, 39
UN Population Fund congressional
  funding of, 44
  UN Women and, 132
UN Secretariat, 7
  composition, 141
  Department of Political Affairs, 5
  Enterprise Resource Planning,
    126
  mandate review and, 125
  Middle East and, 29, 31
  reform, vi, 125-26
  regional partnerships and, 25
UN Stabilization Mission in Haiti,
  See Peacekeeping Operations
UN Women
  AIDS, 131
  budget, 132
  composition, 132
  creation, 131
  potential agenda, 131
United Nations
  2005 World Summit, 32, 125
  2009 Global Trends report,
    93
  arrears, 152
  budget contributors, 151-52
  budget data, 142-50
  climate change and, 96-103
  composition chart, 140
  creation of, 34
  G20 and, 129-130
  Haiti, role in, 26-28
  important dates, 136-139
  internally displaced persons,
    88-91
  international cooperation, 2
  Middle East, role in, 29-31
  Nobel Prize winners, 178-79
  peacekeeping and, iv-v,
    xxiii-xxiv, 16-39
  quartet on the Middle East, 31
  Responsibility to Protect, 32-34,
    123
  reform, vi, 122-33
  "four disorders," 122-23
  prescriptions, 123-24
  rule of law and, 6-7
United Nations Entity for Gender
  Equality and the Empowerment
  of Women, 132
United States
  Black Hawk Down affair, 23, 38
  Chemical Weapons Convention
    and, 12
  climate change and, 96-99,
    102-103

Coalition Provisional Authority
  and, 70
Human Rights Council and, 46,
  79, 85-87
human rights review, 86-87
Iraq, role in, 70-71
Maersk Alabama, 24
Mine Ban Treaty and, 12-13
Northern Distribution Network,
  66
permanent Security Council
  member, 8
peacekeeping and, 17
quartet on the Middle East, 31
Security Council reform and,
  127
Strategic Arms Reduction
  Treaty, 8, 44
UN arrears, 42-44
Urquhart, Brian, 30
US Agency for International
  Development, 28, 71
US Climate Action Network, 99
US-Russian Strategic Arms
  Reduction Treaty, 8, 44
Uzbekistan
  Islamic fundamentalism, 65-66

V

Venezuela
  Nuclear Nonproliferation Treaty
    Review Conference (2010), 8
Vieira de Mello, Sergio, 71

W

Waldheim, Kurt, 29-30
weapons of mass destruction
  biological weapons, 4, 11-12
  chemical weapons, 4, 11-12
  limit of, 9
  nuclear weapons, 3-4
    nuclear states, 8
    use of, 8
  proliferation, 3
Wolfowitz, Paul, 43
Women's Environment and
  Development Organization, 133
World Bank, 27-28
  Global Monitoring Report, 57
World Customs Organization, 6
World Food Program, 28, 61
World Health Organization, 80
World Meteorological
  Organization, 107
World Resources Institute, 102
World Trade Organization, 80

Y

Young, Andrew, 30

Membership Application

Join UNA-USA today and become part of a nationwide movement for a more effective United Nations:

The United Nations Association of the United States of America (UNA-USA) is the nation's largest grassroots foreign policy organization and a leading center of policy research on the UN and global issues. UNA-USA offers Americans the opportunity to connect with issues confronted by the UN and encourages public support for strong US leadership in the UN. UNA-USA is a member of the World Federation of United Nations Associations.

For more information on the organization or how to join, visit www.unausa.org.

To join UNA-USA by mail, please return this form with your payment to:

UNA-USA MEMBERSHIP SERVICES
801 Second Avenue, New York, NY 10017

- ☐ $1,000 Lifetime (one-time dues payment)
- ☐ $500 Patron
- ☐ $100 Sponsor
- ☐ $40 Regular
- ☐ $25 Introductory (first year only)
- ☐ $25 Limited Income

NAME

ADDRESS

CITY, STATE AND ZIP

HOME PHONE / CELLPHONE   BUSINESS PHONE

E-MAIL

CHECK ONE: ☐ AMEX   ☐ MASTERCARD   ☐ VISA   ☐ DISCOVER

CREDIT CARD NUMBER

EXPIRATION DATE

SIGNATURE

Membership in UNA-USA is open to any citizen or resident of the US who is committed to the purposes of UNA-USA, a 501(c)3 nonprofit organization.

SAVE THE DATE

THURSDAY, NOVEMBER 18, 2010

UNITED NATIONS
FOUNDATION

UNITED NATIONS ASSOCIATION
of the United States of America
AND THE BUSINESS COUNCIL FOR THE UNITED NATIONS

2010

UN FOUNDATION / UNA-USA

ANNUAL DINNER

THE WALDORF=ASTORIA • 301 PARK AVENUE • NEW YORK, NEW YORK

HONORING

The Honorable John F. Kerry
UNITED STATES SENATOR

Simon Fuller
AMERICAN IDOL
CREATOR AND PRODUCER

Michel Sidibé
EXECUTIVE DIRECTOR
UNAIDS

HOST

Rick Reilly
ESPN PERSONALITY